READY,

SET,

A Must-Have Resource
for Campaigns of All Kinds

TALK!

**A Guide to Getting
Your Message
Heard by Millions
on Talk Radio,
Talk Television,
and Talk Internet**

ELLEN RATNER
AND
KATHIE SCARRAH

Chelsea Green Publishing Company
White River Junction, Vermont

Managing Editor: Marcy Brant
Copy Editor: Robin Catalano
Indexer: Beth Nauman-Montana, Salmon Bay Indexing
Designer: Peter Holm, Sterling Hill Productions
Design Assistant: Daria Hoak, Sterling Hill Productions

Printed in the United States
First printing, July 2006
10 9 8 7 6 5 4 3 2 1

Our Commitment to Green Publishing

Chelsea Green sees publishing as a tool for cultural change and ecological stewardship. We
strive to align our book manufacturing practices with our editorial mission, and to reduce the
impact of our business enterprise on the environment. We print our books and catalogs on
chlorine-free recycled paper, using soy-based inks, whenever possible. Chelsea Green is a
member of the Green Press Initiative (www.greenpressinitiative.org), a nonprofit coalition of
publishers, manufacturers, and authors working to protect the world's endangered forests and
conserve natural resources. *Ready, Set, Talk!* was printed on Ecobook 100 Natural, a 100 percent post-consumer-waste recycled, old-growth-forest-free paper supplied by RR Donnelley.

Library of Congress Cataloging-in-Publication Data

Ratner, Ellen, 1951-
Ready, set, talk! : a guide to getting your message heard by millions on
talk radio, talk television, and talk internet : a must-have resource for
campaigns of all kinds / Ellen Ratner and Kathie Scarrah.
     p. cm.
ISBN-13: 978-1-933392-21-9 (pbk.)
ISBN-10: 1-933392-21-5 (pbk.)
1. Radio in publicity. 2. Television in publicity. 3. Internet in
publicity. 4. Talk radio. I. Scarrah, Kathie. II. Title.
HF6146.R3R38 2006
659.14--dc22
                              2006014210

Chelsea Green Publishing Company
Post Office Box 428
White River Junction, VT 05001
(800) 639-4099
www.chelseagreen.com

CONTENTS

ACKNOWLEDGMENTS

So many people have contributed to this book with ideas and advice about getting and staying on radio, television, and the Internet. Quick comments and suggestions—sometimes given on a campaign bus or in a radio or television studio—became ideas within this book.

Ellen Ratner

I would specifically like to thank Peter Johnson Jr., Roger Ailes, Darla Shine, and Bill Shine for their great career guidance and support.

Doug Stephan, Mark Bernier, Howard Monroe, Blanquita Cullum, Scott Hennen and Thom Hartmann, and Alan Nathan are hosts who have been very helpful with their insights. Mike Sponder is always ready with fresh ideas. Anne Gehman and Wayne Knoll, Richard F. Miller and Kandy and Frank Stroud, Webb and Suzy Hubbell, and Anna Donovan have endured many dinners with discussions of this book. Patricia de Stacy Harrison of the Corporation for Public Broadcasting has a deep understanding of the talk medium and has contributed her insights.

The staff and talent of *Fox and Friends* are so much fun. Their green room is a perfect example of what rises to the top and makes it on the air. I would especially like to thank Matt Singerman, David Clark, and Fred Cwerner for their guidance and friendship. Chris White always presents great ideas. Jim Pinkerton, my partner in *The Long and Short of It*, has given me great ideas throughout our many years on air. Chris Curich and Darianne Bramberg make Fox's green room a great experience!

The book took a bit of holiday during some eye problems. Drs. Judith Haller and Dr. Thomas Hwang and the staff of the Johns Hopkins Wilmer Eye Institute were wonderful during a very long ordeal. Dr. Gina

Brown and Trish Heller endured many hours in the hospital and in Baltimore taking care of me and being wonderful friends.

Rich Michalski of the International Machinists and Aerospace Workers understands the talk media better than anyone and has always been a listener as well as someone ready with suggestions.

Shari Johnson not only edited this book, but also encouraged it all the way to publication. She is a masterful editor with a keen eye and a great sense of humor. The staff of Chelsea Green are the most wonderful team in publishing. It has been an honor to work with Margo Baldwin, John Barstow, and Marcy Brant. The marketing team, headed by Beau Friedlander along with Alice Blackmer, is the best in the business.

Cholene Espinoza, my life partner, has believed in this project the whole way, even taking dictation and making corrections when I could not see. My family—Bruce Ratner, Pamela Lipkin, Michael Ratner, Karen Ranucci, Charlotte Haynes, James Johnson, and Valerie and Lisa Espinoza—have been great. Chip Espinoza labored over statistics. My nieces and nephews are always fun to talk to during the heat of a project.

The staff of Talk Radio News Service—Lovisa Frost, Greg Gorman, Victoria Jones, and Wendy Wang—have collected stories and information. Adam Sharon spent days finding the latest statistics. The staff at *Talkers*—especially Michael Harrison, Carole Marks, and Shelly Blanchette—is always the best!

Kathie R. Scarrah

I would like to acknowledge those who had faith in me and afforded me the opportunity to perfect my skills as a broadcast "spin doctor." U.S. Senators John Melcher and Joe Lieberman, U.S. Secretary of State Madeleine K. Albright and Congressman Dennis Kucinich. I also appreciate the friendship and support of my political colleagues—Jim Kennedy, Michael Lewan, Bill Andresen, and Eric Federing. For his very frank advice on what he looks for when booking guests, Andrew Yates, who produces the Mike Murphy Show at Talk Radio 710 KCMO in Kansas City, Missouri. He was a great source from the "heartland." Several colleagues from the Washington bureaus of national television networks also contributed to this book. My contacts at ABC, CBS, CNN, and NBC, as you requested, I have not revealed your identity. Throughout the years I have enjoyed working with all of you and I am honored to call you friends. To Bill Ritz for sharing his enthusiasm about talk radio. And finally to my parents, Warren and Pat Scarrah, for understanding that a liberal arts degree wasn't a bad choice and for encouraging me to believe in myself and to keep going, especially when times were tough.

FOREWORD

We are experiencing explosive growth in the expansion and influence of talk media in America. The term "talk media" includes talk programs that are delivered to their audiences on traditional AM and FM radio stations as well as their kissin' cousin, cable news/talk television. But wait, there's more—the high-flying newcomer satellite radio, the steadily improving process of radio on the Internet, and the paradigm-shifting phenomenon referred to as podcasting are drastically expanding the talk media universe. What began as the talk radio revolution of the 1990s has evolved into the multi-platform, electric engine of democratized twenty-first century media. These developments cannot be ignored by any individual or organization involved in public relations.

Public relations make the world go around; whether in business, politics or community activism, we are all traders in the free marketplace of ideas. And free it is. Although broadcasting sales departments will happily sell advertising to anyone willing to pay for it, the opportunities for free exposure of products and causes in this field are infinite. More important, the free messages offered by these outlets of the spoken word are among the most influential in all of communications. The key is to know how to tap in to this persuasive mother lode and vigorously exploit its tremendous potential. *Ready, Set, Talk!* presents a handy set of guidelines to help everyone interested in promoting a product or a philosophy to *get the word out*. This includes grassroots public service groups to national political parties, mom and pop retailers to multinational corporations, self-published authors to major publishing houses.

Talk shows today run the gamut from the big-time network extravaganzas emanating from state-of-the-art radio and television network studios in New York, Los Angeles, Chicago, and Washington, DC, to desktop computers loaded with the latest cool software in the basements and home offices of independent syndicators and podcasters. There are thousands of these entities out there and they all have one thing in common—a nonstop craving for content in the form of stories, information, and, most highly valued, guests.

If you have a story to tell, information to pass along, and someone interesting to talk about it, the odds are good that there are a whole bunch of talk shows out there waiting to hear from you. These shows cover conservative, liberal and independent politics. They deal with the arts and sciences. They talk about home improvement and gardening. They are focused on health issues. Personal finance. Relationships. Technology. Sports. Collectables. The list goes on. Some of them have massive audiences that can make a product or idea the new big thing in one felt swoop. Others have small audiences that can help you build your empire brick by brick. Regardless, research studies indicate that talk show audience members are attentive and act on what they see and hear.

So get going! There is a whole world out there anxious to learn about you, your product, your organization and your message via the dynamic world of talk media.

—Michael Harrison, publisher,
Talkers® Magazine

LET THE TALK BEGIN

I am a dyed-in-the-wool liberal, so it surprised me when the 2004 Bush presidential campaign asked me for advice on talk media—both for the campaign and for the convention. (Among the other hats I wear, I am political editor of *Talkers® Magazine*.) My staff and I offered this same advice to Kerry campaign staffers, but they were not interested in learning how to use talk media for a more effective campaign. I was disappointed and amazed that the Bush campaign "got it," while the Kerry folks were uninterested.

I wrote a shorter but similar book ten years ago because I was tired of hearing that "right wing conservatives" controlled the talk media. At that time, the talk media consisted mainly of radio and cable news. I could see that the liberals were losing out on an important and viable source of help for their campaigns, charities, issues, programs, books, ideas, or anything else they might want to get before the people.

With the exponential growth of the Internet, talk media has reached remarkable heights of influence. Politically, there is now a better balance; many top issues are no longer falling into traditional red state/blue state columns. An informed public wants and needs to know the entire story.

Think of the airwaves as modern day territory ripe for the taking. Many of us tend to think that there is an *inside track*—that taking and retaining the media is the exclusive territory of high-priced professionals. Nothing could be further from the truth. The airwaves and the Internet "talk street" are out there for anyone willing to learn how to make use of talk media to garner effective free publicity.

This book is designed to teach anyone—from a new candidate running for office in the smallest community to the chairman of a Fortune 500 company to a local activist group of high school students to a young publicist starting out—how to craft a message and get that message out there.

After reading this book you will not only know what to say and how to say it, but you will also know where to say it, including innovative technological territories that are still being cultivated.

I have a short attention span so I have written *Ready, Set, Talk!* for like-minded people—those who don't have time to spend perusing a book to uncover the information they need. Many of the pointers are in list form. These range from tips for dressing for a television interview to handling a major crisis (and the press). I also love a good story—or, to be more specific, I like gossip. I use real stories from both sides of the street—the good, the bad, the incompetent, the arrogant, the brilliant—to illustrate the highly effective tricks of a trade that is moving to new mediums, but essentially runs off the same playbook.

To ensure that *Ready, Set, Talk!* covered all the terrain, I asked Kathie Scarrah to add her valuable insight. She has been an on-air talent in both radio and television, and helped make Connecticut Senator Joe Lieberman a national figure by "pitching" him to the national talk media early in his career. Since I receive pitches from public relations firms, publishing houses, and campaigns, I knew Kathie's unique insight in this area would be invaluable. Her work at the US State Department during the Clinton administration taught her how to make complicated international issues resonate at home.

We continue to collect stories, examples and lessons from campaigns, both great and not so great, and invite you to share your experiences with us. We will continually update the Web site www.readysettalk.org and may use your stories in future editions of this book.

Is your non-profit organization your passion, but no one knows it exists? Have you written a book that has the potential of being a best seller, but you seem to be the only one who knows about it? Are you the right candidate for public office, but your campaign coffers are sparse? Are you a publicist in your first job and feeling overwhelmed? You are the reason this book was written. Let the talk media work for you. NOW!

—Ellen Ratner
Washington, D.C.
May 2006

READY, SET,
TALK!

PREPARING YOUR MESSAGE AND CAMPAIGN

Be ready, willing, and available.

Conservative issues and guests have dominated the airwaves because they are ready, willing, and available to be on the air. There are numerous examples of the willingness of Republicans to try new strategies to get their message out. Call it confidence or call it communications savvy, but Republicans have cornered the market on embracing media—especially talk radio, talk television, and talk Internet.

The day after the 2005 State of the Union Speech the Republicans gave seventy radio interviews in less than twenty-four hours. Kandy Stroud at the Democratic National Committee booked several interviews as well, but getting Democrats to do early morning and late-night radio was very difficult. During the 2004 primary season the goal of the Republican National Committee's Scott Hoganson was to have a Republican presence in every radio market and on every radio station in the country including early morning and late night shows.

Arbitron, a company that rates listenership in radio, recently released data indicating that 18 percent of the radio-listening market went to news/talk stations, and a significant amount went to Spanish-language stations. This does not preclude listening on stations that include talk as part of a music format. While the Democrats were running against each other, the RNC steadfastly promoted President Bush and Republican-sponsored ideas and policies. Market share and audience size did not matter. Why? The RNC had a uniform message—every vote counts. One extra Republican vote per precinct can swing a presidential election. It is that simple.

The Republicans are masters of the *rapid response*. Surrogate speakers are on-call and can take orders from the RNC to go on the air, set the faxes humming, and arrange rebuttal news conferences and events at a moment's notice. Even though the Democrats also have a response mechanism in place, the Republicans appear to get their word out more quickly and in a more consistent, organized manner. They all seem to be on the same playing field when it comes to the message. The Republicans are willing to appear on the air because they know that the shows and their hosts will make time available to them.

The war in Iraq presented the most daring example of risking a new reporting practice—embedded journalists. Vice President Dick Cheney was against the idea of embedding reporters, but was won over by media-savvy Secretary of Defense Donald Rumsfeld. No one knew how the coverage from the embedded print and broadcast journalists would be reported. Would embargoes be honored and the locations of troops remain secret? Or would reporters try to report "gotcha" stories and rely on yellow journalism in order to be the first to leak a story—no matter how inaccurate—and would the troops be endangered as a result? As preparation for the Iraqi conflict began and before joining troops on land, in the air, and on the sea, the media went to military boot camps. The government, the media, and the public realized the significant benefits of the embedded journalists who could now give an *insider* angle to news reporting.

Before the 2002 midterm Congressional elections the White House invited more than forty talk-show hosts to broadcast from a tent on the White House lawn, and the event was repeated for the State of the Union Address. The White House made a grand show of this talk-radio event, complete with special souvenir badges and a White House tour. The administration supplied high-level guests to ensure that every host had at least one star. It was a huge success.

On the one-year anniversary of the Iraq War, the Pentagon hosted Talk-Radio Row. At this event three or more talk-show hosts are located in a specific area, each with their own broadcast space. The guests proceed down the row from host to host and are interviewed in turn. At the Pentagon's Talk-Radio Row, not all of the talk-show hosts were conservative; some liberal talk-show hosts were also included.

Republicans reach out to their like-minded hosts with invitations to fund-raisers and other political events. With the exception of Democracy

Radio and Campaign for America's Future, Democrats and liberal organizations seem to fear any mention of fund-raising and politically related events, and make a point of not inviting their like-minded talk-show hosts. They do, however, remember these hosts when they want to pitch a guest—not a good way to win friends and influence the media.

When George W. Bush was a presidential candidate campaigning in 2000, he was asked to speak at the talk-radio industry's May 2000 *"Talkers Magazine* New Media Seminar"*. He left the campaign trail and flew to New York specifically for this event. Vice President Gore's campaign, on the other hand, not only did not show, but also did not bother to respond to the invitation to appear at the Seminar.

Senator Kerry repeated this no-show policy during the 2004 New Hampshire primary. Governor Howard Dean as well as the other candidates understood that talk radio is a powerful medium. But even he came to this realization too late.

At the "New Media Seminar" presidential candidate Bush spent time with the hosts and was as friendly with the liberals as he was with the conservatives. The no-show by Gore set the stage for Democrats and talk radio in the 2000 presidential race. Even when the vice-presidential candidates were named and Joe Lieberman, who was widely considered a friend to the talk industry, joined the ticket, the Democrats continued to be missing in action on talk radio and television.

Throughout his senate career, Senator Joe Lieberman had appeared on more than a thousand talk-radio shows, but when selected as the VP candidate, he was suddenly no longer accessible to the talk shows and hosts. When Senator Lieberman ran for president in the 2004 primaries, although his campaign once again reached out to the talk media, producers and hosts did not enthusiastically receive him.

Despite the advent of Democratic radio initiatives, Democratic strategists continue to argue against putting their spokespeople on conservative media shows. This is a ridiculous argument. A recent study by RADAR, a network rating service of Arbitron, revealed that radio reaches 95 percent of those in the seventy-five-thousand-dollar-plus per year households and that 95 percent of college graduates listen to the radio. Whether the show is broadcast on the Internet, radio, or television, do not overlook or ignore it—it has a following, and it could be an important one. The show's demographics may not be aligned with you politically, ethically, or morally, but if you are trying to sway opinion, change minds, or reach a potential supporter, it is worth reaching out and communicating your message to this audience.

It is amazing how many people avoid appearing on a show that is considered confrontational—even if it has a large audience. A gay physician refused an invitation to appear on John McLaughlin's *One-on-One* television show, and a gun-control advocate did not want to get into a debate with the NRA on *The Montel Williams Show*. Both shows have huge audiences and those audiences reflect the general public's views on many issues. A one-minute advertising spot on these shows costs thousands of dollars. Both of these individuals could have received more than the equivalent of that amount in free airtime to push their causes. Why would a well-prepared spokesperson for each cause turn down all this free airtime? The guests control their talking points—the idea is to get your message out.

One conservative activist said, "If a station is five watts, I'm there." A spokesperson on the left said, "I won't do single-station shows; I only get on syndicated shows." Those two statements sum up the difference. Small stations and media outlets create a critical mass. Their audiences tend to be very loyal. They are impressed if a bigwig is willing to do an interview with the little guys. Be willing to go the extra mile and get on the air on small and large stations. If enough people with a minority viewpoint were willing to go on the air, all sides would be heard.

During the 2004 presidential campaign, the Kerry camp gave talk radio and television the short shrift and did not want to be seen on the Fox News Channel—even for a one-on-one interview with Alan Colmes. John Kerry gave interviews to MSNBC, and John Edwards went on *Larry King Live*, but both avoided *Hannity and Colmes*. These were the ratings:

John Kerry on MSNBC's *Hardball*: 0.7 rating/610,000 viewers

John Edwards on CNN's *Larry King Live*: 1.4 rating/1.267 million viewers

George Bush on *Hannity and Colmes*: 2.8 rating/2.44 million viewers

The Kerry campaign thought they were controlling the media by not appearing on Fox. Because, according to the Pew Center's poll, half of Fox viewers are either independent or liberal, an opportunity was missed to speak to more than one million of their potential voters—more than if *all* the *Larry King* viewers were committed to voting for Kerry and Edwards!

One host inquired about having a well-known airline president on the air. The host was told that the president's schedule was booked one year in advance. No one is that busy, not even the president of the United States.

A government official said, "We only do shows heard inside the beltway [the eight-lane interstate circling metro Washington, D.C.]. We like to hear our work." What this official did not realize is that the radio show was simulcast on the Internet; it could have been heard within the beltway even though the host was hundreds of miles away.

It can take as little as five minutes for a radio or Internet interview, and it can be done from anyplace—your home, office, or the car. A television interview, including makeup time, can take as little as a half hour once you are in the studio or at the remote location. And it is all free airtime; something the industry calls *earned media*. "It is also important to be radio active and ready to get going fast," says Mark Pfeifle, former deputy communications director of the Republican National Committee. Willingness and a rapid-response team are key ingredients that contribute to the success of conservative issues and guests with talk media.

Check 'em out.

If your goal is to get on talk radio, listen to the shows that are broadcast in your area as well as those that are nationally syndicated. Most shows are available via satellite radio or the Internet, making them accessible to an audience well beyond their local markets. If you cannot listen to them live, most shows archive summaries and even entire scripts of previous shows. This preparation is important, even to industry professionals. For example, before developing the very successful Fox News Channel, Roger Ailes locked himself in a room and watched all the news shows and channels for one month. He then knew exactly what was on the air, and what his channel should address.

If news is your goal, listen to the hourly news on your local stations and the all-news networks. Check out the latest from the Associated Press and

Reuters wire services. Monitor Internet news sites as well. Several Internet sites post up-to-the-minute wire stories, providing instant access to the news around the world.

Check the media-monitoring sites such as Mediamatters.com, Fair.org, Aim.org, Newsbusters.org, and Factcheck.org. Mediamatters and Fair are decidedly liberal, Aim and Newsbusters are conservative, and Factcheck can be either. To monitor the blogosphere, Technorati is the current technology. It allows you to create watch lists. Type in *Avian flu*, for instance, and you will find more than two hundred blog references. Google also has Web alerts, called Google Alerts. Video can now be monitored on the Web via Google and other sites.

Find out what excites people, even if you don't share the passion. Writer Andrew Sullivan reads the religious right to understand them. He uses the Internet to go into "a million town halls to understand what makes them excited."

The morning drive is an important time for radio and television, so listen to the "morning zoo" radio shows and the network and cable-television morning shows. According to Arbitron research, people are spending more time in cars, not less. Whatever you are hearing on the radio is the same as what a lot of other people are hearing. Pay attention to the weekend specialty shows. Listen to the guests on these shows and note which topics capture your attention. Monitor the chat rooms on the Web sites you plan to utilize. What are the topics that generate chat response? If you are in a vehicle, use the radio drive test: Can a topic capture your attention while you are driving to and from work with other things on your mind?

You can be creative with the kinds of media you monitor. For example, the most often e-mailed stories can be found on several newspaper sites. Retail information is also available, such as the top-selling items and the range of items that are sold. This information enables you to put your finger on the pulse of popular culture trends and current events.

If you are planning an immediate on-air campaign, listen to the issues of the week. We live in a culture that responds to trends and we tend to have a pack mentality. Your literature and your spokesperson should reflect the mood and theme of the country, as well as the demographics and lifestyle of the people you are trying to reach. (More information on this appears in the section about choosing the right spokesperson.) You will get more attention if you dovetail your issues with current trends so they sound timely, but don't go overboard. Know what you are getting into before you do a show.

Define, create, refine.

In order for a message to be successful it should be rich with elements of conflict, confrontation, and emotion. It should answer the basic questions every journalist asks: who, where, what, when, how, and why? In short, your message should contain a cause and an effect. If you don't define your message, you can be sure your opponent will; be proactive, not reactive. Your message must frame the issue; just as a picture frame directs focus and enhances the visual presentation of a photo, your words should direct the perception of your issue. You may reframe your message depending on what kind of media you are using and the demographic that message is intended to reach.

Make a list of the toughest questions you could be asked about your issue—especially the ones you *do not* want to answer. This is the best way to begin your campaign, because these are the questions that will most likely be asked on the air. A surefire strategy to ensure that you are prepared is to debate your issues with conservative or liberal friends who oppose your issue. This will help you develop both your printed material and your on-air and online campaign.

Your issue should answer these four important questions:

1. How does this affect Joe and Sally's pocketbook?
2. Does this issue fit into Joe and Sally's value system?
3. Why is this important?
4. Why is this important now?

Take, for example, the issue of AIDS. Most conservatives see sexuality as a moral issue and nothing is going to change that. Present these issues from a different angle. Weigh the cost of condoms and sex education against the cost of treating the AIDS epidemic. The way in which you define your issue can enlighten an audience and make a difference. But be careful to acknowledge and support your audience's right to their values.

The issues of prisons and prison overcrowding have begun to unite the right and the left as the comparative costs of housing nonviolent criminals has skyrocketed. Is incarceration the answer? Or perhaps rehabilitation in the community is a more economical and realistic way to look at the problem. This is an issue now being defined by interest groups.

The alternative-food industry has been very successful in their bid against genetic engineering. They have supported many interest groups who have waged successful campaigns against genetic engineering. Recently there has been a successful radio and Internet campaign to redefine the issue and change their message. Junkscience.com is an example of this. Genetically engineered crops can save lives or can damage ecosystems, depending on which side you support of this often controversial issue.

After the defeat of the Democrats, former President Bill Clinton made a speech about *message*. Clinton was the king of message in his day. He said that in order to be a national party you must have a national message that contains vision, program, unity, and clarity. He said that it must contain shared responsibility, shared benefits, and shared community. The message must have longevity (and last beyond one election cycle).

The Johari Window, invented by Joseph Luft and Harry Ingram, is a model used to describe the process of human interaction. It is a four-paned "window" that divides human awareness into four different types:

Open—what you know about yourself and others know about you
Blind—what others know about you, but you are unaware of
Hidden—what you know about yourself, but others don't know about you
Unknown—what neither you know about yourself, nor others know about you

Based on this model, the Democrats developed what they call the Tully Message Box. Divided into four quadrants, Paul Tully defined the four components of *message*:

1. What you say about yourself
2. What your opponent says about herself
3. What you say about your opponent
4. What your opponent says about you

The message must also be characterized by the four Cs: It should be clear, contrasting, concise, and convincing.

Green Media Tool Shed (GreenMediaToolShed.org) has its own Message Development Box. They divide it into:

Threshold Messages—what do people need to know, believe in, or care about in order to become engaged? What obstacles do you have to overcome to get people over this threshold?

Solution Messages—offer suggestions for how, if people do what you say, their lives will be better.

Reinforcement Messages—how do you keep people involved? How do those who are involved convey your messages? What are some statistics, anecdotes, and sound bites we can use to support these messages?

Action Messages—what is the purpose of your message? What do you want the people who connect to you to do? Do you have different goals for different campaigns?

Take several messages from the world of politics, advertising, and advocacy. See how each one fits the Tully Message Box. Do some of your own research by asking people in the local coffee shop what they think of the message. By understanding how successful messages have been developed, you will begin to understand how to develop your own.

Do the research to discover how to reach your audience. For a message to work, your audience must identify with your issues. What is the common ground you share? In the very successful rehabilitation program Alcoholics Anonymous, participants share their "experience, strength, and hope"; this brings the message of sobriety to the membership. You must share your experience, strength, and hope with those you want to influence. You want them to share and buy into your objectives. You want them to remember your message and own it.

How far your message reaches can be summed up in an equation developed by Gordon Allport and Leo Postman in the 1940s. They called it the basic law of rumor: R= i {x} a. They found that rumor strength (R) will depend on the importance of the subject or message (i) times the ambiguity of the topic or message (a), if the message is hot, new, or interesting.

It also makes sense to understand the population of your target audience. For instance, if you want to reach a female urban population you might want to turn to the Arbitron data for that demographic. One Arbitron study focused on the urban adult woman contemporary-radio listener. The study found that worry is a part of everyday life for her; she uses radio to change her mood, especially at work; she wants funny on-air personalities; she likes call-in shows with advice; she is concerned about kids listening to the content; and that money decisions and concerns are her responsibility. The study pointed out many more characteristics of this demographic, but it is clear how understanding a population and using the data available will help you develop your message.

If your target is a younger audience, knowing that 50 percent of college freshmen consider themselves middle-of-the-road politically, that they love self-determination, that they listen to peers from their generation more than to older spokespersons, that they are very cynical as a group, that one in four of them were raised by a single parent, and that they volunteer more than the previous generation, are all crucial to help you craft even nonpolitical messages.

According to journalist Damien Cave, one group who understood this was an antismoking group that did the "Truth" advertisements, which highlighted tactics used by the tobacco industry. It struck a cord with the younger generation. According to Cave, Rock the Vote took the tendency toward cynicism into account when it designed its Social Security campaign with the theme "Don't get ripped off." There is also the red-state alternative to this organization, Redeem the Vote.

A message must also match actions. In an interview with the *New York Times*, Democratic senator Charles Schumer said, "You could describe George Bush's overall campaign message and theme in eight words: War in Iraq, tax cuts, no gay marriage. And these were not just slogans. For better or for worse, he tried to implement all three. And the challenge for Democrats—we don't have to do it in eight words, but we have to have a succinct program; not just slogans like *better health*." People, as Senator Schumer stated, have the ability to look beyond the message and see actions. Make sure your organization's message and actions match, or even the greatest message will fall flat.

Rick Frishman of Planned Television Arts suggests that you have some friends cut headlines from a newspaper and place them in an envelope. Then have them give you the cut-up newspaper and ask you to write the headlines. Are your headlines as simple and clear as the newspaper's? (Maybe they are better.) He also suggests compiling a list of words with impact for use in future messages, keeping the list easily accessible.

Use common sense. If your focus groups tell you one thing but your eyes and ears tell you something else, pay attention to your eyes and ears. Former presidential candidate Gary Hart kept telling the Kerry campaign that Kerry should talk about jobs and energy in the context of security, but the focus groups said something different. As Bob Dylan remarked, "You don't need a weather man to know which way the wind blows."

Steve Rabinowitz, known as the "Rabbi," who coordinated message for Bill Clinton in 1992, says that "when you are developing message it is important to make sure that everything that is going out from the campaign is message driven. Make sure that everything that you say to the press is on message. Some press will work hard to take you off message, but if you are doing your job right they'll be sick to death of it and in no time you'll find yourself answering all sorts of questions about obscure policy issues, your boss's or client's favorite movies, or other trivia. Your job is to be dogged about the message and to remember that anytime you talk to a journalist about any topic it is an opportunity to get some variation of your message out."

Congressman Sherrod Brown (D-Ohio), says the reason the Clinton health plan failed is that it took five minutes to explain. He said you cannot win an election if you cannot explain your issue(s) in one minute.

Think of your media campaign as a physical improvement regimen. First, define the goal (weight loss/gain, healthier lifestyle), then create a program to reach your goal (healthy diet, physical workout, more rest); then constantly refine the results of your efforts in order to stay healthy. Apply this same regimen to your message—define, create, and refine. It is a combination for success.

The ultimate test: Can you define your message in one sentence? People remember sound bites and easy concepts. Think of successful advertising campaigns.

Keep up!

Dated word usage is a sure turn-off. The on-air commentators might make jokes about politically correct speech, but it is usually a safe bet. The elderly are now older persons, waiters and waitresses are waitpersons, stewards and stewardesses are flight attendants, and so forth.

Buzzwords can make your campaign snappy and current. Think of some current buzzwords and how they have become commonplace in speeches, commercials, and news coverage. According to Yourdictionary.com the most defining political phrases of the 2004 election year were *red states/blue states*, followed by *moral values* and *two Americas*. Possibly the most memorable buzzword is *9/11*. People no longer refer to September 11, 2001; just the numbers 9/11 or 911 create mental images of the terrorist attacks at the World Trade Center, the Pentagon, and a field in Shanksville, Pennsylvania. The American conscience and the war on terrorism are embodied by *9/11*.

Along the same line, buzzwords such as *axis of evil, roadmap to peace, and weapons of mass destruction* or *WMDs* have been used to support both sides of the debate on terrorism. Even the words *terrorism* or *terrorist* are buzzwords in this post 9/11 world. Utter those words and you are sure to get someone's attention.

How long did it take you to figure out that *FAQ* means "frequently asked questions"? Have you used the following examples of buzzwords that are so ingrained in our everyday vocabulary?

> **Low-carb:** Remember when the fat content of our food was our primary concern? In the early years of the new millennium, it was all about carbohydrates. Everyone got on the bandwagon— McDonald's, Blimpie, Subway, and even the major beer manufacturers claimed their products were low-carb.
>
> **Exit strategy:** This is an ever-changing policy for American forces in Afghanistan and Iraq. Have a well-defined and -planned exit

strategy in case your campaign message does not have the desired impact or is not reaching your target audience, and don't be afraid to use it!

Reaganomics: Used to describe President Ronald Reagan's economic policies; widespread tax cuts, decreased social spending, increased military spending, and the deregulation of domestic markets.

Sound bite: Generally a seven-to-ten-second, snappy quote that summarizes an idea. If you speak in sound bites, you are guaranteed that at least one of your clever comments will be picked up by the media. The concern is that you might not be able to speak beyond a sound bite and therefore cannot present the backbone of the issue. It doesn't hurt to have one or two well-placed sound bites in your prepared written statement or presentation.

Out of the box: A phrase originally coined by the public-relations industry to describe refreshing public-relations campaigns, ones that used unorthodox methods of reaching an intended audience.

Information superhighway: The "prehistoric" definition of the Internet.

Rules of engagement: Used in the military and in politics. Everyone has his or her own definition of the rules.

You can follow the language trends, and thus make the most of *keyword advertising*, by using Web-based services such as searchmarketing. yahoo.com. It can tell you if people are using the term *mad cow disease* or if they are using *BSE* instead. This way, you will know if the language is changing on the topic that you want to market.

There are several Internet sites that demystify the most common or current buzzwords. Just type in *buzzword* and you will be stunned at the number of sites listed. WordCentral.com lists a daily buzzword. If you are studying for a spelling bee or current-affairs quiz game, it is an excellent research site. LanguageMonitor.com has a "global language monitor" that tracks the use of buzzwords and compiles the information in a quarterly report. The Linguistic Society of America also reports on "words of the year," which is useful to check out.

Prior to the war in Iraq the military began circulating a deck of cards featuring the fifty-five most wanted figures in Saddam Hussein's regime. Saddam Hussein was the ace of spades, and his two sons, Uday and Qusay, were the ace of hearts and ace of clubs, respectively. Presidential Secretary Abid Hamid Mahmud Al-Tikriti rounded out the top four as the ace of diamonds. Clever entrepreneurs created their own cards and sold them on the Internet for as much as fifty dollars a pack. They were an instant sellout. Months later, you could buy knockoff copies in stores throughout the United States for around five dollars. The campaign, although initiated by the U.S. Department of Defense as a visual means to identify their most-wanted Iraqi government officials, was picked up by the media and resulted in millions of dollars of free advertising for several shrewd businessmen. Right-wing Internet sites ran with the idea and published Hillary Clinton decks and other cards that made fun of Democrats.

Sometimes your words or products will create a bounce on their own, or as marketing expert Julianne Corbett says, "You don't want to be a smattering of lights—you want one bold, broad stroke." If a radio ad or a billboard creates a stir, you are almost guaranteed an invitation to talk about the incident.

When Mark Pfeifle was deputy communications director of the Republican National Committee, he spearheaded stunts that were often covered by national media. So many received notice that *George* magazine dubbed him the "master of the modern political prank."

During the 2000 presidential campaign when Vice President Al Gore tried desperately to distance himself from President Clinton, the RNC placed a 14-foot-by-48-foot billboard less than 500 feet from Gore's Nashville head-quarters, depicting President Clinton embracing his vice president. It included a quote from VP Gore saying President Clinton is "one of our greatest presidents." The two-year-old quote from Al Gore commending President Clinton was a reminder to everyone who saw the billboard (and thanks to national television coverage, several million more saw it than would have in the greater Nashville area) that no matter how hard Gore tried to distance himself, he was still part of the Clinton inner circle.

Pfeifle's pranks, wordsmithing, and Internet illustrations have included dismissing poll numbers by saying, "Those numbers are less credible than the figures in Joe Millionaire's bank account." He discounted a Clinton administration's foreign-policy trip that included a stop in Hawaii when he said, "Forty million dollars in taxpayer money and all the president got was a lei." He also called President Clinton's trip to Africa "the forty-million-dollar fund-raising safari."

Be ready to use the smart imagery and phraseology of others. The *New York Post*'s pre-Iraq War front-page photomontage, "War of the Weasels," depicted an image of UN Ambassadors with their heads replaced by those of weasels. The image was picked up by the pro-war talk media and lasted much longer than the one-day newspaper headline. Use current affairs to your advantage and develop campaigns that create their own buzz.

Focus on your goal.

Know the audience you want to reach, influence, and convince—and know what you want them to do. Once you have done that, set your goals.

Make your goal attainable and measurable, especially if you are trying to be part of a news cycle. Consider carefully what you want to accomplish with this campaign. Have a twenty-four-hour plan of action: Focus on the immediate impact of your campaign and on what you hope to accomplish in the news day.

Marketing expert Julianne Corbett speculates that the Republican successes have come about because the Democrats do things the way they have always done them, which basically amounts to taking a guy around the country, working on messaging rather than building a product, and not developing a strategy to speak to a new generation of consumers. Corbett says, "There has always been an ebb and flow of family and values in American politics, but now the Republicans have made it into a marketing platform."

She suggests using OSGM—objectives, strategies, goals, and measurements—for a marketing campaign. Objectives and strategies involve words; goals and measurements involve numbers. While she was working for Valvoline Oil Company, the primary objective was to sell oil. To get Valvoline-sponsored NASCAR driver Scott Riggs name recognition and to sell oil, Corbett needed to find a way for him to relate to the product. She helped build him into a bootstrapper (someone who pulls himself up by his bootstraps) who went from riding motor bikes to being a top-level racer.

Corbett's goals were to use sponsorship to maximize brand value and build a loyalty program that would connect Riggs with his fans. Many racers, she figured, were too far from the fan base. Her strategy was to make her "products"—Valvoline oil and Scott Riggs—seem different from other racers and their sponsors, and thus more accessible to fans. Corbett developed Valvolineteamowners.com and targeted radio advertising. She measured her success by the membership numbers in her program and her pre- and post-surveys of the increased awareness of Scott Riggs and Valvoline oil. (For more on branding see Appendix 3.)

Keep your focus on your goal. Who is your intended audience? Are you trying to sway public opinion or congressional votes? Are you trying to change corporate policy or put pressure on the administration? Are you trying to stop or start something? Envision your end goal *before* you try to get your issue on the air or online.

Find out who the stakeholders are. Who are the stakeholders on your side? Who are the coalitions that you want to reach? Who are the stakeholders and coalitions that will fight you? What is your goal in reaching them? Do your best to understand the stakeholders' minds on both sides of the argument. What motivates each side? What would change their opinions?

Richard Miller, a conservative commentator for Talk Radio News Service, says that there are "only ten zip codes in the United States" that care about issues such as Guantánamo and detainees in Iraq. This changed when Senator John McCain made an argument against it. Suddenly, more zip codes cared, and ninety senators voted against torture. The timing, the spokesperson, and getting to the stakeholders makes the difference.

Bob Newman, a public-relations consultant in Boston, organized a campaign on an aspect of Social Security legislation. The goal he set with his client was to turn certain states by blanketing them with appearances by spokespeople on television and radio. Newman's method was to saturate targeted congressional delegations. Everything the spokesperson said and every media appearance was designed to keep pressure on these congressional districts. The campaign worked and many congressional members in the targeted districts voted in support of this aspect of Social Security legislation.

Sometimes communications professionals will place their spokesperson on a show only if they can fulfill their specific talk strategy. Goals are important, but being rigid in this area may not work for you as a long-term media strategy. You might also want to go for the intangible benefit of filling a request as a matter of goodwill or good faith. It works.

One of the main reasons Senator John McCain resonated with the electorate in the 2000 presidential campaign was because he campaigned like a program producer looking for an audience, issues, and demographics. He wanted to find out what would work. His goal, of course, was to win the nomination. Despite losing it, he won the public-relations battle and respect of those disgruntled with partisan politics. He is still a very prominent Republican voice on Capitol Hill and may take what he learned in 2000 and apply it to 2008.

Move the *middle*.

A general campaign should try to move the middle (those who have not committed to either side) and aim the message at the Influentials in this group. The Institute for Politics, Democracy and the Internet has studied these Influentials, who, as the institute's director, Carol Darr, describes, "tell others what to buy, for whom to vote, and where to vacation." One in ten Americans fits this definition. The Influentials are generally two to five years ahead of the rest of the population. They write letters to editors, call talk shows, and direct watercooler conversation. They are information junkies and love links and resources.

Former Bush/Cheney campaign staffer Matthew Dowd and former White House Media Director Tucker Eskew have said that it is very difficult to find the Influentials. They identified them by using surveys and marketing data.

Because your aim is to move the middle, your entire presentation should be geared toward it. Playing to any other audience is just dead air and a waste of time. However, it is important when playing to the middle that you do not turn your back on your core constituency. If you alienate this group they will not vote with your issue in mind and will not support your cause financially.

There is a reason that the newspaper *USA Today* sells so well. It is designed to speak to the common denominators of American life. If you want to know what folks are talking about, do some street research at school events, pool halls, bowling alleys, beauty shops, and supermarkets. The topics that interest you may not interest your neighbors and friends, and may not speak to where they live or where they are at this time in their lives.

On an Election Day, roughly 30 percent of American voters will vote Republican and 30 percent will vote Democratic. The remaining 40 percent are uncommitted voters who have the power to move an election. They are the nonideologues. Whether your issue is political, social, or personal, the goal of your media campaign should be to sway the person who represents the 40 percent in the middle.

There are times to go negative. Negative advertising works because a voter who is not paying a lot of attention will tend to believe negative ads, and because people are often cynical by nature. The Swift Boat ads in 2004 and the Club for Growth Ad in Iowa are examples. But this is not where the middle lives.

The public may be willing to put up with negative-issue ads, but might feel differently about negative candidate-to-candidate ads. During the 2004 presidential campaign, for instance, the only two negative ads in Iowa were from Howard Dean and Dick Gephardt. They did poorly, finishing in third and fourth place.

People want answers and help with their lives. John Kerry attacked Bush when the middle just wanted some help. Later in the campaign he said, "Help is on the way." However, if he had started with, "I can do a better job; I can make you safer," and then came up with a simple, specific plan, he would have gone a long way toward answering the question, "Who can give me better protection?" He could have pounded away at that and had some really positive results.

According to the nonprofit Committee for the Study of the American Electorate (CSAE), 59.6 percent of the eligible electorate voted in the 2004 presidential election—the highest number since 1968, when 61.9 percent of eligible voters voted. Approximately 120.2 million people voted in this extremely close election—15 million more voters than four years earlier. According to CSAE, this was a presidential election where the centralized, professional, and highly targeted voter identification and get-out-the-vote campaign of the Republicans bested the Democrats' decentralized but equally vigorous mobilization efforts. Their findings concluded that Senator John Kerry proved to be a very weak candidate, running behind Democratic candidates for governor and U.S. senator in most states. Voter turnout increases were greater by an almost 2-1 ratio in battleground states. The 2004 presidential election was a battle between *red* and *blue* states.

More than one-third of the people who walked into the polling booth on Election Day 2004 and voted either Democrat or Republican had not appeared to be leaning toward either party throughout the campaign. They represented the middle. As commentator Mike Sponder remarked, "I imagine they said, 'Maybe this one, or that one,'" without much conviction that either candidate had really moved them.

The Pew Research poll shows that in the past, only 8 percent of voters split their tickets. Why, then, is the middle so important?

A grocery store that was started in the 1930s as a family operation still dominates the Washington, D.C. market. As it grew, family members began to fight. Each faction received 49 percent of the voting stock, and a trusted family friend was given 2 percent. Whichever group the family friend eventually sides with will control the company.

The middle may not be great in numbers, but it can control the direction of a company—or of a campaign. But the middle is always changing, depending upon the issue. The goal for Democrats in the 2004 presidential election was twofold: to reach the 36 percent of voters who didn't make up their minds in 2000 until Election Day, and to reach the 48.8 percent of eligible voters who did not vote that year. Voters cast their ballots on personal issues—money, home, family, education, and security. It was up to the ever-expanding group of Democratic candidates to show how the Bush administration had been unsuccessful in these areas; it was up to the Bush administration to draw on the initiative the war on terrorism has brought to patriotism and the thousands of votes that could be expected from the military community. Let the games continue.

What's your purpose?

Is your purpose to stabilize the grass roots, or is your intention to cast a wider net?

With issues such as abortion and gun control there is very little that will change opinions, so your media campaign might be for the sole purpose of keeping the issue alive in the hearts, minds, and pocketbooks of your supporters.

If you are using your media campaign to mobilize your supporters, be sure that your message is crafted accordingly. If this is not your clear-cut goal, don't spend useful time preaching to the choir.

Who are you trying to reach and why? The following questions should be reviewed and answered by every campaign—whether political or non-profit, before the campaign begins:

1. Do you want contributions?
2. Do you need volunteers?
3. Are you interested in letting your core supporters know what you are doing?

If you want to keep your base but you also want to convince others, you must find those who are receptive to your message and who might move in your direction. Find out how they make decisions. Where do they get their information? How have they arrived at the position they hold at this point in time? What will make them move in your direction? What are the time factors that will influence their decision making? Think about a board and a fulcrum—at some point, the board tips in one direction or the other. Your job is to find the point at which it will tip in your direction and then figure out how to get it there.

The Arab-American vote was important during the 2004 elections, especially in Michigan. This has not been lost on Karl Rove, senior adviser to President George W. Bush. Reaching out to the Arab and Muslim populations around the United States, President Bush has gained both support and criticism from these communities for his war on terrorism. Entire public-image campaigns have been generated by the administration to ensure that various ethnic constituencies understand that the war on terrorism is not against a religion, ethnicity, or people. Public-diplomacy campaigns aimed at the worldwide Arab population have resulted in the creation of a U.S. taxpayer–funded radio and television station: Radio Sawa and Al-Hurra, respectively.

The Jewish vote, usually claimed by the Democrats, has been carefully mined by the Bush administration with special off-the-record briefings and visits to the White House. The president's "roadmap to peace" in the Middle East has resonated with support from some previously Democratic Jewish contributors.

The Internet site MoveOn.org received tremendous publicity in June 2003, more than 16 months prior to the November 2004 election, by staging a primary for the growing list of Democratic 2004 presidential candidates. In a little more than 48 hours, nearly 318,000 people logged on to cast their ballot.

Your media campaign must have a purpose, and part of your strategic communications plan must be to identify your target audience. If you are casting a wider net, do not forget about your base and their possibly negative reaction to your targeting another audience.

Personalize your issue.

Fox News Channel's Brian Wilson calls these *Hey, Martha* issues—the kinds of subjects someone might talk about over the back fence or around the cubicle. "Hey, Martha, did you hear . . . ?" It means framing an issue or a new product or news so that it is exactly the kind of thing that is repeated.

Mark Pfeifle personalized President Bush's tax plan by using what he called tax families. He showed how much an average family would save under the Bush tax plan, giving a human face to the numbers.

When Pfeifle wanted to publicize Alaska's Artic National Wildlife Refuge (ANWR) and demonstrate the small amount of damage oil exploration and drilling would do to this environment, he used the image of a dime on a kitchen table. The table represented the size of ANWR and the dime represented the size of the area to be drilled—a comparison everyone can relate to. The antidrilling campaign countered with a beautiful photo of the caribou elk grazing in ANWR.

Anne Glauber, senior vice president of Ruder Finn, says, "It is important to explain how an issue can impact the 'average' American and affect a family's life directly." In Glauber's work with the Century Council, a non-profit organization funded by the distiller industry, while developing programs to prevent underage drinking they were able to commission surveys of teens and their parents to illustrate the lack of communication about the issue of teenage drinking and the dangers teenagers face. In her work with the plight of women in Rwanda who had survived genocide, Glauber was able to make the issue relevant to women in America by having the women from Rwanda describe their daily lives, their histories and their personal horrors, through pictures and video. The public and the media were drawn to the women's stories. In addition, people were able to purchase Rwandan baskets, helping these women rebuild their lives.

The Pentagon has become expert at personalizing their issues. They now offer The Pentagon Channel to cable and satellite companies. They also have the Army and Air Force Hometown News Service, staffed with an army of reporters who develop news stories focusing on the accomplishments of service members and tailored to their hometown media.

Adam Cohen of the *New York Times* interviewed Dr. George Lakoff, author of *Don't Think of an Elephant! Know Your Values and Frame the Debate*, the all-time expert on framing, who teaches linguistics at the University of California–Berkeley. Dr. Lakoff wanted to frame the issue of the national debt for the 2004 presidential campaign by dividing the interest on the national debt by the number of babies born each year and then billing each baby for that amount ($85,000). His thesis was that people vote their identities, not their interests, and they will vote for people whose values match theirs. Did the Kerry campaign take his suggestion? No.

On the other side of the issues, author Ronald Sider wrote the book *Toward an Evangelical Public Policy: Political Strategies for the Health of the Nation*. It helps frame values for the evangelical community. Looking at both sides from a linguistic point of view will help to frame your argument and message.

Essentially people vote for a president based on who they are willing to have in their living rooms for the next four years. Do you want someone sitting on your couch who is not in sync with your values? This individual might support you and your interests, but do you want them as a member of your household each evening? That is the real question.

Know your audience and reach them with words and images that speak to the demographics you want to target. Let's say your media appearance will reach moms and NASCAR dads—not an impossible or improbable combination. Design your media campaign to reach both groups at the same time by using words and images that piggyback. Each group will feel as though you are speaking to them.

Tucker Eskew of ViaNovo, LP, says, "It's important to be on the same playing field with the same type of bats and balls that your audience is playing with; if they are watching satellite television, that is where you have to be engaged in as well."

Local radio is great for reaching people where they live—emotionally and spiritually. It allows for the dissemination of local color, local issues, and local scandals. Talk radio is now aimed primarily at a thirty-five-plus age demographic. If you are wondering how to frame a hot issue, spend time absorbing local media in several markets. Compare the regional differences. It will give you insight on framing any upcoming issues.

The embed experience during the Iraq War will be talked about in communications graduate schools for the next decade. It is hard to be critical when you are living with and depending upon the subjects of your reporting. Any time the public can feel, see, and experience the issues you want to target, you will have rented a bit of space in their hearts and minds.

The 2003 documentary *The Fog of War: Eleven Lessons from the Life of Robert S. McNamara* resulted in a poignant look at the humanity of Robert McNamara, former Secretary of Defense for Presidents Kennedy and Johnson, and who was despised by anti–Vietnam War protestors for decades and labeled a villain of Vietnam. This documentary personalized a much-debated and contentious issue by making McNamara seem human.

In 2001, partially due to personal problems and partially due to the financial state of the city of New York, Mayor Rudy Giuliani dropped to new lows in his popularity rating. The terrorist attacks on 9/11 showed New Yorkers, Americans, and the world that Mayor Giuliani was a strong leader who was not afraid to display his emotions. He let everyone see and feel the loss and pain of his city. He led efforts to bring New Yorkers together to demonstrate for the world that they could unite in tragedy.

He changed his image. He was not only a hero to New York, but also was named *Time* magazine's Person of the Year.

Paint a picture and make it personal. Can people identify with your issue or your spokesperson? Are they of the age demographic you want? Make sure the picture you are painting is one that people can identify with.

On the March 18, 2004, *Larry King Live* show, Tammy Faye Messner announced that she had inoperable lung cancer. She had survived colon cancer eight years earlier and could not come to grips with the fact that she now needed chemotherapy. As she told King, "My doctor says the treatment will be three days every two weeks. And you know, it's so funny, Larry, because a woman is so vain! And the first thing I thought about was, 'Oh, no—I just got my hair right, got the highlights just right, and now I'm going to lose it all!'" Here was a woman who had survived scandals, public humiliation, divorce—and she was worried about losing her hair. She gave us all a glimpse into the very personal side of cancer treatments. Now in her sixties, Messner is an unofficial poster child for lung cancer. The transcript of her interview was placed on several sites, including a Web site for tobacco news and information. Why would the tobacco industry want this interview on their Web site? Because Messner said she never smoked and never even picked up a cigarette in her life. The tobacco industry was using her interview to promote smoking!

Ask yourself if your issue has an impact on your targeted population. Whenever possible, put a human face on every campaign document. However, it is important when making your issue personal that it does not focus on *I*—make it clear that there is a *we*. Use phrases like, "Our members tell us . . ."

Simplify, simplify, simplify!

If you want to sell Valvoline oil, you do not want to spend time describing its complex chemical formula. According to marketing expert Julianne Corbett, people could not care less that it is a high-friction modifier— what they want is something simple like, "Your engine will last longer."

The intricacies of the Medicare debate made the public's eyes glaze over. In order to make your campaign understandable, you have to use visual images. They are crucial, especially to radio audiences. Explaining the proposed gap in coverage made more sense when it was described as a "doughnut hole," an image that depicts nothing in the middle—some coverage, then no coverage, then coverage again.

An entire book could be devoted to the confusion caused by conflicting campaigns on the future of Social Security. Will these programs be around for today's thirtysomething population or the aging baby boomers? Is privatization good or bad? Both sides on the issue financed tremendous campaigns, and in the final analysis, most taxpayers have no idea who wins or what they should support.

In February 2004, then Federal Reserve Chairman Alan Greenspan urged Congress to reduce the growth of Social Security and Medicare, or the nation would face one of the most difficult fiscal situations in its history as seventy-seven million baby boomers begin retiring around 2008. What does this mean? In the end, have the complexities of Social Security been answered?

President Bush scored well with the under-thirty generations by talking about Social Security in terms of an ownership society. However, he needed some help in terms of getting spokespersons other than himself so young that people could identify with the issue. It is all about finding the right salesperson that can put it in clear, understandable language. Jack Schnirman, who is working on the issue, says that the idea of Social Security is very abstract—you can't taste it or touch it. So this means finding a way to make the abstract concrete and important in people's lives.

President Clinton's health-care plan was defeated simply because it scared people. Republicans capitalized on the fear of too much government control in the lives of ordinary people. The Clinton health-care plan seemed beyond the reach and understanding of the average person, because the debate never focused on simple pocketbook issues for individuals and the nation.

Is your issue something everyone is familiar with and can envision? Who can forget the battle strategy for the Iraq War? "Shock and awe" made it into video games, and even entertainer Dolly Parton used the phrase to refer to her large chest at the National Fourth of July celebration on the U.S. Capitol grounds. Use words that create an image and tell a story.

Instead of overloading people with statistics, the liberal Web site costofwar.com compares the overall cost of the Iraq War with what the same money could buy in terms of preschool and public housing needs. This makes the numbers easy to understand.

Before the Iraq War, former Republican National Committee Communications Director Cliff May started an organization called The Defense of Democracy. In order to gain support, television was saturated with women from Iraq telling their stories of rape and abuse. What woman could not sympathize with other women telling these horrible stories?

When trying to get the American public to understand the now infamous mistake of disbanding the entire Iraqi army after the official Iraq War ended, an on-air reporter, Cholene Espinoza, used this analogy she was given from an Iraqi: "Imagine you have a man who has trained his entire life to be a soldier. This is his profession. Now you take away that livelihood, [but] you let him keep his weapon. If you didn't have an enemy before, you have created one now."

The following, a public service announcement (PSA) from the U.S. Department of State, is an example of making a simple message complex:

> International Education Week, [dates] will provide your school and community the opportunity to engage in a global dialog on the value of international perspectives in your local education institutions. This dialogue will demonstrate the Department's strong belief that international education and exchange—public diplomacy—have a critical role in U.S..foreign relations in the next millennium.

Whew! Who can understand what the above script is trying to convey? When was the last time someone asked you to "engage in a global dialogue"? What is "the Department"? Who is going to produce this PSA? It was actually written for Secretary of State Madeleine K. Albright, but nowhere in the script (keep in mind that this was a radio PSA) do we identify who is speaking.

This PSA for International Education Week was intended for a domestic audience, to explain how international education benefits their community. This thirty-second PSA as originally written was (a) too long, (b) too wordy and wonky, and (c) not intelligible to the general public—the desired audience.

After several rewrites, the PSA below aired across the country and represented a change in the method of doing business at the State Department. Suddenly it was easier to reach a domestic audience and it was well within the guidelines of the law.

> This is Secretary of State Madeleine Albright inviting you to join me in celebrating International Education Week [dates] to recognize the importance a global education has on your community. For more information visit the State Department's Web site at www.state.gov.

Public-relations expert Jay Byrne says that you should tailor presentations so that a sixth-grader could understand them. If your goal is to reach a wide audience, cast a wider net, simplify your message, weed out the complexities, and make your campaign understandable.

Timing is crucial.

You have probably heard the real estate adage "location, location, location." There is another saying that is equally as witty and every bit as important: "timing is everything."

An important factor in your goal should be timing. News happens in a twenty-four-hour cycle—especially if you are aiming for a national or international audience. If your audience is local or regional, remember that not all markets have drive-time radio news, local breaks in national TV morning shows, or evening newscasts at a standard time. Generally, the evening news (including national and local news shows) airs from 4:00 P.M. to 7:00 P.M. and from 10:00 P.M. to 11:30 P.M., depending on the market. Your audience may be living in several time zones and your interview may be prerecorded, so it is important to keep time references generic.

A joke with a poorly timed punch line isn't funny. A speech with a reference in poor taste is a flop. Mike Schur, a writer for *Saturday Night Live*, says that after 9/11 they declared a moratorium on Bush humor. They tested the jokes in dress rehearsal and would get negative responses. It took several months to return to the Bush jokes.

Although many have spoken and written about the connection between global warming and recent hurricanes, one person wrote an article titled "For They That Sow the Wind Shall Reap the Wind," as Hurricane Katrina devastated the city of New Orleans. The city's residents were still trapped. The timing could not have been worse.

When planning your campaign, pay close attention to other events, holidays, or annual observances. Obviously, there are slow times of the year, such as the Fourth of July, Christmas, Labor Day, and so on. A media campaign that is ill timed is a disaster. Many public-relations campaigns have been ruined by poor timing. A creatively written campaign, however, can also work to your advantage at these times—especially if your issue fits into these themes.

If your issue is political, it is easier to get attention when Congress or your state legislature is in session. But there are times when it is worth pulling a campaign, even at the last minute, when breaking news is far more important. On 9/11, several Congressional news conferences were canceled at the last minute, mostly due to the uncertainty of what was going to happen. No one was interested in Congressional news. Everyone was glued to their television sets to watch the disasters in New York City, Pennsylvania, and the Pentagon. Events that are totally out of your control may draw attention away from your media campaign, no matter how carefully you have timed its launch.

On July 11, 2001, Congressman Dennis Kucinich, D-Ohio, unveiled legislation to create a cabinet-level Department of Peace. Supported by the Congressional Progressive Caucus, the news conference on the grounds of the U.S. Capitol was large—due in most part to the number of congressional members participating. The media presence was relatively small but impressive. (When members of Congress announce their intent to introduce legislation, it generally isn't newsworthy, although it is usually mentioned in the weekly *What happened in Washington this week?* columns.) However, this new legislation was unusual, was covered by local and national newspapers, and was mentioned on several news and talk-radio shows. It wasn't given serious mention, but was instead reported in a tone of, *Can you believe what they're trying to do in Washington now?*

At the same time the Department of Peace legislation received tremendous positive coverage from the newly emerging Internet press. Two months later, on September 11, 2001, journalists renewed their interest in the legislation and gave it serious mention. After the events of that fateful day, interest in a Department of Peace expanded beyond imagination and fueled Congressman Kucinich's run for president in 2004.

There are other timing concerns, such as when to roll out certain aspects of a campaign. You don't want to move directly to your issue without the public having had an introduction to the problem or situation. Another is when and where to use your spokesperson. Lay out the campaign in stages and be sure you have considered how fast-paced you want it to be.

The "Vote for Change" tour featured a lot of well-known pro-Kerry rock stars, went to several swing states, received a lot of publicity, and was wonderful—but it did not do what it set out to do, which was garner votes. Why not? It was close, but not close enough, to Election Day. It was just a couple of weeks off the timing mark, and that was enough to lessen its impact.

Every year several senators join with the National Institute on Media and the Family to release this nonprofit organization's annual video game report card. The news conference marks the beginning of the holiday shopping season and is held during either Thanksgiving week or the following week, when the news cycle in the nation's capitol is slow because Congress has adjourned. The networks and news organizations are hungry for news—especially news with visuals. At this news conference, the members either hail or condemn the video game industry, marketing, and retailers. It serves to educate parents who might be purchasing video games for holiday gifts and may not know what they are buying. The annual coverage is incredible. Even after several years, the video game campaign still warrants a news conference because it generates so much coverage.

Piggyback your issue on hot news and current events.

Your issue will have more clout and relevance if it is tied to some hot news. Do your homework to find books that are about to be published, movies that are about to be released, and recent magazine and newspaper features relevant to your campaign or issue. If you are planning a local campaign, identify something on a national level that can be tied to the local situation.

Long before the Iraq War and before citizens of the United States were buying huge quantities of duct tape to include in their terrorist survival kits, Henkel Consumer Adhesives, Inc., marketer of Duck brand duct tape, began sponsoring a "Stuck at Prom" scholarship contest. Scholarship money was awarded for the most creative use of duct tape for prom attire.

In 2003 the company received millions of dollars in free advertising—first, because the Department of Homeland Security recommended stocking up on the product, and second, due to the company's creative prom campaign. Many journalists did not realize it was an annual event and thought it was tied to the terrorist alerts. The image played during the antiwar marches in 2003, and "Duct and Cover" (referring to the 1950s atomic bomb preparations) was visible on several posters and signs. The image was also aired on television and discussed on radio.

Liberals had a field day, marrying the arts with antiwar activism. *Lysistrata*, an ancient Greek play about wives who refused to have sex with their husbands if they went to war, had a strong Web, television, and radio presence before the Iraq War began.

The "prayer in school" supporters and the immigration lobby were able to gain sympathy for their causes after 9/11 as well.

Piggybacking your issue or campaign will require research on your part. Take the time to determine how you can adapt the current news of the day to your agenda. It requires out-of-the-box thinking, but it will pay off by getting your agenda out there when others are left behind.

Repetition, repetition, repetition.

Two months after the terrorist acts of 9/11, President Bush signed the law that established the Transportation Security Administration. Originally under the Federal Aviation Administration, the TSA is now under the Department of Homeland Security. Confusing, yes. Changes happened rapidly in the post 9/11 world. The TSA tried to educate the public and made its case before Congress about the evolving list of prohibited carry-on items on flights. Every day new items were prohibited—eyebrow tweezers, chopsticks, scissors (even small cuticle scissors). Because the list of allowable items changed constantly, people weren't kept informed as well as they could have been. The TSA told people to check their Web site before heading to the airport to learn what items were not allowed in their carry-on baggage. Reality check: Who has time to log on to the Web right before heading out for a flight? And even though this is the twenty-first century, not every household is wired for Internet service. TSA did not do a good job of message saturation because the message changed too frequently. These days, before going through magnetometers, people are used to taking off their shoes, emptying their pockets, and taking batteries out of laptops and cameras and cell phones, but it has taken several years to reach this point. Every trip to the airport involves new challenges in getting from the ticket counter to the gate!

Getting your message to the masses is not a one-shot opportunity. To make your message memorable you have to give it time. The message will work with repetition and continuous plugging. While an occasional campaign produces an immediate reaction, such as a new Super Bowl commercial, most campaigns take real saturation and blanketing of the markets.

One member of Congress, who produced a weekly radio feature, wanted to know after just one month why he had not received much reaction. Think of how many decades it has taken for the president's weekly radio address to be included in the Saturday news shows. All forms of media involve continuous repetition if you want long-lasting results. Have you seen an ad for Coca-Cola once, twice, a million times? And every time the company introduces a new flavor—lemon, cherry, vanilla—you still see the same ads for the original Coca-Cola, right?

Keep in mind that talk radio and the Internet can lengthen your campaign. Talk radio can keep an issue alive long after the mainstream media have moved on to other campaigns. For example, an issue that was difficult to understand was the marriage penalty tax. People had heard about it and wondered what it was, but did not know what it meant to them personally. Given time and a repetitive media campaign by several organizations explaining the pros and cons of the marriage tax, the general public agreed that the marriage tax should be eliminated.

Don't let your message get stale. It is important to rejuvenate an old message with a new angle. You can't just keep recycling the same old stuff and expect to see results. As media consultant Aric Caplan points out, "TV is limited by the size of the screen. Magazines and newspapers have detail and graphics but lack timeliness. The talk media is limited only by a listener's interest in a topic." Give your message time and let it saturate, but keep it alive with fresh information.

Being *right* does not always guarantee a spot in the winner's circle.

What is the right side? You might perceive your side to be the moral one, but someone else may think that yours is on the wrong side of the moral compass.

During the heat of the 2004 presidential election Sinclair Broadcasting thought they were morally correct when they planned to air the anti-Kerry film *Stolen Honor.* The pro-Kerry camp thought differently. They accused Sinclair Broadcasting of using the airwaves without balance by promoting their own point of view. This negatively impacted Sinclair's relationship with the Federal Communications Commission, caused their advertisers to drop them because of the controversy, and their shareholders stepped in with concerns of Sinclair becoming front-page news. The lesson here is to think about the long-term implications of your campaign being on what you consider the moral high ground.

All across America people are more aware of security, or lack thereof, since 9/11. In 2003 Secretary of Homeland Security Tom Ridge introduced Americans to a new system of terror alerts. Red, orange, yellow, blue, and green—what did it all mean, and how could an average citizen feel safe from potential terrorist attacks?

After Secretary Ridge unveiled the color-coded Homeland Security Advisory System, the country was transfixed on the security color code of the day. March 17, 2003, to April 16, 2003, when the security threat was moved from Elevated (yellow) to High (orange), schools canceled field trips to the nation's capitol, parking garages in the District of Columbia went into lockdown mode, and missile launchers were strategically parked around metro Washington. The news media pointed out we should not be in a panic, but that we should be aware of these changes. When no real danger followed these inconvenient security codes, they no longer made an impact on our daily lives. The administration did not make clear distinctions about the security threat. Although they had great graphics and eye appeal, there was nothing to connect a security color with an image of what it really meant. In other words, people stopped paying attention. Even though the government thought it was a good idea, it should have been field-tested to see if it would actually work

Environmentalists are always on the side of conservation. This is their *right* side. But conservation sometimes interferes with development or infringes on personal property. Any time you hear that a tree hugger stands in the way of a project, you know he is not going to get a lot of public sympathy, even though he may get a lot of media attention. Until recently, environmentalists have had a difficult time explaining their case to the American public.

Your campaign will be more effective if you use the operative concept of control. Does your audience perceive they will be more in control of their lives with your plan or issue, or less? If you are in an interview situation and the caller or interviewer does not like your position, you can begin by agreeing with them. "I think there is a lot of evidence to support your view, but let me give you some other facts." This takes you off the moral stance, allows the other person to be right, and keeps you in control of the interview. Agreeing to disagree is diplomacy in action.

Make your story *today's* news.

Remember, news is only news if it is new. Most shows are looking for a story that is hot today. As mentioned before, news is a twenty-four-hour cycle. If you are unveiling a great campaign, determine what news cycle or cycles will work best for you. Fridays are generally good days to release information that can go through the weekend. Unless there is a catastrophic event, your issue could carry through Saturday and, in some rare cases, even through Sunday. Many media outlets have fewer people on staff on the weekends, so rip-and-read journalism, (content taken directly off the wire and read almost verbatim), is more common on weekends.

You can get a lot of mileage from one story if you report the results of something that you have covered previously. News organizations like to do follow-ups. Listeners, viewers, and readers of blogs like to know out-comes. Even after the initial story is out, find a way to report results.

In order to get the attention of the editor, program director, or web-master, your news has to have an effect on people and their lives. It must be of local interest or have a clear impact. Sad to say, but one local car pileup is worth five car pileups several states away. News gets attention if there is a celebrity involved. News gets attention if it is strange or unusual. News gets attention if it is new and/or the first of something.

There are several definitions of *news*. It doesn't always have to be infor-mation that is earth-shattering or shocking. News can be light and fluffy. News is best when it can elicit a strong emotional response. It can be about a hero or it can be about someone on the edge of death, as in the Terry Schiavo case. It can be about two sisters who have not seen each other in fifty years. Strong emotions equal news.

Who would have thought that ice cream, the all-American treat, would be part of a presidential campaign? The "Ice Cream Primary" began in summer 2003 when the famous Ben & Jerry's created the Maple-Powered Howard Sundae, a New England tribute to former Vermont Governor Howard Dean. The twist in the new flavor was that Ben Cohen, founder of Ben & Jerry's, actually endorsed another candidate, Congressman Dennis Kucinich. Not to be outdone, the Puritan Backroom Restaurant in Manchester, New Hampshire, created flavors in support of Senator Joe Lieberman; Cup of Joe was a cappuccino treat containing caramel and a streak of chocolate, and Heavenly Hadassah, named after Lieberman's wife, offered a chocolate base with almonds, chocolate chips, and marshmallows. Ice cream was in the news and it wasn't about fat grams or calories!

Federal Reserve Chairman Alan Greenspan testified at a senate com-mittee hearing in July 2003 that natural-gas prices would go down if more sources for domestic natural gas were discovered. Senator Mary Landrieu (D-Louisiana) jumped on his comments and said, "The supply imbalance we face has been years in the making. Quite simply, we have pursued a policy that is in conflict with itself. On the one hand we encourage the use of natural gas in this country to meet our energy needs and environmental goals. However, we have ignored the supply side of the equation. We pro-mote the use of natural gas but restrict its production. I am glad that Chairman Greenspan recognizes this discrepancy."

Senator Landrieu's position, one she had long championed for her Gulf Coast state, was suddenly making as much news as Chairman Greenspan's. Noting that the U.S. economy had thus far escaped harm from rising natural-gas prices, Chairman Greenspan also suggested that we are not apt to return to periods of relative abundance and low prices anytime soon. To consumers not interested in natural gas, a ho-hum day for news—but to the rest of the country, an incredible news hit.

During President Clinton's impeachment trial, a Washington, D.C., law professor began taking apart some of the constitutional issues of the trial. He then faxed his ideas to radio, TV, and Internet talk hosts. He quickly found himself on the air all over the country as an expert on the subject. This was quite an amazing feat for someone who normally would not have had a hot angle that could get him on the air. If you can't think of anything that makes your issue connect with what's hot, get some people in a room and brainstorm. Identify, identify, identify.

Craft a sound bite or catchphrase.

Your message is the crux of your campaign, and the manner in which that message is crafted will stick in the mind of the media consumer. This is the *brand* of your product or organization; it will be what you are known for—your trademark. Consider Animal Planet's "living, breathing entertainment," or Fox News Channel's "we report, you decide" and "fair and balanced."

During the 2004 presidential debates, the public felt Senator Kerry had communicated his message well concerning his agenda, with a rating of more than 51 percent in one poll. This was a dramatic increase from his predebate numbers, but it was not good enough. President Bush's rating was 76 percent. When we asked people on the street, many were able to articulate something about the president's message.

The Gore camp was accused of having too many messages in the 2000 presidential campaign. Try to think of one campaign slogan from that race. Nothing stands out. However, the Bush campaign chose to go with a few messages and they stuck—phrases such as "No child left behind," "I'm a *uniter*, not a divider," "I'm a compassionate conservative." These phrases resonated throughout the campaign. Not only did the Republican ticket win a Supreme Court decision and a ride to the White House, they also won the media campaign for creating the best campaign slogans. Al Gore did redeem himself during his acceptance speech at the 2005 Webby awards. His sound bite? "Please don't recount this vote."

Go with a few phrases that are well-honed and clear. Make your sound bites create an image that is something people can identify with and remember. For example, few Americans will forget the "axis of evil" or the follow-up, "axis of weasels."

As President Clinton defended his position on affirmative action, he came up with the saying "Mend it, don't end it." Corny as it was, it was repeated by a multitude of talk-show hosts and it stuck as a phrase that embodied his administration's philosophy. The president is also widely quoted as talking about "those who work hard and play by the rules."

Chuck Lewis of the Center for Public Integrity coined the term *career patrons* to describe groups who give huge amounts of money through political action committees. And who could forget the phrase from O. J. Simpson's trial, "If the glove doesn't fit, you must acquit." Millard Fuller, the founder of Habitat for Humanity, gives a good illustration of hypocrisy in the phrase, "He's not a Christian; he prays to God once a week and preys on people the rest of the week."

Phrases that stick are the bread and butter of public-relations agencies. If your budget does not include hiring professionals for this purpose, spend the time to craft a phrase that works—it will pay far bigger dividends than buying full-page newspaper ads.

Statistics don't have to be boring.

Spinning statistics is common sport. Consider the battle of unemployment figures. When the unemployment rate rose to 6.4 percent, Labor Secretary Elaine Chao issued a press release stating that it was "disappointing." The release went on to say that tax rebates would stimulate the economy. This was a missed opportunity to make the statistics come alive.

It would have been a great time to release stories about the unemployed and personalize the issue by giving unemployment a face. Experts could have been booked on local radio shows and B roll could have been sent to television stations. (B roll is the secondary footage for a video. In order to string together two interview clips that were not shot consecutively, an editor will cut away from A roll to B roll.)

Statistics and facts will help you. Statistics and facts will empower you. Statistics and facts are hard to refute. It is amazing what a few well-placed and well-illustrated statistics will do. The American Jewish Committee (AJC) sponsored a trip to Israel with talk-show hosts. They spent ten days touring Israel, and the hosts were able to come up with incredible insights and material for their shows. About two weeks after their trip the AJC ran an ad in the *New York Times* presenting information on the number of Jewish refugees who had left Arab countries, providing an interesting counterargument to the Palestinian refugee problem. One host remarked that this small chart had done more to explain the problem than what was learned on the trip. If the AJC information had been given to the broadcast media or to select Internet sites, it would have had a much greater impact than that one expensive ad in the *New York Times*. A show-stopping statistic used sparingly can make all the difference.

Another good way to use statistics is to mix them with stories. Give a statistic, then tell a story or anecdote to illustrate it. Be creative; come up with other indicators. Sometimes the statistics themselves say all that needs to be said. Look at the index of *Harper's* magazine for ideas.

Pros and cons.

Can you list the merits of each point you are trying to make with your strategy or message—or the risks if you stray from the message? If you are going negative by knocking a person or organization, have you considered the impact it will have on the popularity and believability of your message?

Envision your media campaign. Explore all issues that could be generated from your message, both good and bad. Think weapons of mass destruction (WMDs) here. Long after the official end of the Iraq War, WMDs still haven't been found. Secretary of State Colin Powell put his credibility on the line when he delivered a 90-minute presentation to the

UN in February 2003 stating that the United States had every reason to believe Saddam Hussein had WMDs. But no one asked the question, "What if we don't find them?" The Bush administration was criticized by the mainstream media and talk-show hosts around the country—even those who supported the war—questioning why there had been such an urgent need to invade Iraq. The administration had lost some credibility with the American public.

You might think you have a really clever and hard-hitting idea, but be ready for the fallout. You are likely to raise the barometer of someone's passion on the issue. Calculate the risks before undertaking your campaign. Sometimes not responding to a negative reaction will make it go away faster. On the other hand, responding quickly with a product recall, or the public-relations equivalent, might win the public over to your side.

Identify your audience and *speak* to it.

Whatever your media campaign, it is important to keep the specific audience in mind for every interview or ad placement. There is nothing wrong with reaching out to several demographics; if done correctly, it will be a successful campaign. However, if you keep the same message in the same tone for every audience, you might receive an unexpected and unfavorable response. Know your audience—know the demographics.

Because Wal-Mart knows their customer base so well, they knew that customers bought Pop-Tarts at seven times the normal rate before a hurricane. Before the next probable hurricane Wal-Mart trucks bound for Florida were loaded with Pop-Tarts. Whenever you are in a local news market or doing a niche or specialty show, you need to load your *talk inventory* with items that will be of interest to that audience—the types of language and ideas they will put into the basket of their mind.

You must also understand consumer and voter behavior. This involves working diligently to understand what motivates people. What and how are they thinking?

If you have been booked for a talk-radio show, do you know the audience profile? If you don't have a media expert booking shows for you and you are doing this without professional media guidance, don't be intimidated—ask. Producers would rather you ask about their audience than have you assume who the audience is.

If you are doing a morning radio show, consider the many formats on the air:

- The "morning zoo" mixes music, entertainment, and oftentimes sophomoric interviews.
- Sports radio is geared toward sports fans. Are you sure your issue is appropriate for this audience, or will you be roasted by the hosts?
- News radio is straight news. Is your issue really a news topic, or can you spin it to become newsworthy?
- Religious radio has a strong presence. Never underestimate the power of the religious format.

It takes time to get to know the market. Kandy Stroud, former director of radio for the Democratic National Committee, was at the task for more than seven years. She knew every producer, host, audience, and the demographics of the audience. Former Republican National Committee radio director Scott Hoganson was brought back to the RNC for the 2004 campaign because he knew everyone in the radio business, including the talk media in every county. Both Kandy and Scott are fifty-plus years old. Young twentysomethings who would not have known the industry and the audience demographics just could not have cut it.

People in traditional news markets were surprised to hear how younger people are getting their hard news. *The Washington Post* reports that Comedy Central's *The Daily Show* has more than double the audience of MSNBC's *Hardball*. The Pew Research Center found that one-half of the viewers in the eighteen-to-twenty-nine-year age range sometimes learn about their news from *The Daily Show*.

Public radio's audience is about twenty-seven million. In any fifteen-minute period it garners an audience of about 1.8 million people. Like most formats, it plays to a very specific audience.

After you have identified the format, identify the age range of the audience. Again, ask the producer or guest booker for this information. If you feel the producer has not given you enough information, make a follow-up call to the station. Receptionists can be very helpful as you investigate the pros and cons of doing a particular show. Will you be speaking to an audience between the ages of eighteen and forty-five, or are they senior citizens? No matter what age group listens to the interview program, don't sound patronizing—but also don't sound foolish by trying to be hip for a younger audience.

If your issue is political, it is important to know that some polls have indicated that 77 percent of Americans feel the federal government controls too much of their daily lives, and 81 percent feel that government is wasteful. A *Times Mirror* survey revealed that callers to talk-radio shows can have the most extreme antigovernment sentiments. Before coming up with solutions that involve the government, remember these statistics. Acknowledge the general feeling, quote the statistics to show that you are at least aware of the general concerns of the population, and then make your argument.

Keep the demographics of your target audience in mind. This is as important as the age of the audience. Are the listeners affluent? Are they streetwise? Are they white-collar workers or blue-collar workers? Will this radio campaign reach women in their thirties driving BMWs in northeastern cities, or will it reach men in their fifties driving trucks in the rural South?

James Gilmartin, an expert on the baby boomer generation, says that products are the gateway to experiences. It is no different on the air. What people hear or see is the gateway to their personal experience—of an issue, a political personality, or even a product that you want them to buy. One radio host actually puts a photograph in front of his microphone that illustrates his audience. It's not a bad idea. Cut out photos from magazines and newspapers representing your target demographics. Enlarge copies of them and put them on your walls, desks, and computer screens so you will remember the audience you are targeting as you craft your message.

An audience will often tune in to a program because they like the message. For Andrew Sullivan's blog site, the first year people liked what they were reading, and in a very short period of time he had raised eighty thousand dollars. He began to disagree with the administration about the policy in Iraq, and the second year he raised twenty thousand. By the third year it was down to twelve thousand. While it is true that people tune in for controversy, they also tune in for confirmation of who they are and what they believe.

There is a basic cynicism of the American public at this stage in our history. A *Times Mirror* survey showed that the greatest level of cynicism occurs between people age thirty and thirty-nine, followed by those in the forty-to-forty-five age bracket. As you define your audience and plan your message, allow for this cynicism.

Stereotypes and misconceptions.

Does your issue have any baggage? Can your opponent exaggerate misconceptions or stereotypes to the point where your audience may not be able to distinguish fact from fiction? The world of politics is a perfect example of where the *perception* of misconceptions has financed hundreds of local, regional, and national campaigns.

There was a lot of focus on NASCAR dads during the 2004 elections. The Democrats thought they had lost them as voters because of the misconceptions about them. There are seventy million NASCAR fans and they have an average yearly household income of seventy-five thousand dollars. They could not have all been conservatives. The Republicans marketed them heavily because they understood that NASCAR fans are loyal consumers. They went beyond the stereotypes to get to the voters.

Examples of some perceptions and misconceptions about Democrats:

- A Democrat is liberal. Any politician who leans toward the middle or the left is characterized as a liberal.
- Democrats are whiners and hate America.
- Democrats are not strong on defense.
- Democrats are antibusiness.
- Democrats want to raise taxes.
- Democrats support overregulation.
- Democrats want to take all the guns away.
- Democrats are anti–family values.

Examples of some perceptions and misconceptions about Republicans:

- A Republican is conservative. Any politician who leans toward the right is characterized as a conservative.
- Republicans are Christian and pro-life.
- Republicans are usually white males.
- Republicans are intolerant of alternative lifestyles.
- Republicans support big business, especially oil interests.
- Republicans are antienvironment.
- Republicans support isolationism.

Be prepared to confront how your issue dovetails with these common stereotypes. Your media plan should address common assumptions in a way that is believable to your audience. Remember to anticipate how the public will react to the position you have taken and balance that with sensible, reasonable responses to their concerns. Be able to give concrete examples of how your position will make their lives better. Be sure that your message appeals to people who work for a living. If you can afford it, invest in focus-group research prior to releasing your message. If not, conduct your own man-on-the-street research. Survey people in coffee shops, malls, supermarkets, and so forth as to what they think. A few hours spent in different locales, conducting your personal research will do wonders toward ensuring that your message will reach your intended audience. When surveying people, remember that your interpersonal communication is as important as the words you use. Keep your tone, eye contact, and body language in check. Don't confirm a stereotype by the way you present yourself.

2

MARKETING YOUR CAMPAIGN, ISSUE, OR SPOKESPERSON

Be creative.

The grassroots political Web site MoveOn.org produced a clever campaign ad called "Child's Pay." There was no dialogue for the ad, only shots of children doing adult jobs as maids, factory workers, garbage men, assembly line employees, and dishwashers. The only words in the thirty-second ad were, "Guess who's going to pay off President Bush's $1 trillion deficit?" The CBS network refused to air the ad during the Super Bowl in January 2004. The ban from CBS made news and resulted in countless free airplay on other networks. Kathleen Hall Jamieson, an expert on political advertising and head of the Annenberg Public Policy Center, told *Newsweek* that the ad would be remembered as "the ad that has achieved the most airtime with the least dollars expended of any ad in the history of the republic."

Target Corporation had a preholiday effort in which customers registered for wake-up calls from one of a number of kooky characters on the day after Thanksgiving—what is known now as Black Friday, the busiest shopping day of the year. Target did this to involve their shoppers, and in 2005 they even added a bedtime call with sheep. People like to be part of the fun, and Target's strategy addressed this.

BillionairesforBush.com, a liberal, satiric Web site, put the Social Security program up for auction on eBay. It was taken off quickly, but not before they got their message out that Wall Street would, according to them, get $279 billion dollars in fees. They then took the eBay auction and sent it to every media outlet they could find.

The Democratic National Committee gave its first Chicken Little Awards, replete with stuffed-animal chickens, for comments Republicans had made that the sky would fall. It was well conceived and made it on the evening news.

The Republicans sent out thousands of mouse pads during the 2000 election with Al Gore's photograph and a quote: "I took the initiative in creating the Internet." It didn't matter that it was taken out of context. It served as a constant reminder to the press that the Republicans painted Al Gore as a liar. He did not *invent* the Internet.

An environmental group staged a twenty-one-chain-saw salute in front of the Department of the Interior to protest logging.

Several years ago, the sugar lobby gave media outlets an all-day sucker along with their pitch about the price of sugar.

In the same way, you can develop games and giveaways to get your project noticed, to get people to interact with your Web site, to answer poll questions, and to collect e-mail addresses. Almost a decade ago, during the long and arduous 1995 budget debate, Empower America developed a "Balance the Budget Game" in paper form and later on the Internet. It made the point for the organization in a way that involved the public. It was effective because hosts could use the questions on the air and the organization was able to drive home their message by leading people to the answer on their own.

Your strategy should also be geared generationally. Brander Peter Arnell says that the younger generation likes the hunt. They don't want everything put right in front of them. They want to be part of the experience to build the message and the brand.

For the couch-potato generation Dr. James Rosser developed an interactive movie that has viewers attempt to rescue an overweight guy who has diabetes and high cholesterol. The title? *Escape from Obeez City*.

Both the right and the left have recently put Social Security calculators on Web sites. Although the calculations differ, it provides a simple way to illustrate the points each side is trying to get across and involves people on a personal level.

A labor advocacy group brought bumper stickers to shows for hosts to give away. The stickers said, "The Labor Movement—the folks who brought you the weekend."

One cell phone company positioned staffers with camera phones in public places to take photos of people on the street and then e-mailed them their photos. They made it personal and not just the same old verbal sales pitch.

This kind of sales and messaging has spawned an entirely new form of marketing that uses people who are trained to go places such as bars, sporting events, and the Internet to create buzz. There is now a Word of Mouth Marketing Association (WOMMA) and a group that signs up individuals to become BzzAgents.

The Republican National Committee and the Democratic National Committee sponsor a steady stream of games on their respective Web sites.

Elaine Angel and her AngelWorks team are experts at radio giveaways. They have worked with stations to give away CDs with budget kits, MP3 players, and so forth. She has no problem getting her guests on radio. Stations and producers pay attention to her because she is always there with something that is going to attract listeners to the programs.

As with most professions, many in the media business, especially those in television, have huge egos. Use those egos to your advantage. During most of the 2000 presidential campaign, Al Gore did not hold news conferences. Appealing to the egos of the reporters, the Republican National Committee issued a daily fax with a photo of a different reporter in a stockade. The fax was titled "Reporters Held Hostage," and every day, as sure as the sun came up, a photo of a different reporter came across the fax wires and appeared on the Internet. It got the reporters' attention, and Al Gore finally had a press conference. The RNC received a lot of free publicity and the reporters were amused by the antics. Learn how the media operates and take advantage of that knowledge. (More on this later.)

Go ahead and do some wild things that will attract attention. Send out great cartoons—those that make *you* laugh about your issue. Both major political parties have some excellent cartoons that have circulated around the world on the Internet.

When the Hooters restaurant chain opened in Chinatown in Washington, D.C., they developed a creative tactic to make their case for their trademark females-only waitstaff. Hooters Frisbees flew all over Washington, D.C., depicting photos of male waiters dressed in drag. The Frisbees created their own buzz; everyone wanted one. Capitol Hill staffers were leaving their offices in pursuit of a free Hooters Frisbee. Hooters understood that people want to be part of something—they want to be part of the buzz. The Hooters event made for a great PR campaign, and somehow the Equal Employment Opportunity Commission lost its intense interest in the Hooters case.

Be clever. Have fun with your pitch and campaign. Chances are the people who are the intended recipients of your message will too.

Put together a great press kit.

A great press kit is essential. Many people make the mistake of creating press kits only for those reporters attending the news conference or event. Don't forget press kits for those who do not attend the event. There may be a very good reason why the reporter said he or she would attend but could not. The number one issue is often time; there are only so many column inches, or so many broadcast seconds, available to fit into a newspaper or a newscast. Also when a newspaper or station is budget crunching, there are fewer reporters available to cover all those issues. The bottom line is to remember who is *not* at the event and to get your press kit to them.

Your press kit should tell the story, inform the producer or host, include sound and pictures that illustrate the story, give access to your spokespersons, and have links and information to support your story. Most of all it should be *interesting* and *different*. Would you stop something you are doing to hear or watch a story? That is your litmus test, and you want it to stand out in your press kit.

Press kits come in all sizes, shapes, and formats. Take a look at other press kits before you assemble yours. Spread them out on a large surface. What works? What jumps out at you? What gets lost in the sea of paper? You may choose to have more than one press kit—one or more for local markets, one for national, one for print, one for television, and so forth. Richard Strauss of Strauss Media Strategies says that if you are targeting your release to radio only and are alerting producers and hosts that you have a guest ready to be booked for an interview, do not send the same release to television. Write your release so it is targeted to each medium.

Being clever with a press kit or mailing may prolong the recognition of your issue, but it does not guarantee impact. There is a very fine line between being clever and being *too* clever.

Let's focus on a standard press kit in a typical pocket folder. The assumption here is that the press kit is not for an immediate story. Remember that the number one concern is time. You don't want to burden producers, hosts, or reporters with too much information, but you want to provide enough for them to cover your issue completely and correctly.

Your pitch should appear on the outside of the kit. Do you have a quote, a one-liner, or an image you are pushing? Make sure it is the first thing a producer sees.

Inside the folder, you should include an up-to-date press release. If you are recycling a press release from a previous campaign, make the release sound fresh. The fastest way to ensure negative coverage is to try to pretend this is new. Don't. It could backfire on you. Make sure you type ### at the end of each release so people know not to look for a second or third page. Include an FAQ (frequently asked questions) sheet and to-the-point answers. Have questions and answers that provide a complete picture of your issue. If there could be a negative side, bring it up in the FAQ and turn it into a positive. Provide a current bio of your spokesperson and her connection to the campaign, as well as talking points. Summarize your issue in a one-page sheet and highlight with bullets or quick headers that a producer can use to promote your issue and spokesperson.

Press releases should be written as well as a news story. Each release should have a lead and then the story that answers the basic questions. It will often wind up in the local newspaper untouched, so make it interesting. Make it is as brief as possible, still providing the basic information. They are often called one-sheets for a reason. Keep the formatting easy to use and make sure that contact phone numbers will be answered by someone knowledgeable. If it goes to a second page, make that clear. Use *The Associated Press Stylebook* for formatting and grammar.

After your materials are gathered, check their placement in the folder. Is the most important piece of information on the right side of the folder as you open it? The person who opens that folder will more than likely look at the right side first. Also if the left side is weighted down, the materials may fall out when the folder is opened.

Don't forget to produce an Internet-based press kit (EPK) as well—one that is easy to download in various formats. Whether you include JPEG, pdf, or wav files with your basic press release will determine how much extra play you receive.

Public-relations strategist Susan Solomon says that a virtual press kit should provide the same material as the paper version, and then some.

Solomon's guidelines for online press kits recommend including:

The absolute latest news. Journalists who have come to expect the most up-to-the-minute information from your site will seek out your virtual press kit; it's a matter of consistently fulfilling expectations.

Downloadable high-resolution pictures. Take a cue from Sony, which provides specs for all the downloadable images in its press kits.

Audio and video clips. Definitely include multimedia. For extra punch, include a transcript for time-starved reporters.

Backgrounders. Make sure the information in the backgrounder is relevant to the latest announcement/product you are pitching. Some backgrounders are too generic and simplistic to fill journalists' needs.

Up-to-the-minute event calendars and timelines. Keep your calendars and timelines updated to the point of changing them daily.

Make it easy for the media to retrieve information, and you won't be disappointed with the response you receive. On the day of your interview, if scheduled late in the day, resend your talking points to the producer. Many people still fax—some news organizations prefer to get that piece of paper—but also have an alternative method of sending out information. Send an e-mail, text message, or a CD with the highlights of your press kit.

If grass roots are your target, give them the kind of press tools they will need right on the Internet. A group called DontAmend.com had numerous materials ready for downloading from their Web site. Included was a poster for a rally (complete with instructions for copier settings), a ready-to-go handbill, a sample news release, a talking-points issue, a sign-up sheet for volunteers, a step-by-step guide on how to organize a rally (including a shopping list for supplies, such as an office stapler), a timeline for the day of the event, local people to contact, and so forth. Of course, this was readily available for the opposition also, but you could password-protect this information if you consider it too sensitive. It was completely idiot-proof.

If your organization's affiliates need a press kit they can adapt locally, put your materials in a cut-and-paste format and they can just add it to their own material. Again, if you don't want the world to see what you are doing, password-protect your material or develop an intranet site.

Sometimes your press kit is the only communication you may have with the media. Make a good impression. Fill your press kit with useful information and facts, and you may be rewarded with good coverage. However, be careful not to put so much material in your press kit that the press won't need to attend your event.

Make your sound and video easily obtainable.

Since the advent of the computer age, there is very little use for an *actuality line*—a line radio stations could call and access sound or a quote they could use in a newscast or talk program. Although there are still stations that are not computer savvy, most radio stations are capable of using MP3 files, which are best for sound-only clips. These audio files can be added to your Web page and e-mailed as a wav file to the broadcast outlet.

It is interesting to note that during the 2004 Iowa primaries, Howard Dean's campaign called each radio station with audio that they fed over the phone because several stations did not have the ability to retrieve audio files over the computer. In large regional and national campaigns this is not an issue, but when each district or vote counts you must be able to reach all the media. Give them what they need in the way they can receive it.

The Dean campaign hired a consultant, Maria Leavey of January Communications, to offer radio actualities from candidate Dean on the campaign trail. According to Leavey, Dean believed in making the big issues local—like what the war in Iraq meant to voters in Iowa. It was very successful, especially when he included the town name in his actuality. Leavey said, "Sometimes it's easier to get on local radio because there has been a decline in local news due to a media consolidation of radio news. Make your actuality local and you will have a better chance of having a station use it." She also recommended making sure you know what the hot issue is in the city or state, and then developing your message to address that issue. When asked for the secret to her success, Leavey commented, "I don't pitch audio.

I offer actualities. They have to be timely and they have to be local." She made it her business to understand the needs of the station and the news director, for example, talking to each news director and finding out what type of audio they use or were looking for. She can tell you the personal concerns of every local station and how it relates to the national agenda. Her research pays off in her ability to place guests and sound.

To get sound only, the best method is to use the MP3 format. These audio files can be added to your Web page and e-mailed as a .wav file to the broadcast outlet.

In the olden days of actualities, they were kept short because editing was time consuming and difficult. Now with programs such as Adobe Audition, it is affordable, fast, and easy to edit digital audio. The decision you need to make is to either control the message with short sound bites (ten to twenty seconds) and risk not having your entire message used, or to do longer clips of sound that might be edited but might also have a greater chance of being used. This is one of those catch-22 situations. Many stations do not have the staff to reedit audio, and they will use the shorter sound bites rather than the longer ones. You can upload the entire news conference or speech on your Web site, plus a transcript if you have had someone transcribe the event. Otherwise, add the statement with the caveat *as prepared* near the headline to distinguish it from *as delivered*. (For example, the prepared State of the Union speech is released a few hours before it is delivered, but it may change during the actual delivery.)

Some tips:

- Make sure the quality of the sound is consistent and good. If you put out bad sound, producers, hosts, and webmasters will be hesitant to listen again.
- Listening takes time. Maximize yours by offering crisp and clear audio. If the audio is questionable or muffled, provide a transcript of the quote. For longer pieces, if you do not have the exact transcript, provide a description of where specific quotes can be found.
- Be certain that what you are offering has news value; don't cry wolf. When a news organization sees your material, you want them to use your audio. If the audio is boring or old news, it

won't be used and you may not get a second opportunity to pitch the audio. If you want repeated contact with the media, offer them usable audio.

- If you are using an actuality line as opposed to an MP3, or if you happen to be in the middle of Iraq and can't send an MP3 file, send each actuality twice so the sound levels can be adjusted.
- If you have an event scheduled, find out from the news organizations what interests them. They might tell you exactly what they are looking for—"We are looking for a reaction to . . ." If you can deliver, it will ensure placement.
- Fax, e-mail, and phone the news organization once you have your sound. Tell them what you have and be willing to edit what they need.
- Any sound you send should have the total time written beside it.
- If your spokesperson speaks another language, such as Spanish, consider sending a translation or the primary sound in that language.

For the older stations that still do not use an MP3 format and use an actuality machine, you will want to send out instructions that say something like the following:

> The actuality is available by calling: 800-XXX-XXXX, then dialing code X, then:
> Enter 1—Back up five seconds
> Enter 2—Replay the message
> Enter 3—Pause and press play to continue
> Enter 4—Advance 5 seconds
> Enter 5—Forward to end of message

Robert Stone, former Hill and Knowlton executive, states that there are more than ten thousand radio stations burning up material (music and words) at the rate of six thousand words an hour. He says a one-minute script will result in hundreds of placements.

Video can be sent via satellite for a video news release (VNR) and B roll. You should make it available to video journalists at your news conference as well as placing video on your Web site. Technically it is still somewhat difficult to get broadcast-quality video from the Internet. Most television networks use the Intranet to grab and edit video. The upside of providing Web-based video is that broadcast venues can add your video to their Web site. Some Web sites have almost as much traffic as their broadcast venue.

You can also provide a satellite feed of your televised news conference. Include B roll and sound bites if you do not have the budget to send the entire event over the satellite. Call your broadcast media in advance to determine a good satellite time for them to downlink the feed and what satellite their station can *see*. Often they have other commitments for their satellite time, and sending a feed right before their newscast is a wasted effort. Confirm the satellite time and coordinates well in advance of the actual satellite window.

The bottom line is to provide audio and video that is easy to access, download, or downlink. The burden is on you to provide it. Take the pressure off the media!

Let your history give your credibility a boost.

In the never-ending search for relevant ways to bring up your issue, don't forget your organization's or candidate's history. Think about creative and timely ways to highlight your credentials.

A great example is one the Republicans employed during the anniversary of women's suffrage. The Republicans sent out massive amounts of publicity that the Twenty-First Amendment was introduced by a Republican. Most people were completely unaware that Republicans had promoted women's suffrage.

Even if your organization is new and does not have a history or your candidate does not have a political pedigree, using other historical references gives instant credibility if used correctly. No matter what your issue, you can refer to some historical connection. Be creative, but don't stretch beyond reasonable limits.

Be aware that your opposition can use your organization's history to make it appear unstable or to be changing with the winds of perceived fortune. History gives your issue prominence and respectability, but be aware of how it could possibly hurt your message.

Find other ways to bolster your credibility.

Credibility can be a problem if you and your organization are not well known. Therefore, you must be ready to bolster the audience's confidence in you. List speaking engagements and any broadcast programs on which you have been a guest. Don't embellish. If you haven't made any other public appearances, don't fabricate any. Getting caught in a lie will definitely hamper your credibility!

A company can promote the respect it gains from consumers in other ways. This would also be a good time to highlight the mission and values of your organization or your campaign. If appropriate, use it when you are pitching your spokesperson. Have it available for all staff members who talk to the media.

Several years ago, when Tylenol bottles were tampered with, Johnson & Johnson immediately took these products off the shelf. This act helped tremendously with their corporate credibility.

Utilize the research you have gathered using techniques defined later in this book, and find ways to make the information accessible to the public. Take your information on your opponent's arguments and put it on a chart, side by side with your information.

During the 2004 primary debates, a few of the campaigns had their research on the opposition at hand. While the debate was taking place they were handing out rebuttals to the press and sending them via e-mail. All systems were ready to go; they just had to plug and play. Note: It is best to counter the *points* made by the opposite side, not the personality of your opponent.

Relate to the needs of the audience by supporting their existing belief system and experience. Make allowances for the diverse nature of the audience. Tie it into something you have experienced that was similar: "I've been there" or "I know where you're coming from." Quote experts— especially if those people or organizations are household names. Provide recent positive examples of what you or your organization have promised and provide the results, including concrete examples and references. If you have had specific measurable results, then by all means use them. Weave them into your delivery, but do it in such a way that you don't sound like a statistics geek.

Be prepared to address scandals or troublesome history in a nondefensive and simple manner, and then move beyond the issue by focusing on current activities.

Control the *chyron* (the printed name/title or other information that appears on the television screen under the person on camera) and the introduction. Discuss beforehand how you or your spokesperson will be labeled: John Doe, Spokesman for Organization, or John Doe, CEO of Organization, or John Doe supports this issue. On the radio or in a chat room, the right introduction is essential. How the audience perceives your credibility at that time can make or break you.

Do something fun or interesting and do it regularly.

The Congressional Progressive Caucus came up with a "Gilded Lily" award for the group that benefited the most from congressional corporate welfare. Republican Congressman Joel Hefley of Colorado began a "Porker of the Week" award (as in government pork). He made a name for himself and, more importantly, he was willing to get on the air outside of his Congressional district. Congressman Hefley announced his winner on radio stations all over the country.

Citizens Against Government Waste has a "Pink Pig Book" that details all kinds of government waste. CNN's Lou Dobbs has written a book, *Exporting America*, about jobs going overseas. Fox News Channel's Bill O'Reilly has his "No-Spin Zone" nightly talking points.

When something is touted on a regular basis on television, radio, and the Internet, people will begin to participate. Creating an event that is a regular campaign ensures regular radio and television bookings and participation in ongoing chat rooms on the Internet.

A few senators have regular coffee chats in Washington in the morning so visiting constituents can have a meet-and-greet opportunity with their senator and get their photo taken. If you are from outside the beltway and you know that your U.S. senator hosts a coffee chat every Thursday morning in Washington, why not stop by while visiting the nation's capitol? Why not promote the chat on the air and invite folks to stop by? Some politicians make regular stops at local diners. The media is invited and these outings become a regular, dependable way to generate publicity. If there is too much hard news at the time and the media doesn't show up, it still builds a loyal constituency.

When the American Meat Institute hosts their annual hot dog give-away on Capitol Hill, People for the Ethical Treatment of Animals (PETA) has a *veggie* hot dog giveaway at the same time. One year their invitation read, *Lettuce Entertain You*, complete with information that Playboy Bunnies dressed in lettuce leaves would be giving out the veggie dogs. True to their invitation, Playboy Bunnies dressed in lettuce leaves gave out veggie hot dogs fresh from the grill on the steps of the Rayburn House Office Building. It wasn't even Easter, yet this bunny sighting was the talk of town!

People love predictions. They love to guess with you and also be able to take you to task when you are wrong. Liberal economist Paul Krugman made a prediction in his column about the lies that would be told at the debates. It was a fun piece and got good talk-radio attention. On the same theme, one group gave out lollipops with *Lies Suck* written on one side of the candies, with a reference to their Web page on the other.

Jon Stewart of *The Daily Show* created a hilarious guide to the news. He called it "New Calculus: A Cheat Sheet for Reporters." It had a decoder with such items as: IR (Investigative Reporter) = TV Reporter + Leather Jacket; and TP (TV Pundit) = Fired Advisor + 2 years + Mounting Debt. It was distributed during the New Hampshire primary, and the traditional press, along with the Internet and talk media, loved it!

The Dean campaign gave reporters a Democratic debate "pre-buttal" that read:

> Today _____ (candidate, candidate, candidate,
> etc.) continued their _____ (adjective, adjective) attacks on
> Governor Dean's record on _____(vital Democratic issue).

It went on like that for two pages and was met with smiles from the press.

During the 2004 election cycle political humor was everywhere on the Net. JibJab.com had more than 50 million hits for "This Land is Your Land," (a satirical take on the traditional song). Why was it so popular? It was poking fun at both sides.

Picking up on JibJab's success, Consumers Union developed a song with animation aimed at the drug industry and used JibJab's Web site to distribute it. Using all the media they could, they also used the public-relations acumen of the magazine *Mother Jones* to direct people to JibJab's Web site.

For Thanksgiving 2005 AmericanGreetings.com developed an e–greeting card of a turkey singing "I Will Survive." As of Thanksgiving Day, AmericanGreetings.com had 36 million hits.

Tucker Eskew, founding partner of ViaNovo, LP, and former G.W. Bush White House media director, says, "The challenge is still old world eyeball aggregation [the number of people who are viewing the animation]. What gets really interesting is if you are able to track through purchasing behavior as a result of those impressions."

With tongue in cheek, Katrina Vanden Heuvel launched "The Republican Dictionary" to discern what the words used by the right really meant. The Weekly Standard has funny parody every week. Humor works on both sides of the aisle.

The Republican National Committee has a regular feature titled "An Elephant Never Forgets." It features quotes from Democrats that contradict their current positions. Whenever possible, they attach sound or video to it. Newsrooms notice the features because the format is easy and fun.

The Democrats have their blog, "Kick Ass." It has star billing on their Web site. Some of this is just for fun and some is to take an opinion poll or to garner voter registrations.

House parties, Meet-ups (using the Internet to organize people with common interests to meet personally), and conference calls have changed the way organizations get the word out. A one-time media push should generate media coverage, but regular events should generate consistent coverage. Avoid being crude, and have fun.

Have some class.

It pays to do things with style and grace—people won't forget being treated well.

When *Talkers Magazine* announces the 100 Most Influential Talk-Show Hosts each year, the Republicans in the U.S. House of Representatives respond with congratulatory letters and phone calls to these hosts. Yes, it takes time, and someone needs to organize the letter writing and phone calls, but what an incredible payoff this effort generates. The hosts mention on the air that they have received a note or call from Republicans. They also mention that they have had no contact from the Democrats. Who looks better in the eyes of the public? Obviously the Republicans do—for being classy, for reaching out without an agenda, and for simply congratulating hosts on a job well done.

If one of your regular hosts has an anniversary, a wedding, or an important birthday coming up, note it, call in, and congratulate the host. The same is true if there has been a death in the radio family or another tragedy—send a note or make a call. Manners matter. Above all, be genuine. Never do something expecting a return on your investment of time. Everyone will see right through that.

The *New York Post* reported on the classiest guy of all, Roger Ailes from Fox News Channel. According to the *Post* in an April 8, 2001, column, "Roger Ailes had a warm welcome for a handful of protestors who showed up Friday in the rain. The radical members of Project Blackout believe the media has conspired in a vast cover-up, refusing to report the 'truth' about how the Republicans 'stole' the election of George W. Bush. So Ailes had a message for the rain-soaked demonstrators posted on the electronic billboard zipper of the News Corp Building: *Welcome Project Blackout protestors. . . . The most powerful name in news is glad to provide something for you to do today. . . . Rest assured, we'll give a fair and balanced report as always.* Ailes then provided the demonstrators with pots of coffee and Fox News umbrellas, which they gladly employed.

Mayor Michael Bloomberg had an unobtrusive photographer follow him while doing his radio row interviews during the Republican National Convention. A couple of weeks later each host received a personally signed picture of the host interviewing the mayor. Very classy!

Following your interview send a thank-you note to the host. Even if you disagreed on the air or felt that your performance wasn't as good as you had hoped it would be, thank the host for giving you the opportunity to inform the public about your issue. If you took calls, comment on how well informed the audience was. You don't have to go overboard with your thanks, but do keep in mind that the show could have spent time promoting another issue during your airtime. Start and finish your pitch with class.

Be *the* source for information.

The goal is to become the go-to person or organization. You want to become not only the person they can call if they need a last-minute guest, but also a fountain of information on a particular topic. Become someone who can give reliable information about your views and the opposition's views. You are the person who knows where all the data is buried, the clearinghouse and the search engine for the media on your topic. But be fair; don't become a media hog and clamor to be in the spotlight. And do not fabricate your opponent's position on the issue.

Mike Collins of Mike Collins Public Relations says that many reporters are cynical and by nature resist authority, but all reporters are lazy. You must do their job for them. Go to producers with a story with a bow wrapped around it: What would their editor want? How many sources can you provide? Offer information on people who might talk against you. Provide them a story *in a box with a bow on top*.

If you want to be the source of information, give it away. The National Association of Evangelicals decided to play off the November 2004 elections and have a half-day forum at the National Press Club titled "What Is an Evangelical?" They brought in people from all over the country. This was a great idea for a very interesting event designed to provide real information from the source. It was spoiled, however, when they charged a nominal fee of twenty-five dollars. In a town where information is provided to the press at no cost, why would someone choose to pay even a nominal fee? If you want to be the resource for information, give it away.

Keep a send pile by your desk. If you know that a host or producer is interested in a topic, clip and mail or e-mail them important information you know they will want to read. The keyword here is *important*. No one wants to have her desk or e-mail cluttered with information that isn't relevant, so pick and choose carefully. If you offered a guest to a program and, due to time limitations, the guest was unable to tell the entire story, send the producer or host additional information.

If talk professionals think that you are including them beyond just sending them your regular press releases, they will be more inclined to take your call and your pitch. The Republicans send the same memos to hosts that they send to their high rollers and insiders. The hosts appreciate being on the inside. Hosts do not like to feel like they are being spun, so any inside information is always welcome.

Good hosts and producers always do their own research, but any information you provide will be welcome. If you send graphs, charts, sources, or statistics be sure your information is clearly sourced. You don't want to be accused of fabricating information. That mistake could prove to be more newsworthy than the issue you are trying to promote.

Programs will often continue to discuss issues for weeks after you have been on the air, so keeping fresh material on the desks of the hosts and producers is essential. Do not send so much material that you give away your punch line. Send good information, but make it enticing so a producer will want your spokesperson to come on the air and fill in the blanks.

Be available during a time of crisis—even if you are not an expert on the issue. If you have interesting comments or insight, or if you can contribute real information in support of your issue, do not overlook any opportunity to bring that position to the air. You may discover that your new position as a source of real information leads to other opportunities.

Make your message work in today's world.

Keep up with words and style. One female politician appeared at a television interview right after 9/11 wearing a beautiful suit with the bold, bright colors from the 1970s. Her appearance was inappropriate during this somber time and it contradicted her verbal message. During the 1970s she was a very popular politician and mistakenly thought her image didn't need to be updated for the new millennium. The same holds true for your words and message—they must not be out of date.

Use culturally sensitive words and language that work. Political and cultural correctness has taken on new meaning in the post-9/11 world. Even the words *us* and *them* can be used against you if you are trying to distinguish between two groups or two ideals.

Look at Searchmarketing.yahoo.com/srch/index.php and other Web sites to find out how an issue has been searched and what buzzwords people are using. To discover how people are talking about an issue, look at Usenet.com and groups.google.com.

Be cautious when crafting a message for today's audiences. As stated before, don't make a fool of yourself or your organization by trying to sound hip. Do not overextend by attempting to reach highly diverse audiences with the same message. Be certain your words, image, and press kit can be understood by each audience. Unless you are hoping to get a quick mention on Comedy Central's *The Daily Show* with Jon Stewart, or to be ridiculed on CNN's *Late Edition* with Wolf Blitzer, stick to what you know and what works. If you are not sure that your words, message, and appearance are current, get an image consultant or a media expert to help you.

Know what works locally. Several candidates in 2004 in primarily Republican or Democratic districts did better than did their respective presidential candidate—Kerry or Bush—and they did this by understanding their local communities.

The *Financial Times* tells the story of a man in Clark County, Ohio, who won his race by fifteen points, but President Bush had won by only two points. How did he do it? When he saw that the race with his Democratic challenger was getting closer, he ran an ad with his five grandchildren and his two dogs that said, "I'd like your vote so that I can continue to make Clark County a great place to live for my grandchildren [the children waved] and my grand dogs [the dogs barked]." He knew his demographics and what would work.

Make your event unique and open to the media.

The pressure is on. Only you can make your press event so interesting that the media will want to cover it, whether they attend on their own or if you host them.

When the New Jersey Nets announced they were moving to Brooklyn, New York, it was not just a press conference, it was a gala event. It had all the elements of a party, complete with political stars such as the mayor and the governor, plus community leaders, basketball stars, and basketball fans. Refreshments were served for all those attending, including the press. There were basketball shirts in packages available to everyone there—again, including the press. The press corps was not shunted behind ropes and they had access to anyone in the room. It got great press because the event was newsworthy and everyone had a good time.

As a converse example, there was an exhibit of hydrogen cars toured by President Bush. Reporters in the press pool were allowed on the tour, but otherwise the press was limited. As far as promotion goes, having the president show up at your trade fair is about as good as it gets—but opening the exhibit to the press and inviting some talk shows and television stations to watch a demonstration would have generated publicity beyond the presidential stop-by.

If possible, do your event early in the day, to give all the media time to get their stories on the air. Tell press where they can park. Make sure the local garage leaves plenty of parking spaces available, and if it is a really big event, make it clear where satellite trucks are to be parked.

Midmorning is always a good time, as it gives the morning-drive radio teams time to leave the station, yet it's early enough to help other media outlets meet their deadlines. The next best time is early in the afternoon; otherwise you are competing with deadlines for print and broadcast. If you are planning a series of events or press events, scatter the times and days so that different members of the media can attend. Find a way to get the sound, video and any other material to members of the press who could not attend.

If you are holding a news conference it should not last longer than thirty minutes. Anything that needs to be said can be said in that time period. If you have too many people prepared to speak at the podium, reporters will quit taking notes and cut off tape recorders and cameras until the Q&A section starts. There should be no more than four speakers, they should be introduced at the podium, and their comments should be brief. The other participants can be available for questions as part of the program or for interviews after the news conference. Do not have a lengthy panel discussion, no matter how many egos you bruise. You can make it up to them by booking interviews for them.

Presidential-advance genius Lindsay Stroud suggests the following rules for every news conference:

- Get it in the daybook (a listing of events for the day used by media outlets). Most areas use AP, but in some areas of the country there is more than one organization putting together a daybook.
- You may have to make hundreds of calls to get twenty reporters to show up. Get a phone bank together just for this purpose. Make sure the people who are pitching this are not interns—your senior staff is an important element here.
- Make the news conference exciting. Pick a news topic that people want to hear about, and be sure that it really is news. Ask yourself if you would be interested in hearing and seeing the news that you are presenting. Is it just a restatement of something you already have in print? Make news!
- Invite everyone. It should be open to all media, not just your known friendlies.
- Bring enough materials for the press. B roll and sound clips as well as photos on DVD are wonderful supplements to your printed media.
- If you are planning an event and you have promised media they will get individual interviews, keep that promise.
- Have a clear agenda and plan it to the minute. If possible, practice with your spokespersons ahead of time.
- Is your place easy to find? Easy to get to? Close? Well marked?
- Select a room that fits the size of the media you are expecting— better a bit crowded than to have a room that is not filled.

- Be sure it is a visual product. Use the background to convey your message. How often do you see President Bush with an American flag behind him or a slogan that supports his message when he does an event on the road? The background of the podium should always be part of the story. Position the press conference so that the sun is not ruining your beautiful, camera-ready background. Cameras cannot shoot into the sun.

- Spend the time to look at camera angles. If you are going to use risers, know how high they need to be. (Three to four feet is common.) Have a good podium. You must have press access near the front for cutaways. (If there is only one camera, it will cut away to something else of interest—perhaps the audience, and then back to the speaker.) Be able to get a good head shot of your speaker. Head shots can be uninteresting, so the background should support your message. How are the camera shots if a wide-angle lens is used?

- Find out if any members of the press have a disability, and be ready to accommodate them.

- Do you need to have an interpreter for hearing-impaired press or attendees?

- Have easy-in, easy-out access for your spokespersons or candidate

- Check on the need for and parking of satellite trucks.

- Have hold rooms available for major speakers or candidates. These rooms can be used for private interviews and preparation time.

- Always have something available for the press to drink and nibble on. They have to mind their cameras and tape machines and can't always get to the refreshment table. Also, find out the dietary needs of your spokespersons or candidates.

- Do not have nonpress asking questions. It looks, acts, and feels like a setup.

- Do not give up control to another group if your name is on the event. If it does not work out well, then your group is in the mud too. They may have attracted the media, but you are hosting the event and you must maintain control of it.

- Have enough electrical outlets available and a mult box (a device for plugging in the recorders) that reporters can connect to to get sound.
- Wireless Internet access is always a plus, as are free phone lines in case there is not good cell phone coverage.
- Work with the press folks of your marquee names to ensure that there will be time for interviews following the news conference.
- Don't promise a crowd. A lot of different things can happen to cause journalists to not show. You can take care of the problem by getting videotape and sound to them.
- Make a schedule of prearranged interviews and stick to it. Treat them as if they were the family jewels.
- You are the monitor. It is your responsibility to handle the press so the event doesn't turn into a free-for-all with an unhappy press as the end result.
- Consider streaming the event so more people can participate. Add a chat room if you think you can get the traffic.
- For press that cannot attend, send the sound via the Internet and arrange a way that some off-site press can get in questions. But be careful not to alienate the press that has made the effort to show up.
- Find a quiet place where interviews can take place. A noisy room will make it difficult to get good one-on-one interviews after the official event is complete.
- Have your own sound, your own video, and your own photos. It would be a waste to have a great event and have no record of it.

Make your event news-friendly by working with a professional who knows how to advance it. The Howard Dean organization, Democracy for America, had all sorts of guidelines for event preparation on its Web site, including accessibility, restrooms, and so forth. Check out their Web page for the latest guidelines. They are familiar with the exact technical and visual requirements needed for television, radio, and Internet reporting.

In addition, work with someone who understands how the event is going to look on television, using both wide-angle shots as well as close-ups. You want to make your event visually interesting and have sound that is clean and usable. The press advance team for President Clinton, led by Steve Rabinowitz, made this into an art form. Their amazing attention to detail included ensuring that the colors of the pom-poms matched the theme of the day. The advance team for President George W. Bush has improved on this even more.

Your advance person should know such things as where to place a mult box, the height of the risers, the best camera angle, the best placement of chairs for the audience, and where news conference participants should be when they are not speaking.

If you can't get television press to your event, then have someone record it. Send out your video from the event and, with proper pitching, you may be able to get coverage.

You can also create your own talk event. *Talkers Magazine* and *Talk Radio News* have created many of these. During the 2001 and 2005 Presidential Inaugurations, a radio row was set up in the hotels that housed all of the big financial rollers. A radio row is a unique event where many radio hosts are invited to broadcast—all they have to do is show up. The telephone lines are ordered, tested, and ready to go. An engineer is on hand to test lines and equipment. Broadcast equipment is often provided by the host of the radio row. (The industry standard for broadcast equipment for remote broadcasts is Comrex.) Hosts simply sit at their spot and guests come down the line. Big-name guests love it because they can get on many shows (and hundreds of stations) in a short period of time. There is often a festive atmosphere and the best benefit is that the group hosting the radio row has control over the guests and therefore the agenda.

Talkers Magazine created the concept of a virtual radio row—you can essentially have transcript and audio selections of all the interviews you and your spokespersons have participated in posted on your Web site so it is available to both the public and the media.

Since the 2001 inauguration the Bush White House has made great use of radio rows, including one before the 2002 election and one right after a State of the Union speech. Both took place on the White House lawn and included all the top figures in the Bush administration. The radio staff at the White House tried to honor all special requests for guests, making sure that even smaller market stations had someone *big* to interview.

Radio rows can be done for nonpolitical events as well. The Inter-American Development Bank and Liz Claiborne have held them on the issues surrounding domestic abuse. Expenses were paid for the talk-show hosts. Although not all guests were celebrities or household names, they were substantial in their decision-making power in their respective countries.

The radio industry often hosts their own radio rows in connection with conferences and events. A radio row was held at the Embassy Suites Hotel at Ground Zero during the first anniversary of 9/11. Guests went from broadcast suite to broadcast suite. This made it easy for any of their affiliates to be a part of a meaningful historical event.

Talkers Magazine has radio broadcast availability at its annual conference and sponsored the first presidential primary radio row at the 2004 New Hampshire primary. A national event could be a great time to sponsor a radio row or to get your spokesperson to an event that is already planned. *Talkers Magazine* has also developed RadioRow.net, so listeners can see the radio row hosts and guests *live*.

Radio Rows are not made for television, but if you can get marquee guests, invite television crews to cover the event and book an interview for the media outlet. Internet broadcasting is a natural addition to a radio row because a broadcaster can do an interview and get it immediately onto an Internet site, as well as book a chat for the guests on the row. If you build it, they will come; keep your event open to the media to get the coverage you are looking for.

Have a full debriefing when an event is over—don't just pat each other on the back and go on to the next event. Take the time to find out what worked, what went wrong, and what could have been better. Discuss the logistics, the room, and the lighting. Who attended? Who did not attend? What questions were asked? What questions did not get asked? What feedback did you get? What else made the news that day? Write up your notes and make a checklist for the next event.

Multiply your message.

There are ways to multiply *any* media you do. One press shop developed an ad they knew would not be accepted by any television stations or networks. The ad was graphic in its depiction of refugees. Because it was rejected by the networks, it was not played as an ad. But it was discussed on television shows and talk-radio shows and was the subject of much discourse in print.

During the 2004 presidential primary season two groups ran ads that benefited from the media-multiplier effect. AmericanFamilyVoices.org ran an ad about the Bush administration and Halliburton Corporation. It was not designed to support any candidate but it had its desired effect by raising money for the organization.

The Republican Club for Growth ran an ad directly targeting the Democratic front-runner at that time, Howard Dean. The ad depicted a farmer and his wife. The farmer said, "Howard Dean should take his tax-hiking, government-expanding, latte-drinking, sushi-eating, Volvo-driving, *New York Times*–reading . . ." and the farmer's wife then finished, ". . . Hollywood-loving, left-wing freak show back to Vermont, where it belongs."

No one knows whether that ad was part of the undoing of Howard Dean, but one thing is for sure—it was the topic of many television and radio shows, and the Republican Club for Growth didn't have to foot the bill for the extra publicity.

Public relations guru Jay Byrne worked on a congressional race early in his career. He seeded talk shows by having the candidate's supporters call and relate stories about his candidate on virtually every show on the air in that congressional market. If the host was talking about scenic bridges, he had people calling about infrastructure. Some local newspapers would not publish articles about radio programs, and he handled this problem by making transcripts of the shows, then writing about what had been discussed. He sent out press releases stating, "It is just not *Denny's* [the opponent's] week." It was not long before the newspapers picked up the expression.

Radio and Internet, if used properly, can give you entry to other media. **Think of the talk media first—not last—when planning your campaign.**

You should always plan on transcribing sound and making it available; it becomes searchable on the Internet and allows media easy access to quotes. A small-market interview can turn into a larger one if you carefully plan where to send the sound and the transcript.

Your campaign strategy should answer the question, "What media can we get that does not require a lay-out of cash?" If your message is hot, capitalize on it; don't look a gift horse in the mouth. You can piggyback your message in many ways if you are creative and on your toes!

Capitalize on controversy.

Sometimes an otherwise cut-and-dried issue will become controversial. For example, there seemed to be general agreement that because it was available to anyone, including children, pornography on the Internet was wrong, illegal, and broke an array of laws. But as soon as enforcement issues surfaced, pornography on the Internet became a hot topic. The most important part of your pitch is to highlight the areas of controversy. These areas need to be clearly stated so they are immediately obvious. Examples to look at are fuckedcompany.com, internalmemos.com, and thesmokinggun.com.

Producers love negative and controversial e-mail. When someone is mad enough to get off the couch, go to their computer, and write an e-mail—or perhaps even write a letter—you know you have engaged the audience. They are no longer passive viewers or listeners; they are part of the conversation.

Before going on the air make a chart or graphic that puts your position and the opposing position next to each other. When pitching your issue think about including quotes from your opposition. "The environmentalists say logging is wrong, but logging helps the economy and creates jobs." Or, "Loggers say the environmentalists are tree huggers, but the environmentalists want you to know that animal and plant species unique to our area will disappear if this land is logged." You get the idea. The more facts and quotes you can use, the stronger your case that it is a controversial issue.

When former Senator Bill Bradley, D-New Jersey, would not endorse Vice President Al Gore during the 2000 presidential race, Mark Pfeifle of the RNC put a photo of Senator Bradley on the side of a milk carton, similar to the campaign used for missing children. The message alluded to the fact that Bill Bradley was missing from Gore's endorsements. If you highlight the controversy, it should make it easier for producers to sell your idea to the host or management.

Media expert David Horowitz plays into controversy and says, "It's about being the people's friend and defining your opponent as the force that holds the people down." He uses this example: "Republicans fight for you, fight against big government, high taxes, and the bureaucracies that keep you down." Do not be ignorant of controversy surrounding your issue.

Look at me, look at me!

There are many ways to get your organization or event noticed. The key is to keep your organization or spokesperson in the minds of the hosts and producers. Everyone receives a multitude of e-mails and faxes—most of them comparable to unsolicited electronic telemarketing messages. In order to keep front and center in the media's mind, try something a bit different. Environment2004.org sent out postcards of a fish with the word mercury stamped on it. The American Society of Civil Engineers sends out regular postcards with maps of the United States and photos of crumbling bridges, roads, and the like, saying, "Greetings from America's Crumbling Infrastructure." It then refers recipients to their Web site. One group headlines invitations to their press conferences with the words "Television Friendly."

Here are three suggestions for getting a group or event noticed:

- Send a postcard with a great graphic on the front and some of your talking points on the back. This is short and simple and has impact. You can also send an audio postcard. Different from just an MP3 file, it can also contain some graphics, so it is fun to open. Just keep in mind that everyone has different amounts of mail storage space.
- Send out a modern-day version of the Burma Shave Sign via Web, postcard, and so forth, with messages that engage the viewer/listener in anticipating what might be coming next. Burma Shave had signs along the highway with a different message on each one. The Eisner Museum of Advertising and Design describes the effect: "The public saw the signs almost whenever they traveled. The breadth in placement (7,000 signs)

give rise to the notion that Burma Shave was a national firm. It also gave the motorist and potential customer a personal, emotional relationship with the signs." Burma Shave became the number-two-selling shaving cream in America. One modern-day version of it is free postcards, made popular by GoCARD.com.

- A variation of the Burma Shave technique can be started online. Some very successful books have "teased" their content by putting up interesting material from and about their book before publication.

The other, more expensive option is to send out what is known in the business as a VNR—video news release, a prepackaged story lasting between one and five minutes.

The VNR serves as a commercial for what you want the media to know. A good VNR includes B roll. There are at least two parts to a VNR—a total, packaged story with voice-over and interviews on one channel, and natural sound on another channel. There is no need to add further layers of audio, such as special effects or music. The second piece on your VNR should include only the sound bite audio and all natural sound. You simply *strip* the voice-over narration from this piece so the local station can use its own talent.

Always provide the script for the story. You'd be amazed at how often small-market stations use the prepackaged story or rewrite it using all of your sound bites and B roll, but with their script. Without clear attribution, it can appear that a VNR is news, not "paid for by. . . ." The government and newsrooms have taken a lot of heat for VNRs that were not properly attributed by some stations that ran them.

Use a professional to produce your VNR. Make it something that the newsroom can clip and view. This is similar to the old rip-and-read that radio stations use for news and their morning prep. You will not need a professional to send out B roll if it is shot well, although there are companies that specialize in sending out VNRs, such as Medialink Worldwide, which distributes more than a thousand VNRs per year. These companies know how to notify television outlets of the satellite coordinates if you choose to send it out on a satellite instead of on individual broadcast-quality videotapes or DVDs.

Additional tips for VNRs:

- Keep it under two minutes—unless it is a compelling story needed and wanted because of its news value.
- Make sure that a news organization has the tools to customize the story. There has to be enough footage and sound to allow them to do their own editing.
- If you are not using a professional company to send out the VNRs do the homework about what format to use and the best time to send it.
- Find out the possible calendar in which the VNR might be used; it could be the same day or *evergreen* (can continue to be used) during the next month or longer. Make your VNR accordingly.
- The better the quality, the better the chance that it will be used.
- There is also a radio version of VNR. Medialink is probably the most well-known of the companies producing VNR for radio.

When creating tools to help you get noticed, the main question is, "Does it make it easier for a producer to book my guest, or for a reporter to cover my event, if I provide the media with a print or broadcast post-card or VNR?" If it does, it is a good investment for your campaign PR budget.

Make your event calendar available to the media.

The more heads-up the media is given, the better they can plan to cover your event. Murphy's Law prevails here and the best-made plans for a news event can go out the window at a moment's notice if there is a late-breaking story. Congress plans its calendar a year in advance and it is common knowledge which weeks they are in session and which they are out of town. The entire city plans around that calendar. The Republicans take care of their talk media by circulating the congressional calendar, with notations and additions, so talk-show hosts can plan programming around it. They also send weekly updates. Print and broadcast daybooks and calendars are great sources for publicity, but you cannot always rely on them to publish your event—announcements occasionally get buried on messy desks and in overfilled e-mail boxes!

If you have planned a conference, an event, or series of events, by all means let the media know. It will help them to plan and they will appreciate it. You can get the word out through fax, e-mail, or by keeping your calendar updated on your Web site. An outdated Web site could come back and bite you. If you expect the media to follow your activities, keep them informed.

If your budget can't accommodate a media planner, there are several Web sites that can help get the word out. Some of our favorites are Protest.net and Mediamap.com. In addition, Meetup.com is great for finding where and when like-minded individuals are gathering. If you do not make your calendar available to the media, how can they cover your event? Think about it.

Do your research.

Knowing the medium dovetails with what we discussed earlier about knowing the audience. Let's explore a little further, with some tips on learning more about the market.

The first place to start is the Internet. You can find the local AP bureau and local media by going to ap.org and capwiz.com/aauw/home. If you are in the dark about a particular station, or even an entire market, an invaluable resource is the *M Street Radio Directory*. This directory has current information on thirteen thousand radio stations in the United States and Canada; it is especially helpful when you suspect a station has changed formats. Your issue or spokesperson may not be as successful on some formats as on others. Based out of Littleton, New Hampshire, you can order the *M Street Radio Directory* online at MStreet.net, by calling 800-248-4242, or by logging on to the InsideRadio.com Web site. For talk radio, *Talkers Magazine* puts out an annual directory of the top talk stations market by market at Talkers.com.

The Bush 2004 campaign made it easy. If you entered your zip code, out popped the talk media in your area. You can find the AP bureau nearest you by accessing it on their Web page. Make sure your list contains assignment editors, producers, and the editor of the local *Penny Saver* or its equivalent. Hosts of local Web sites should be added, although there is still no media directory for that. Every media outlet has a webmaster and often has a content editor or even a news editor. Make them part of your media list as well.

In addition, check *Bacon's MediaSource*, the *Broadcasting and Cable Yearbook*, and the *Radio and Television News Director's Association and Foundation*. Many congressional offices also list the radio and TV stations in their districts on their Web pages. They will often have a transcript of a recent appearance by the congressman.

You might be able to discern whether the station is friend or foe to your issue by reading a few transcripts. The best place for information is the station's Web site. If the show is an in-your-face program, they will brag about it. If the host has won an award for best newscast, best anchor, or best show, you will find out about it on their Web site. If you are going to be on a syndicated show, the Web site should list the stations that carry it.

Find the niche-market programs. Some are ethnic, some are shows where the host has purchased the time, and some are topical shows that will challenge you to find where you and your issue might fit. Design your outreach to meet the needs of the producers and hosts of those programs.

Chances are the station you are interested in has its own Web site. Once again, a good place to start is the Internet. Use one of the major search engines and type in the station call letters. An interesting bit of trivia: All stations east of the Mississippi River usually begin with a *W*, such as WABC in New York City. The one exception is Pittsburgh's KDKA. All stations west of the Mississippi River begin with a K, though there are exceptions: WDAY in Fargo and WDAZ in Grand Forks, North Dakota.

The station's Web site should provide you with a lot of information about the shows, the formats, and the hosts. Many of the hosts have their own Web pages that feature excerpts from previous shows as well as musings and tips. These Web pages may also have links to chat rooms or have some blogging (Weblog) action. But do not rely on directories or the Internet for your only sources of information. Look up the Web site for the local chamber of commerce in the city where the station is located. This can serve several purposes. For starters, you learn more about the community and the character of the station, information you would not find on a station-hosted Web site or in a national radio directory.

It might seem like the research is a lot of work for a short interview, but you may be able to stay on the air longer if you can make a local appeal to the audience and host. The more often you can localize an issue with specific examples, the more effectively you will be able to get your message across to listeners. Have your staff or organization research the basics about the area or host, and use it in your discussion. Read the local newspaper online if possible. As former Speaker of the House of Representatives Tip O'Neill, D-Massachusetts, said, "All politics is local."

Establish your organization or event in your community. Read the trade magazines and online updates to determine where you want coverage for and about your event. Subscribe to *Publishers Weekly*, *Talkers Magazine*, publications of the National Association of Broadcasters, and broadcasting and cable publications that focus on the Internet. Attend trade conventions. Get to know the people capable of putting your issues on the air. If you are attending an event, do not pester people to put you on the air; those attending these events are there to do business and/or to let their hair down. Be likeable and be seen as a resource.

If you represent a national organization or branch of government, call like-minded organizations or government agencies to get a sense of the local political mind-set.

Learning about your potential audience is a perfectly acceptable preinterview practice. If you have exhausted all avenues to determine the audience of a particular show, ask the show's producer. Be prepared for the producer to say, "We have the best listeners in the world." Every station does. You can come back with something like, "I would like to tailor my comments and thoughts to your audience, and would appreciate knowing more about your audience demographic." When you know as much about your audience as you do about the host, your message should have a greater impact and will hopefully provide watercooler chat long after the interview has been broadcast.

Reinforce your message.

Although the Internet reigns as king of information dissemination these days, the printed word still has the look and feel of legitimacy. If you are planning a campaign for the long haul, think about writing a book. It will give you instant credibility. The Internet and print can work together.

If your campaign timeline will not accommodate a book, think smaller scale with a pamphlet or booklet. You can give them away at press events or appearances. Both are tangibles that can be kept for referral. As we stated previously, a press kit is great, but how many press kits will find a permanent place on someone's bookshelf?

The Center for Constitutional Rights in New York City printed a booklet called *When the Agent Knocks*. Although the media often dismiss the center as "one of those left-wing organizations," the booklet garners interest on both sides of the aisle from those who are fearful of government power. And Citizens Against Government Waste releases a *Pink Pig Book* every year. It is a great giveaway and is widely anticipated.

Your literature can be distributed in a newsletter or an e-mail if you do not have the budget for a book, booklet, or pamphlet. The information you release to the public must always include the reason for your program or campaign, as well as your mission statement. It is helpful to circumvent potential arguments by highlighting the costs and benefits of your program and campaign.

Your Internet site is your calling card. Keep it updated and monitor all of your links and page sites to ensure that they work. When you release new information, don't forget to update your Web site at the same time. If you want your readers to help you get your message out, include a form letter with suggestions on how to personalize it. Make it easy for people to take your information, absorb it, and then act on it.

If you can afford pop-up ads on the Internet, they will provide a great graphic that will reach targeted districts. If you had logged on to the Web sites of most major newspapers of the seventeen targeted states during the 2004 presidential race, you would have been inundated with pop-up ads for the candidates or the party platforms. At first glance it looked like those papers had endorsed the candidate, but they were actually paid ads.

Also, do not overlook the cross-pollination effect of releasing your information in several formats.

If you have a sense of what your opposition might be releasing about you or if you know someone is digging up dirt, have your crisis materials ready to go. Include all questions you think might be asked, plus your responses. Hopefully you will never need to use them. Keep them under lock and key. Do not give a disgruntled employee an opportunity to take this information to your opposition.

Seed the audience.

There is big difference between using a shill and having a supporter planted or seeded in the audience. A shill is usually obnoxious, tries to take over, and is too rehearsed. Someone who is planted in the audience is a participant and takes part in the discussion without steering it. They are real listeners/viewers who are part of the regular audience and community. Many folks may be willing to do this for your issue or campaign. Parents home with small children, employees on a day off, commuters with cell phones, and students are all possibilities. Having a cadre of people call in regularly accomplishes several objectives. It ensures that the airwaves and cyberspace are exposed to your issue and that it gets regular mention; it can engage the host and other audience in legitimate conversation; and if the host perceives interest in your topic, it can make booking your spokesperson easier. In addition to calling, these folks can also fax and e-mail letters and questions about the issue. Again, the goal is to keep your issue or spokesperson on the front burner.

During hot campaigns remember that *for every minute one of your people is on the air, the other side is not*. Even if your callers are not great on the air, the viewpoint of your organization is the one being presented—not that of your opposition. Since the 1996 presidential election, various campaigns have used the talk format to help fill the airwaves and the Internet. The International Association of Machinists and Aerospace Workers (IAM) has been very forward-looking. For almost ten years they have been training their members how to call into talk shows and even to develop their own cable-access television shows. They put the resources into the training and it has paid off for them.

Train your people. It is free airtime and it can turn public perception around instantly. Beware these two caveats:

1. Do not issue written talking points. They could be leaked to the other side or to news organizations.
2. Have your supporters speak in their own words. By the second caller, a host can tell if they are seeded and operating from a script or a sheet of talking points.

A local station in Tennessee received several calls the morning of the 2004 presidential primary. The first call sounded legitimate to the host, but he became suspicious after the second call, when the pro-Clark agenda sounded the same. As the calls came in he began to look at his caller ID. They all had the same agenda and they were all out-of-state calls. From that point, he and his co-host had a field day discussing how Clark couldn't even get Tennessee supporters to promote his agenda. The entire morning show suddenly turned into a thrashing to embarrass the callers for shilling from out of state.

Covering forums, chat rooms, and the like is as important as being on the air. You can look at ForumFind.com, chat.yahoo.com, and the AOL and Google groups. Google bought the Usenet data bank so it is now possible to monitor some topics dating back to 1979.

When training the troops on making calls, provide them with these tips:

- Keep a list of stations and phone numbers; talk programs and airtimes; and Internet addresses, chat rooms, and forums. Do your homework ahead of time and find out which programs are live, which ones are archived on the Internet, and which ones have chat rooms. There is seemingly no end to programs and chats to call or write to.
- Calling very popular programs usually means you will have to wait before you are put on the air. Call in at the top of the hour and during breaks. Many hosts or anchors love to talk even if they have callers backed up. It is a self-promoting opportunity for them to announce, "We have ten lines blinking."

- If a station is trying to reach a young demographic they might screen callers who sound older. The same goes for younger people calling a station targeting an older population, men calling a program directed at women, and women calling a program directed at men. You might want to arrange to have your calls made by those who fit the demographic of the station.

- Relate your personal experience to the topic. If the discussion is about education have a teacher make the call. If parenting is the topic, there is no better expert than a parent. If job loss is the issue then all the experts in the world do not equal one person who recently lost his or her job.

- Address the host, anchor, or chat room guest by name. Make it obvious that you have been listening to them or have been following the chat. Never call a show you are not listening to and do not just jump on a chat and start expounding on your point. Producers, call screeners, and chat room managers are wise to such tricks.

- In the world of caller ID, it is nearly impossible to fool anyone by changing voices or giving different locations. Even if you block your calling number, remember that most producers have been around the block a few times.

- Once your call is answered turn off the radio or television to avoid annoying feedback. You will experience a short delay, so listen to the questions over the phone, not on your radio.

- Never use a speakerphone, and never have someone on an extension of the same phone line.

- If you are a first-time caller or chatter, say so. Hosts love first-time callers. Say something complimentary about the show, but only if you can be genuine about it. You do not have to agree. You can say, "I have a different perspective, but I find your show informative and entertaining." Don't be or sound phony.

- To bring the other side into the discussion, really listen to what **you** are saying. Draft what you are going to say, then practice and shorten it. Write your comments from the heart. Do not read from your notes. Speak naturally. Remember that your comments are part of a conversation or written Internet discussion. You don't read your notes when you are talking to a friend—right?

- If you are going to ask a question, just ask it. Don't say, "I want to ask a question," and then go into a long monologue. Ask your question or make a statement. Again, speak as you would in a normal conversation with a friend.

- If you have backup for your point, such as a book or a statistic, use it. If you saw something on television or the Internet, be specific about where you saw it. The host and audience will be grateful for the information. Avoid vague gossip or hearsay. Hosts will be all over it and you will sound foolish. Be very careful when you mention another television network, radio program, or the call letters of another station. Hosts do not like that and neither do their bosses!

- This is a conversation, not a sermon. Let the preachers preach, the hosts give monologues, and the news anchors read the prompters. Your job is to be part of the conversation.

- People on the outs make the best callers. The standard party line gets overused and tunes people out.

- Do not be offended if the anchor or host is abrupt with you. They must keep the conversation flowing, the ratings up, and entertain the audience. They are not on the air to develop a new best friend.

- Turn off your call-waiting. It is very annoying on the air.

- Pick a quiet place to make your call—no kids, other conversations, or background music. It is you they want on the air, not your whole household. There are those times, however, when you are driving down the road and you get enthused about the topic on a program. When you call, tell the host that you heard something on their show that made you pull off the road to call in. You will be forgiven for the traffic noise.

- Car phones still usually get priority, so tell the producer if you are on one, and be certain you are not in a black-hole area where your service is sketchy.

- Remember a rule of assertiveness training—you can be a bit of a broken record and repeat your point, just don't overdo it. If the host tries to throw you off guard, stick to your point and do not back off.
- No one can argue with you about how you feel. Remember, a feeling is not a fact and it represents what you really believe. Use personal examples—it is hard to argue with experience. Other callers will be more accepting of your viewpoint if they can identify with your situation. Be someone callers or Internet chatters can relate to.
- Never lie to a screener to get on the air. Most hosts and producers will throw someone off immediately if they suspect they have been lied to. If you have a different viewpoint, say so.
- Do not insult the host. It is not politic. One guest on a recent radio row told the host he was an idiot. It did not go over well, and it created a lot of tension among the other guests and hosts.

Seeding the audience is an ideal method to steer the discussion in favor of your issue. It is also an opportunity to hear what points the opposition raises. You will then be armed with additional responses to attacks at your next appearance.

Provide easy access.

Make your Internet address one that is easy to remember. You no longer have to give the http://www—most people understand that is the prelude to Internet addresses. Try to avoid addresses that require a hyphen, could have several spellings, or are difficult to spell. A toll-free telephone number is always welcome, especially if you want that retail caller you might get from being on the air or in a chat room.

Your information should be printer-friendly on your Web page so that directions or information can be retrieved easily. Work with your Web page designer. Can you easily e-mail information from it to a friend? Can you print vital information? Give it a test run and have someone who is not necessarily Internet savvy try to reach you or print something from your Web page. Also, do not overlook those who are not on the information superhighway; provide an alternative way to get information to those without Internet access.

If your appearance on a program will be either early or late in the day, think about hiring someone to answer the phones during that time. Give the contact phone number often during your interview. Ask the producer if your segment is going to be rebroadcast. If so, have phone coverage when the rebroadcast airs. If this is not feasible, provide your office hours every time you give your phone number so you will not have frustrated callers.

Before you begin your campaign make a management plan for handling inquiries. Scott Hoganson, formerly with the Republican National Committee, uses his background in management to set measurable goals for responding to calls and e-mail requests. Decide who is going to answer inquiries and set measurable goals on paper before you begin your public campaign.

If you are the press contact, be available 24/7—weekends and vacations are included. If you can't be available have backup help, because the twenty-four-hour round-the-world news cycle is a reality, especially if you participate in chat rooms or the show is simulcast on the Internet.

If an event is planned, write out directions and add them to your Web site. Post signs in the area. Alert the switchboard concerning important details about location, time, and directions. Have on-site contact numbers available during the event

Accessibility to information about your issue, campaign, or event is an important marketing tool.

Cross-promote.

It is difficult to ignore an issue when it is brought up again and again, especially when presented in different ways with different spokespersons. Coordinate your campaign with other groups who support your stance and can cover the specific areas in a way that is relevant to the audience. Let it be known that you are working with like-minded groups. Mention them when you are on the air; list them in chats online and in blogs. Don't forget to mention their support on your Web page or news releases. Provide links on your site to Web pages of like-minded organizations. Make it clear that you are sharing information and resources. Competition should only exist between opposing groups. Working together with groups who are on your side is a great strategy.

Be creative and make alliances with groups and people who differ slightly from what your position offers—homeless groups with hunger groups, crisis pregnancy centers with child advocacy groups, pro-choice groups with libertarians. The possibilities are endless.

Anne Glauber, senior vice president of Ruder Finn, teamed the pro-peace Middle East group A Different Future, with the group Walk the Road to Peace and put together a press conference of religious leaders from around the United States. It was an amazingly diverse group that included presiding bishops of the Methodist, Lutheran, Presbyterian, and Episcopal churches; two Roman Catholic cardinals; the Greek Orthodox primate; three well-known Evangelical ministers; rabbis from every major Jewish sect; and seven major Muslim clerics. The goal of this news conference was to ensure that the Israeli-Palestinian peace process was back on the table of the Bush administration. There were more television cameras there than at "Monica Beach" during the height of "Monica Gate" during President Clinton's administration. The organizers of this "Peace in the Middle East" news conference really had to work the press, but the event generated a lot of media coverage.

Following are some ways to make your event successful with the media:

- Work with other groups early in your media-planning process. Including other organizations in your event should guarantee wider coverage.
- Meet with the groups to divvy up the media territory. Work together when it makes sense, but also work separately so you can make maximum impact.
- Plan your joint events and make a calendar.
- Let the media know that your event will be visually interesting. Tell them what will be there for the camera to film
- Decide what will be in your B-roll package as well as any VNRs so the press can grab and go if your event day turns into

a busy news day. The editing of your VNR will affect the outcome of your coverage, so include the images and sounds you want to see on your final package.

- To avoid misunderstandings, plan the news conference agenda and decide upon the speakers before the day of the event.
- Set up your interviews before the conference and get absolute agreement with your partner organization about who is responsible for what. Leaving these important issues to the day of the event could ignite turf wars.
- Make your pitch calls to the media. Walk the Road to Peace, for instance, made six hundred calls to get the media to their press conference.
- Connect the issue to the news of the day. That means preparing your spokespersons the day of the event and having your affiliate organizations all on the same page. Get up at 6:00 A.M. and have a conference call about the day's news.
- Start and end your event on time.
- Lighting is crucial. A poorly lit news conference looks terrible and has little chance of getting on television.
- Invite some talk shows to broadcast from your event and arrange to have your speakers available to them for interviews.
- Fill the space. An empty news conference setting does not provide good video. Have your supporters on hand, but they should not look like they are there to fill space!
- Publicize your event on Internet chat rooms.
- Stream audio and video and add MP3/podcasts/videocasts of your event on your Web site as soon as possible after the event is over. If you cannot put the entire event on the Internet, pick the best sound bites. Make a transcript of the event available.
- Agree on the follow-up plan with your affiliate organization. Make measurable goals.
- Have a postmortem meeting to assess what went well and what needs to be improved.
- Including other organizations in your event should guarantee wider coverage.

Be willing to debate.

You may be able to get your side of the argument on the air with greater ease if you set up a debate and offer it as a package to media outlets. This can be done on the air and on the Internet. Of course, this may mean dialoguing with the enemy, but it might astronomically increase your chances of getting your issues publicized. You may need to work with an intermediary who is not associated with either organization to book the media. The most important idea to remember is that a debate is better than not having your issue heard at all. In fact, you cannot have a credible discussion of an issue if it is one-sided. Every issue has another side.

Rarely will a Republican refuse to debate a Democrat, whether in person, on the air, or in a chat room—even if the debate forum is liberally oriented and assumed to be skewed toward Democrats. Surprisingly, Democrats often refuse to debate. Since the dawning of Democratic radio initiatives, this is an issue that has been hotly debated in Democratic and liberal circles.

There is just no reason not to go on the air with a host who is willing to give you a free and fair debate. So what if they make remarks about you when you leave the show? Just remember the childhood maxim "Sticks and stones may break my bones, but names will never hurt me." A debate is a great forum to have your say, to speak to your supporters, and to hear what your opponents are saying. Debates are pure democracy.

Fox News Channel's viewers are comprised of approximately 18 percent liberals, 32 percent moderates, and 46 percent conservatives. Viewers are mostly male, age twenty-five to fifty-four, with college degrees and annual incomes exceeding seventy-five thousand dollars. CNN's viewers are approximately 16 percent liberal, 38 percent moderate, and 40 percent conservative. Fox News Channel caters to a powerful audience, yet many liberals refuse to debate their opponents on FNC. They are ignoring a chance to reach their own constituency and to possibly move the middle—a major missed opportunity.

In the final hours of the New Hampshire primary on January 27, 2004, presidential candidate Howard Dean took a spin down radio row, vowing to his press people that he would not go on the nationally syndicated Sean Hannity radio talk show. However, several people in the talk-radio industry and a leader of a supporting advocacy group encouraged him to do so. His handlers had to be convinced that Democrats listened to the show. Hannity was a gentleman and came up during a break just to talk with Dean. Governor Dean went on the show and held his own, and his campaign got several e-mails and blog mentions from supporters telling him he did a great job. It was a win-win situation for everyone that day. In addition, Dean had a very friendly exchange with Hannity off-microphone. When he bowed out of the race a few weeks later, Hannity put the audio of his entire speech in the most visible area on his Web site.

At that same time, several of the other Democratic candidates refused to go on Sean Hannity's show. As a result, they missed out on a huge amount of free airtime.

If you choose to go into the lion's den keep in mind that reaching the audience, not the host, is your goal. It is also a chance to reach new demographics other than your regular constituency.

If your spokesperson is not always up for the job, take a hint from the Republicans. One of their former chairs was not as passionate as he should have been on the air. During *radio rounds* (being on several radio stations at the same time, one after the other—similar to a satellite tour), the Republicans initially placed him with a very liberal Democratic host. It got him so revved up he was good for the next ten interviews. The moral of the story: Know how to prepare your spokesperson for debate.

There is such a thing as *attack radio* (read Howard Stern's *Miss America*). Some guests go on the air, roll with the punches, and do very well. But attack or shock-jock formats are not for every issue, every campaign, or every spokesperson. If your spokesperson is quick on his or her feet, it is worth exploring these shows; just check the closet beforehand for any skeletons. Be willing to debate and you will gain respect from your opponents, your audience, and the talk-show host.

If all else fails and the other side will not debate, issue a challenge in print, on the air, and on the Internet. The media hates cowards, and if the other side will not debate, people need to know. Save all the documentation and correspondence of your challenge so you can make political hay out of the opposition's refusal to debate. When Florida sugar farmers refused to debate Nat Reed, a south Florida conservationist, he brought an empty chair to the studio and referred to it as his opponent throughout the interview. It was quite obvious that his opponent was not in attendance.

Internet chats can be handled in the same way. When it is time for the response of the opponent you simply type in, *Still refuses to debate.* Those four words are pretty powerful—especially if they are the response to every question posed in the chat room.

After Senator Robert Toricelli, D-New Jersey, dropped out of the U.S. Senate race 2002 just more than one month before Election Day, Senator Frank Lautenberg, D-New Jersey, at first refused to debate his Republican challenger, Douglas Forrester. Mark Pfeifle of the Forrester team secured Lautenberg's campaign schedule, borrowed two podiums, and placed a cardboard likeness of Lautenberg in front of one of the podiums. Candidate Forrester then "debated" Senator Lautenberg. It provided great visuals for the media covering Forrester's campaign.

When you are issuing a challenge and your opponent does not respond, be sure that you control the visual of the ignored response. A news conference on the steps of your opponent's office always makes for an interesting photo—especially if there are some of your banners in the background. And you are not breaking any laws if your supporters place those banners.

In the world of public-relations and campaign fund-raising, it is not uncommon for a coalition of divergent groups who normally would never publicly speak to each other or endorse each other's issues to join forces and challenge the opposition. Both teams are then in the spotlight. Sometimes opposite organizations need each other, and issuing a joint challenge can work to your advantage.

No free hits.

In other words, don't just sit there—fight back! An example of *don't let this happen to you* took place during the 2004 presidential campaign when the Kerry campaign gave the Bush campaign a free hit by not responding adequately or quickly to the Swift Boat Veterans issue. This will undoubtedly be remembered as one of the biggest blunders in campaign history. After the election, Kerry campaign manager Mary Beth Cahill said they initially thought there would be no legs to the ad from the Swift Boat Veterans. Had they been open to advice from the talk media they would have understood the potential damage. It really did not matter what the assessment of the campaign was; what mattered was that they allowed a free hit.

A group well prepared for free hits is v-fluence.com, which responded to the hysteria surrounding mad cow disease. They were ready to go when the issue came mooing at their door. First, in one day, they identified and evaluated who the stakeholders were. In other words, who were the players who were seeking to influence the discussion on mad cow disease? They monitored talk television and talk radio; they mined the Web and monitored Web sites, chat rooms, forums, and blogs. They found out who was seeking to participate and what their perspective, content, and tactics were.

V-Fluence was able to discern between earned media and paid media. Through their work with mad cow disease they found that the entry point of information for professionals in the television and print industries was oftentimes radio. They would get story ideas from listening to the radio on their way to work in the morning and driving home at night. Therefore, they chose to make sure that their no-free-hits campaign for mad cow disease made it to radio first.

Moving into action, v-fluence.com diluted the debate by sending out as much information to as many different online channels as possible, such as newsgroups, supportive stakeholder Web sites, and supportive blogs. They used the Internet by optimizing friendly Web sites and ensured that they had search-engine visibility. They overwhelmed the opposition and confused them at the same time.

Linkages among allies were recommended and content was recreated by developing columns and editorials. This all translated into v-fluence.com's point of view being easily found online. They were able to show real-world results, thus the site they created became the number one Web site for anyone searching the topic of mad cow disease. Their campaign was so successful that *USA Today* contacted them to write one of the point-counterpoint editorials on the subject. By identifying the stakeholders they became the early warning system for the next hit.

With the Internet and a twenty-four-hour news cycle, ignore free hits at your peril. Don't be a victim—be proactive, and make your motto, "No free hits!"

Big is not always better.

Small markets and Web sites can be just as effective as large satellite markets. Small markets are great for getting your feet wet and for trying out new approaches. You can reuse their material (with permission) on your Web site.

Even the smallest radio station has a listening audience of at least five hundred people. If you had an invitation to speak at a banquet for five hundred people, would you accept? Most of us would—in a heartbeat! In the 2004 presidential election, the Republicans did not take anything off the table. With states as close as they were in 2000, five hundred votes could make a huge difference in electing a president.

Find hosts, producers, anchors, and newsroom workers in smaller markets and develop a relationship with them. They will bask in the attention and remember you and your issue throughout their career. Professionals in the media move around and move up. Just imagine how your star could rise if an unknown you've worked with for years is now the hot new nationally syndicated radio host.

What about Web sites? Some companies spend millions on their Web sites, but who can doubt the moneymaking ability of Howard Dean's initially inexpensive Web site? He might not have won, but he pulled in a lot of money. His fund-raising capabilities spawned imitations by most of the candidates running on the national and state level. There is a world of money and press available; you just have to know where to look.

3

SELECTING A SPOKESPERSON

Personality plus is a plus.

It is important for people to like your spokesperson. What is the response when this individual enters a room? Is the air electrified, or does the energy level take a nosedive? Either will come across on the air.

One progressive group's spokesperson sounded like the annoying party guest everyone avoids. Although the campaign was for a great cause, no one wanted to listen to the spokesperson.

First impressions are important. There is evidence that we form our ideas about someone within the first twelve seconds of meeting them, and that the first five minutes of any personal interaction structures our overall viewpoint of that person. Any doubts? Sit with a man who is holding the remote control in front of a television set. How many seconds does it take before he changes channels? Ask him how he made his decision.

"Credibility is key," says marketing expert Julianne Corbett. You need to find your own scale of credibility. Who will the public trust? The gender of your spokesperson is important. Women are perceived as having empathy, but they may need to establish credibility. Men might be seen as having credibility, but they may need to establish empathy.

If the purpose of an organization is for a great cause and not an ego trip for its director, then the director should be open to getting the right spokesperson. The best way to market this person is to first do your own profile—conduct your own interview as if you were the editorial board of the newspaper, or a local television reporter doing a profile piece, or a writer with the Sunday magazine. This may be the best way to find great marketing material on your spokesperson. It may also help you discover potential pitfalls of your most out-front personality.

In one study news directors were asked whom they would want to interview after a crisis or disaster. Their first choice were the individuals who were directly involved, followed by the families of the affected individuals, then employees and management effected by a crisis, and last was the spokesperson for the affected organization or government agency. Visuals are always more compelling than talking heads.

Of course, you must try to preinterview these individuals. CNN interviewed three fishermen who were dramatically rescued in a midwinter sea. All that CNN was able to get out of these men were one-word answers—no emotion. The interview was a total bust. The only time the fishermen became animated was when they were asked about their predictions for the Super Bowl. They should have had the rescuers on television, not the rescued.

Do you want your organization or issue to be associated with a recognizable voice or face? In other words, do you want celebrity attraction? Think of some of the obvious campaigns that have used celebrity appeal.

Subaru has Paul Hogan, star of the *Crocodile Dundee* films, as spokesman for their Outback sport utility vehicle. Viagra will forever be associated with former senator and presidential candidate Bob Dole. When thinking of the Outback SUV or of Viagra, you visualize the campaign as well as the spokesman. If Subaru had chosen Hugh Grant, a Brit, instead of Paul Hogan, an Aussie, for their campaign, it would not have been as successful. If Viagra had chosen someone young and virile as their spokesman, that campaign would have flopped. The campaign was successful because it featured an older, former presidential candidate who suffered from erectile dysfunction.

When choosing a spokesperson, and especially if you are going after celebrity appeal, choose someone that crosses generations or is appropriate to the product or campaign. It does not need to be a hot celebrity—a well-recognized former star will often work quite well.

Keep the other endorsements and personal or political beliefs of your celebrity in mind. Do they sound sincere when pitching a product, or is it just another endorsement fee to collect? Do people like and respect your spokesperson? Although everyone might want to meet and be seen with the Hollywood crowd, you have wasted time and money if your spokesman is not believable or energized about your product or cam-

paign. No matter how worthy the cause, if the spokesperson lacks believability, most media will not listen to the message and will focus more on
the celebrity than on the campaign.

A celebrity spokesperson gives your issue instant appeal, but a celebrity
may be available only for the initial launch. You need someone who will represent your issue throughout the campaign. You may not be able to afford or
to obtain a celebrity spokesperson, but there could be several other people
from which to choose. If time is on your side, take an approach similar to
what a stage director or movie director would take: hold auditions.

Record someone you are considering for the position on tape, both
audio and video. Play the tapes for people in your organization and listen
to their feedback—the positive as well as the negative. Try to be impartial
when you are asking for suggestions. Do not lead your control group to
select the spokesperson you want.

While reviewing the tapes, critique body language. Pay close attention
to the candidates' voices—the tones, quality, pitches (the highs and lows),
speech patterns, and rates. Analyze the rhythm of speech as well. Where
are the pauses? Are there too many? Not enough? Does the pause rate
match that of the show's host? How does both body language and voice
work when your spokesperson wants to emphasize a point? What gestures
do they use? Do they work for or against the message you want to
convey? Do they look uncomfortable on camera? Do they have a difficult
time focusing? Do they look up, down, or away from the camera?

Do they sound believable, at ease, and professional? Do they speak
thoughtfully, which can be perceived as being hesitant? Do they speak in
sound bites, which can sometimes seem too polished, depending on the
audience, the host, and the show format?

Avoid people with grating, whiny, or otherwise irritating voices, unless
it will support your issue. For example, in an antismoking campaign, a
gravelly, raspy voice would be an asset. Also avoid someone with a
regional accent that may be difficult to understand outside that region.
However, if your campaign is going to air only in a select region or
market, your spokesperson's performance should compliment that area to
prevent sounding like someone from the outside.

A well-known publisher with a pretty good track record for placing
authors on talk shows pitched an author with the worst voice known to

humankind. The author was a transsexual whose appearance and characteristics had nothing to do with the book he had written. Unfortunately his appearance on one television show resulted in the cancellations of all his other interviews. He was sending too many messages—most of which had nothing to do with the book. Many of the radio producers the publisher had lined up for the author were not aware of the television debut, so those interviews were not canceled. In addition to a not-for-broadcast voice, the author could be heard chewing during the radio interviews. Eating while being interviewed is a definite no-no. The publisher's credibility suffered for a long time after this fiasco.

The head of your organization may want to be the spokesperson. This is not a problem if you are representing a political candidate or an author. Otherwise, your communications person may want to gently suggest employing additional voices and faces as spokespersons.

The spokesperson must be a good conversationalist as well as articulate and quick. The media rely on you to adequately prepare your speaker. In the world of media, perception is reality. If your spokesperson sounds like a failure, it is not a far stretch to imagine that your campaign will sound like one too. Choose a spokesperson who is a winner from the start.

4

PREPARING THE SPOKESPERSON

Coach your spokesperson.

Be sure that your spokesperson knows and understands your issue. As obvious as this seems, during President Clinton's radio initiative for the Crime Bill, Attorney General Janet Reno admitted on the air that she had not read the legislation. The host and listeners made chopped liver out of her.

During the 2000 presidential campaign, both major political parties used celebrities from the worlds of entertainment, sports, and public service as surrogate spokespeople for their platforms. The Democratic National Committee quickly signed Cher to rave about Al Gore and his running mate, Joe Lieberman. What the DNC did not know was that Cher didn't even like Joe Lieberman and she was not shy to admit that on national talk radio. She did not agree with his position on violence in the media; she thought he was going overboard on morals in Hollywood. The interview was supposed to tout the Democratic platform; instead, it set up a continuing debate on violence in music, movies, and on television. Unfortunately, the Democrats did not learn their lesson the first time. Once again, during the 2004 campaign, Cher was available and willing to speak in support of Democratic initiatives and candidates. And once again, no one screened what Cher would say before she went on the air— a big mistake.

It is also important that your spokesperson's information be up-to-the-minute. Long after the Swift Boat controversy had done its damage, the Kerry campaign put forth a spokesperson who kept talking about Kerry's record in Vietnam. The host just sat there, wondering what planet this spokesperson was on.

Following is the actual transcript of an exchange between Secretary of

Defense Donald Rumsfeld and a reporter at a Pentagon briefing immediately after the war in Iraq:

> **Reporter:** Mr. Secretary, I'd like to ask you about a couple of words and phrases that keep popping up in the commentary about what's going on. One of them is guerrilla war, and the other one is quagmire. Now, I know you've admonished us not to . . .
>
> **Rumsfeld:** I never have admonished you.
>
> **Reporter:** . . . Not to rush to any judgment about a quagmire just because things are getting tough. But can you remind us again why this isn't a quagmire? And can you tell us why you're so reluctant to say that what's going on in Iraq now is a guerrilla war?
>
> **Rumsfeld:** I'll do my best. I guess the reason I don't use the phrase guerrilla war is because there isn't one, and it would be a misunderstanding and a miscommunication to you and to the people of the country and the world. If you think what I just answered on the first question . . . looters, criminals, remnants of the Baathist regime, foreign terrorists who came in to assist and try to harm the coalition forces, and those influenced by Iran . . . I would say that those are five, if that was five items, five different things.
>
> They're all slightly different in why they're there and what they're doing. That is . . . doesn't make it anything like a guerrilla war or an organized resistance. It makes it like five different things going on that are functioning much more like terrorists.
>
> I mean, if you think of what the Baathists and the remnants are doing, well, think what they did during the war, the Fedayeen Saddam. They put civilian clothes on, went around, and took women and children and shoved them in front of them in Basra, as I recall, during the early part of the war, and attempted to use human shields and that kind of an approach. Now, that is not . . . it doesn't fit that word.
>
> So I think I think that if one analyzes what is going on in that country, they would find a different way to characterize it. I know it's nice to be . . . have a bumper sticker, but it's the wrong bumper sticker.

Reporter: Well, I know. But appreciating, as I do, your apprecia-tion of precision in language—

Rumsfeld: You've got the dictionary definition?

Reporter: What the DOD [Department of Defense] definition of guerrilla war.

Rumsfeld: I was afraid you would have. . . I should have looked it up. I knew I should have looked it up! [Laughter] I . . .

Reporter: According to the Pentagon's own definition . . .

Rumsfeld: I could die that I didn't look it up!

Reporter: . . . Military and paramilitary operations conducted in enemy-held or hostile territory by a regular. . . indigenous forces. This seems to fit a lot of what's going on in Iraq.

Rumsfeld: It really doesn't. [Laughter]

Now, the other part of your question. Quagmire. Quagmire. We have had several quagmires that weren't thus far, and I don't know . . . I didn't look that word up either. I should have, knowing you. But why don't I think it is one? Well, I opened my remarks today about the United States of America. Were we in a quagmire for eight years? I would think not. We were in a process. We were in a . . . we were evolving from a monarchy into a democracy. What happened in Eastern Europe? Were they in a quagmire when the Berlin Wall fell down and they started struggling and working their way towards democracy? Was Afghanistan in a quagmire as they went through that awkward stage of trying to schedule a Bonn process and then a Loya Jirga, and now they still don't have a permanent government, nor is it perfectly peaceful there.

If you . . . you call it what you want, and then be held account-able for it. My personal view is that we're in a war. We're in a global war on terrorism and there are people that don't agree with that . . . for the most part, terrorists. And our goal in each of those countries is to get the terrorists out of Afghanistan, get the Saddam Hussein regime out of Iraq, and allow the people of those countries to take over their countries and put their countries on a path towards something approximating a representative, civil society that's not a threat to its neighbors.

If you want to call that a quagmire, do it. I don't.

Secretary Rumsfeld might be able to entertain and can therefore get away with a lot, but most spokespeople cannot and their credibility will suffer. Secretary Rumsfeld skated by, but he had the reporters murmuring for days.

Do not be afraid to suggest questions and topics for your spokesperson to producers and guest bookers, or even to the hosts.

Can your spokesperson back up what is in the material? It is important that he or she knows it cold. Most hosts do not have time to read the books or lengthy articles and rarely follow any issue as closely as an advocate does. Instead, they rely on the pitch material that is mailed or faxed to them. To keep the conversation going, *your spokesperson must be able to carry it.*

It is wise to give your spokesperson a source pack that includes additional information on the topic to be covered. Many producers, hosts, and anchors regularly run Internet searches before a broadcast. You should do this as well to search for anything pertaining to your issue to ensure that your spokesperson will be well informed. This will also allow you to see what information is available to others—you and your spokesperson will then be better prepared for anything that might come up during the interview.

Monitor the media before the interview.

This is especially important the day before and the day of the interview. By monitoring the talk media and the Internet, your spokesperson will know what issues the audience is interested in at the moment and may be able to anticipate some of the call-in or write-in questions. This exercise enables the spokesperson to become familiar with the format. The best way to avoid a surprise is to monitor the exact program scheduled to understand the style and rhythm of the show, host, format, and audience. Give your spokesperson the extra confidence that comes from knowing what to expect, rather than sending him or her on a show cold.

If the program is on the radio, listen to the style, voice, and cadence of the host. If it is a television show, observe the body language of the host and notice how he or she is dressed. If participating in a live chat on the Internet, take note of the written delivery style. Your spokesperson should adapt a style comparable to the show. Right before the interview, confirm that your spokesperson is still monitoring the show or, if the interview will be taped instead of live, listening to other shows of that particular host.

Many talk-radio shows are simulcast on the Internet, which makes it easy to monitor a show that originates in a distant city. If your spokesperson is a politician or someone who cannot take time to listen, prepare a briefing memo about what is being discussed on the airwaves.

Again, try to find a way to tie your issues to topics the audience and other guests have been discussing. It is not absolutely necessary to connect your issue with previously discussed subjects, but at least try to make an intelligent segue from what was discussed to what you will now be discussing.

In the spring of 2004 when allegations of abuse of Iraqi prisoners by several American military prison guards surfaced, there was little else to talk about on the airwaves for weeks. If a spokesperson had not monitored the talk shows, it might be assumed that the debate about these human rights abuses was divided along party lines. Surprisingly, in many markets it was not.

Even if your campaign issue has nothing to do with something as horrendous as the above example, be prepared to address the issue if only to say something like, "My personal opinion is to be thankful we live in a democracy where it is expected that we will pursue truth and punish those found responsible." Then continue with your reason for being a guest on the show and discuss your campaign. An uninformed spokesperson could hurt your campaign. A well-informed spokesperson can help promote your issue.

Debrief your spokesperson.

This step is often overlooked, but it is important to determine immediately after an interview what conversations your spokesperson had in the green room and makeup room and with whom. Make some reminder cards as to any interests the media staff may have so that you can send them something of personal interest. This is good information to have on hand for the holidays. They will be amazed at the personal touch. This is especially true if you ask about a new baby or their daughter's soccer team during the next visit. It makes the spokesperson seem less egocentric and more like the caring, thoughtful human being you know they are.

5

BOOKING THE SPOKESPERSON

Think outside the rut.

Look beyond your usual scope of programming. See what you can do to get your issue and spokesperson on different kinds of shows and formats. Radio and television newscasts use short stories (packages) with quick interviews that provide a lot of bang for the buck. They might repeat the segment several times during the day or over a weekend.

Christian stations are often overlooked by progressive organizations, just as progressive radio is often overlooked by conservative organizations. Both offer a rich source of interview possibilities.

Richard Strauss of Strauss Media Strategies says ethnic stations, sports stations, and specialty stations are additional sources that are often overlooked. The "morning zoo" type of radio programming and television shows such as *Fox and Friends* are light, funny, and yet very topical—and they have large audiences. Accept any amount of time these programs will give you.

Don't forget weekend and late-night programming. Most people think about booking their spokesperson on shows that air during business hours, Monday through Friday. For radio, the second-most-listened-to time is between 10:00 A.M. and 3:00 P.M. on Saturdays. There is a wealth of programming available on the weekend, which makes it a great time for your issue to be heard. *Fox and Friends* on Saturday mornings often has double the ratings of other cable news and information channels aired during prime time.

On weekends people are in their cars, they are up early with the kids, they are watching television, and they are checking out the Internet. This is an ideal time to get their attention. But remember that the family is around, so orient your presentation accordingly. Several of the overnight hosts have a multitude of listeners, so have your spokesperson set the alarm clock and be ready to talk.

The trick is to watch and listen to all kinds of shows and then find a hook for your issue. You may have to really stretch to find it, but it will be worth it. A hip-hop morning-drive show may be a perfect match for your message and the audience you want to reach. Kandy Stroud booked Richard Miller, author of *Harvard's Civil War*, on several shows. It was not exactly a cutting-edge type of book, but she found the hook. The book was released right after Hurricane Katrina, and she was able to book it on the issue of the largest displacement of American citizens since the Civil War. The author was able to connect content in his book with the current issue of the hurricane. Producers were happy, and so were Stroud and the author.

Internet radio is catching on, as are the satellite distributors XM and Sirius. They all produce shows that are part of a unique delivery system. Many of these shows have more listeners than traditional radio, and those listeners are devoted to the satellite medium. When you think beyond your regular business hours and recognize the vast amount of airtime available at night and on weekends, you can double and triple the amount of exposure available for your message or issue.

Bite the bullet and budget for a radio and TV *satellite* tour.

There are two methods of media satellite delivery. One is the radio satellite tour, which does not involve any extra equipment, expense, or even a satellite, and uses nothing more than telephone lines. The other is the television satellite tour, which requires the booking of satellite time.

A radio satellite tour involves scheduling radio shows so that in one or two long sessions your spokesperson can sit down and be on twenty-five to thirty shows in one morning or afternoon. Unless you have a great booking department, know the media, or have a superstar spokesperson, you may want to hire a public-relations firm specializing in media tours. As in performing open-heart surgery, the success of a drive-time tour depends on how many times you have done it.

Great back-to-back bookings are difficult to secure if you have never booked shows in this manner before, so it is wise to invest in a firm that can do the bookings for you. They know the shows and the scheduling times that will add up to a very successful tour for your message.

If you prefer to do this yourself, here is how it works:

- For a national message, identify fifty or sixty markets that you want to reach. If you are interested in a statewide or regional message, adjust the number of markets appropriately.
- Identify the intended demographic. Twentysomethings don't usually listen to traditional talk radio, but they do listen to morning zoo programs, music formats, and sports-talk formats.
- Learn who the producers are for the shows that interest you.
- Set the date and times your spokesperson will be available. Remember, early morning is a great time for interviews.
- Begin blocking off three-to-ten-minute interviews as early as 5:30 A.M. EST. Offer the stations set blocks that will fit into their interview format time.
- Plan to do from five to seven interviews per hour. Understand that most stations have news at the top of the hour and several minutes of advertisements to fit into that one hour.
- Send confirmations to the stations and follow up with a phone call the day before the interview.
- Choose a live interview instead of a taped interview whenever possible. You can never be 100 percent certain that a taped interview will be utilized or will air in its entirety.

On the day the radio satellite interviews take place you will need the following:

- Two telephone lines in two rooms.
- An assistant to make the calls necessary to connect the spokesperson to the station.
- Newspapers and Internet clips from the regions you are calling. Know what local news the listeners are waking up to.
- Food and drinks to keep your spokesperson going.

- Any background you can provide your spokesperson about the host, the station, and issues pertaining to the region.
- Some radio stations would like to be called via an ISDN or Comrex Blue Box. It would be an added benefit to you if you have the equipment or can borrow a studio and producer.

Satellite television tours work very much the same way except you really need a satellite hookup to get your spokesperson into the newsroom or on a program at the television station. A satellite hookup can be very expensive. There are two components to a television satellite interview: the actual time on the satellite (called the bird), and the time it takes for someone to book the tour and to make sure that the completed interview is used. Some of your interviews will be live and some taped. The time of taping will depend on what other programs or satellite feeds the station must downlink on a daily basis. Stations and networks are accustomed to dealing with PR firms and will usually run their material. Your only concern should be when and how the interview will be placed—in a newscast, as a packaged story, or on a local talk program.

You can use satellite tours to cover a large section of the United States with millions of potential viewers and listeners, or you can downsize your satellite tour for a regional and statewide campaign. The bottom line is, the results and placement you gain from a satellite tour usually outweigh the expense.

Make your call count.

Sound fresh and excited every time you make a call. This can be a difficult task when you have to make several calls. This is one reason why it is worth your time to establish a friendly relationship with the people you will be calling. When you know someone personally you can engage in conversation and your call becomes a friendly, social call in addition to satisfying the original intent—to get your spokesperson on the air.

If you are leaving a voice-mail message, be brief. Your task is to make your pitch sound interesting without taking up a lot of time on an answering machine. The following is a transcript of an actual pitch call

that was placed and left on an answering machine. Obviously, the names
have been changed:

> Hi, this is Judy Pitcher and I am calling with the Women's
> Science Club of Washington. I am calling to be sure that you
> know about the news conference we are having next Tuesday the
> tenth at ten o'clock in the morning at the Hilton Hotel in
> Ballroom C. We are releasing a report that looks at the progress
> and the advances that have been made by women and girls over
> the last three decades in the areas of science, technology, and
> engineering. It also examines the barriers they still face in those
> areas; and highlights programs that have been very effective at
> helping women and girls to get more involved in and more
> invested in science, engineering, and technology; and has recom-
> mendations for employers, for schools, and for colleges and uni-
> versities, for the entire gamut of places where women and girls
> come into contact with these fields. The news conference is
> going to feature the former astronaut Sally Ride as well as
> Congresswoman _____, who has introduced legisla-
> tion on science education for girls and the director of the
> National Science Foundation. If you didn't get the advisory or
> would like an advance and private copy of the report please give
> me a call. Again it is Judy Pitcher. I am at _____ .
> Thanks, bye-bye.

Read this aloud while timing it. You will have the producer's attention
for about ten seconds. This was entirely too much information for a
phone call and it sounded like she was reading an advisory. Not only that,
but the message was annoying. She could have given the main information in one sentence and led with the bait that Sally Ride was attending
the news conference.

Always give your name and phone number twice. Enunciate and speak
slowly so your name and number can be understood. No one wants to listen
to a message again and again just to get a name and phone number.

Follow the same format for pitching your message as you do for writing
your campaign message—sound fresh and excited. Your voice-mail message

or phone call could be the first impression you make on the media. Don't lose the sale on the telephone!

Provide good service.

Think of your campaign as providing a service. Your job is to be of service to your customer—the producer, host, anchor, chat room convener. Again, this involves establishing a relationship with that person. They need to know how to reach you and to know that you will be helpful beyond your immediate interest.

If a producer is not interested in your guest or says there is no time for an interview, offer sound, B roll, or even some graphics to illustrate your message. Offer an alternative that can accommodate the window of time that is available. Be creative. How have local people previously treated this issue? How are they treating it now? How has this affected the local area? What legislation is being offered at this time? If you can provide a creative response to any of these questions, you may be able to present a new angle to the story using your message.

A producer's time is valuable and the last thing you need is for the producer to look at you (and, essentially, your message) as a pest. One way to avoid this is to begin a call with an apology. "I am really sorry to bother you. I know you have a busy show to produce, but if I can have a few seconds of your time I'd like to tell you about an issue that might be of interest to your listeners." Or, "I know you're very busy, but I have to get my spokesperson on the air." Let them understand that you have a job to do, just as they do. However, keep in mind that faxes and e-mails do not have voices. The above could come across as rude and pushy without the benefit of voice inflection.

Call more than once, but not every day. Producers can get as many as seventy-five calls a week. Wait a few days before you call back. Remember "The Gambler"—the song written in 1976 by Don Schlitz and performed by such great country music entertainers as Kenny Rogers and Johnny Cash? "You've got to know when to hold 'em and know when to fold 'em." If you don't receive a response after three attempts to contact the station, give up. But remember this before pitching an idea, message, or campaign to that station or person again.

Ask the important questions.

Why is your campaign an issue? Why does it matter? Why does it matter now? Why does this issue mean something to your target demographic? Does it mean something to Tina Teenager or Joe Lunch Pail or Sally Soccer Mom or Glenda Gardener? Why is this particular spokesperson the best person to represent your campaign on radio, television, or an Internet chat? Why is this person or issue going to impact the audience? Why should the station or Internet site devote time to your campaign or issue? Why will your issue make an impact on the listeners? Does it pass the so *what* test?

When you are preparing the pitch ask yourself the most important question, "Who cares?" Who cares about your issue, and why should they care? If no one would care, why have an issue at all?

Andrew Yates, producer of the *Mike Murphy Show*, KCMO Kansas City, says his pet peeve is getting a call saying, "Hi, I'm with So-and-So Public Relations Firm and boy do we have a great guest for you! Just call me back at 1-800-LOUSY GUEST and I'll tell you who it is." Don't expect a return call. Yates says, "Us old codgers in the radio business spend a lot of time teasing listeners, and we don't fall for the teasing pitch."

If you can answer the question of why your campaign or issue is important to the audience, chances are you will be rewarded with airtime for your spokesperson. Do not leave any unanswered questions out there for the host, producer, or guest booker to answer. Give them the answers up front about why your issue should be heard.

Utilize conference calls.

Conference calls are being used more and more in the media. An important aspect to remember is that conference calls are not live. Why would one station want to give airtime to another station's reporter? Consider arranging a conference call when you want to inform people on a regular basis, or you have breaking news and don't have time to arrange a news conference, or it's late at night or on the weekend, or you just don't have time to place a lot of individual phone calls to stations or shows. Conference calls allow you an informal method of reaching a large number of media outlets.

White House officials make use of conference calls for late-breaking news or for clarification of bills or positions. Senator Hillary Clinton hosts a conference call almost weekly with media all over the state of New York. Political campaigns use them to discuss scheduling or to place the expert or surrogate speaker of the day on the air.

Conference calls can include both print and broadcast reporters. However, when you include both, make sure the print reporters put their phones on mute. When print reporters type the answers on their keyboards, the clicking sound drives radio and television reporters crazy. It interferes with clear audio and it might render it useless. Many great conference calls have had unusable sound because of background typing.

There are several ways to operate a conference call. The most common is the free-for-all, and that usually works well. Just ask reporters to identify themselves before asking a question. Another is for the originator of the call to control who speaks when. The more organized conference call will do a roll call and let each reporter or host ask a question. It allows even smaller news outlets to get their needs met and it is the fairest way to give everyone on the line an opportunity to ask a question.

Conference calls are a quick way to assess the mood of the media. A conference call can be your very own media focus group. It allows you to understand where each host, producer or anchor is coming from. It also allows you to find media markets you would not have mined otherwise, and to get your experts on the air before they need to be on television. This does not mean that you can just put an expert on without preparation, but it allows you to clarify a point or to step in if your expert says something that is not on message. Since conference calls are taped instead of live, your interruption will not be taken so negatively.

You can also arrange a backgrounder conference call by providing a spokesperson on background—meaning that their comments will not be aired or attributed to your background spokesperson. However, always be mindful that even if the media participants have agreed to your on background rules, they are usually recording anyway. Many stations may not be interested in participating in a backgrounder. You will only know that after you approach them with the idea.

If there is an ongoing story that you want to comment on, such as budget hearings, you might want to arrange for a daily update conference call with different experts you have selected. Even if reporters are not able to get on the call, a transcript or sound bite highlights can be sent to them. You can also send out sound from the call via MP3 files.

Be aware that you might encounter market competition. Some stations in the same market may take issue with their competition being on the conference call. Every situation is different, and if the stations realize the conference call is their only opportunity for audio about your campaign or issue, they might overlook the fact that their competitors are on the line as well. You will be the one to determine the merits of including competitors on the same conference call.

When sending out information on your conference call, include the following in your release:

- What is it? Make this a one-line header.
- When is it? Give the date or the event it follows and the time in each time zone.
- Give the call-in number. Make this easy without having to make reservations. You can find out who is on the call by having the operator take roll call.
- Who are the participants? Give exact titles.
- What is the anticipated length of the call?
- Who is the contact person for follow-up or questions?

Honesty is the only policy.

Media people know each other and they talk. It is a very fluid profession. People change jobs, they socialize while on the road, and they see each other at media events. They will know if you decide to upgrade (change the program that your spokesperson is booked on for a better or higher-profile one). Don't lie about it. If you have booked someone on a show and Tim Russert comes along with an invitation, be honest with the first show's producer. You may never again get booked on that show, but at least you won't make an enemy for life.

Use care when granting first dibs or exclusivity to programs and producers. You do not have to tell the producer that you are operating on a first-come, first-serve basis, but it doesn't hurt to mention something like, "We were on your show last Monday and we'll do it again, but we want to give others a chance."

If you plan to give a show, producer, or host an exclusive interview, make certain that this media outlet is the best match for your publicity needs. Follow up in writing that you are granting them exclusivity.

Keep *them* honest. Always bring your own recorder to an interview. This is not as important for radio or television, where there is usually a recording made of the interview, but it is the *only* way to make sure that you are not misquoted.

Provide a choice.

Providing a choice of spokespersons is a key to getting on the air. If you have a hot issue, don't overuse one spokesperson. Offer a spokesperson of a specific gender, age, or ethnicity to the show or geographical region. A spokesperson on a station with a large Hispanic audience should be able to communicate to the audience in their language, especially if the show is broadcast in Spanish. The head of your organization might want to be the media star, but remember that you are promoting the goals of the organization, not necessarily the spokesperson.

Different spokespersons can offer different approaches. Former President Bill Clinton is the master of letting his audiences know he "feels" their pain or "understands" where they are coming from. On the other hand, Senator Hillary Rodham Clinton is more "policy oriented."

The Institute for Public Accuracy is a Washington, D.C.–based group that understands the importance of a choice of spokespersons. They are prepared as issues come up, providing a paragraph that explains who the spokespersons are, their positions on a topic, and the phone number to call. If there is an election somewhere in the world, their spokespersons are immediately ready to go. They are fast and effective; they fax, they e-mail, and their phone numbers work. They provide a choice, and their pitch paragraphs actually say something, enough for you to really understand what the potential guest is going to say.

A list of spokespersons made available to the media is worth its weight in gold. Many producers have databases, and if they cannot use your spokesperson now they may be able to at a later date. Give the producer an opportunity to choose. Put together a short biography on each person that humanizes the issue. Include your list of spokespersons on your Web site and attach audio and video as part of the bio package. If your spokesperson is energetic and well-spoken, the producer will be able to get all the information they need. Often, just one detail will catch the producer's eye.

Offering two choices at the time of the pitch can be effective. For example, you could suggest an executive director of an agency who could speak intelligently about a broad range of issues related to your central goal, and you could offer someone who can tell a compelling personal story that relates to your issue. For example, if your issue concerns AIDS, you could make at least two suggestions: One might be the director of a local AIDS service organization who knows about many service-delivery issues, and the other might be an AIDS patient who can talk in real terms about what it is like to live with the disease on a daily basis.

If your group of spokespersons is large, consider publishing a guide to possible guest experts and send it to media outlets. Booklets can sit on shelves, so be sure your webmaster is able to pull out the sections you need when a hot issue comes up, then e-mail the relevant section of the guide to producers and bookers. The think tanks have made tremendous use of published guidebooks listing different experts. Not a day goes by that you do not see or hear one of these experts on the air, expounding on the most current hot issue.

With Web pages being the go-to place to look for information about guests, the best way to capitalize on this is to attach sound and video clips of your experts so producers can see and hear the potential guest. New audio and visual can be added as it becomes available. With the source's permission you can put a thirty-second clip or even an entire interview on the Web. You can also e-mail the video and sound to producers. It is best to save the e-mail tactic for something really spectacular—you want the next one you send to be opened, so don't overdo it. Always provide a written transcript of content; no one will open up a sound or video file without one.

Be able to offer guests for radio or Internet chat on a five-minute basis, and for television on a half-hour or hourlong basis. If you let producers know that you have someone available for the length of time they need to fill, you will have better success placing your spokesperson. If you are offering a choice of spokespersons that can be available on a moment's notice, make sure your talking points are up-to-date and that even on dress-down day, your spokesperson is prepared with suitable, professional clothing to wear for television interviews.

Availability counts!

Your research department should be willing to help news departments, hosts, producers, webmasters, and anchors find answers to their questions. When a media outlet calls, it is best to share the wealth and not be proprietary with information. The most important part is to be viewed as a helpful source of information. If you have weighed the pros and cons and feel that you can share your opposition research with producers, do so. You will have friends for life and may get tips that will help your organization or issue in an even exchange.

Offer information that makes the news department or host look good— it will buy you loyalty. It also allows you to get information on the air without needing to book a spokesperson. If you provide good, reliable information it will help you gain credibility for your issue and spokesperson.

Tell the producers that your spokesperson is available to them for background information. Give out other like-minded contacts when it makes sense for your organization. Think long-term, not just short-term. Does your issue have an evergreen effect—will it grow into other stories?

Get your facts straight.

Many people use media directories for their only source of information; they should be used only as the start of research. Check the phone book and the Internet. Get the phone numbers of studio lines (for radio), booking producers, and on-air producers. If you are booked for a television satellite, make sure you have the direct cell phone number of the person who is actually shooting your guest. Call all the numbers ahead of time to check for their accuracy. Double-check every name, address, fax number, e-mail address, and phone number before you pitch something.

If you operate on the two-source rule (having the same information from two different sources), then your information should be correct. It's embarrassing to pitch a show that used to be on the air, or a station that used to be a news format. Avoid being uninformed.

Learn the time zones and clarify them. Producer Andrew Yates says that he would be a wealthy man if he were given a dollar for every time there was a time zone mistake. He said he cannot count the times he was told, "I thought that was ten o'clock Eastern." Then he would have to reply, "No, I'm in the central time zone."

Be clear about the length of the interview. It sounds terrible for a guest to say, "I have to go." Know what your time windows are and put them in writing.

Avoid a conference service that has one show moving into the other. It is a prescription for disaster if one station comes on the line before another is finished. It is not worth upsetting the host or the big-name guest.

Send a confirmation in writing. If appropriate, send an e-mail and a fax. Follow it up with a phone call. Be sure to include your backup numbers in case you need to be reached. Keep a copy with you and in your booking file, and write down the names of all those you have contacted. It is helpful to refer to the person by name when you are speaking with them. In addition, if you have spoken with someone not authorized to take the confirmation, you will at least have a name to back up your story.

Cancellations—make lemonade from lemons.

No one likes cancellations—not hosts, not producers, not even the guests. If you must cancel, do not leave the producer in the lurch. Many shows promote guests on the air or in the newspapers prior to an interview. If you have to cancel, try to provide an equivalent substitute. Always offer to rebook. If a big-name guest cancels, sending a plant or box of candy will go a long way.

U.S. Senator Ted Kennedy (D-Massachusetts) was scheduled to do a show with actress Whoopi Goldberg. Unfortunately, at the last minute she had to cancel. The interview was arranged as a joint appearance, so Senator Kennedy apologized on the air and offered to help the host rebook Ms. Goldberg. This helped with the host's promotion problem and showed that the senator was sincere.

If you mess up, apologize in writing immediately. A congressional leader was booked on several talk shows over a three-week period. At the last minute he canceled several shows. There was no apology or viable explanation given. Unfortunately for the politician, several of those hosts were together at a national forum. While comparing notes, they discovered that they had all been stiffed by the same politician. The hosts are still waiting for a letter of explanation and have all vowed never to book that politician again.

If you think that, for some reason, your spokesperson might not be able to make a radio or television appearance or may be late, then tell the producer the parameters and let them make the decision of whether or not to cancel. If you must cancel, be gracious and apologetic. No one can afford to risk negative publicity.

Here are some other suggestions from booking guru Cheryl Stein:

- Pay attention to headlines. Tie what you are trying to book to something in the current mainstream. Don't pitch the book or the specific issue, but pitch the idea; then say there happens to be a book or organization available on this subject.
- Most talk shows are considered entertainment. You must be willing to compromise what you want to talk about.
- Have your client participate in giving you ideas and angles that can be pitched.
- Develop good rapport with the media bookers and the studio people so that you make the mechanics of their job easy.
- Joke with the media bookers; they like to have fun and have a laugh too.
- Bookers are always in a rush—if they are on the run, let them be.
- Find out what they want—some only want e-mail, some only want a phone call.
- Be persistent.

If all else fails, review the public file.

The public file is one of the least-understood aspects of getting on the air. It should be used as a last resort only, when nothing else works. Each radio and television station is required by the Federal Communications Commission to have a public file. It contains the basic information about what that particular station is mandated or allowed to air. Should there be a set amount of commercial time per minute? Is the station licensed to air religious programming only, or licensed to broadcast certain hours of the day at a certain power level?

The public file must be made available at the station's main studio and it can be obtained on a computer if the computer terminal is available. Licensees are encouraged to post their electronic public files on the Internet. The file must be made available for inspection by any member of the public, free from harassment, at any time during regular business hours. An employee of the station may remain in the room while the file is being examined. No appointment is needed to view the station's public file, but as a courtesy you may want to call beforehand.

The public file must also include all letters and e-mail received from the public that were sent to station management or to a publicly advertised e-mail address, and that contain comments and suggestions regarding the operation of the station (unless obscene or confidential).

Letters may be provided to the public on diskette. All stations must make a quarterly list of the station's most significant treatment of community issues during the previous three-month period. Did the station provide public service time to an event or issue? Commercial radio stations must have a copy of every contract or agreement involving time brokered, excluding financial information.

By law, copies of the public file must be made available at a reasonable cost. In addition to agreements, ownership reports, and contour maps, the public file must include any records of political broadcast requests, charges made (if any), and any records of free time provided to or on behalf of the candidates.

So—how does all this translate into time on the air for your issue or spokesperson?

If a radio or television station is not being responsive to community needs, when that station comes up for relicensing they could be in jeopardy if enough community members make enough noise.

Recently five hundred locals from San Antonio, Texas, showed up at the FCC's town hall hearing to protest the decision to weaken the media ownership rules. Their main issue was how local radio and television can serve the local community.

Once you have assembled the information, talk to management about their responsiveness to your issue and the need to give it some airtime. If you still get no response you may want to talk to the local advertisers and the local newspaper. You might eventually make a friend of the manager if the program or segment you propose is a hit—or you could make a permanent enemy. This is a last-resort strategy.

6

PREPARING TO BE ON

Scan the media before your interview.

When told to look over the Drudge Report a couple of times a day, an influential campaign staffer for presidential candidate Howard Dean replied that he didn't have time. He didn't have time not to.

Scanning the media used to be a matter of reading the morning newspaper and then turning on a television news show. It has taken on a whole new meaning since the age of the Internet. It is a good idea to read the major papers online—the *New York Times, L.A. Times, Wall Street Journal, USA Today,* and the *Washington Times,* as well as the local paper.

Also look at the Internet sites that others read, such as The Drudge Report, Salon.com, and "Morning Papers" on Slate.com. Other helpful sites are the homepage of Yahoo!, AOL, or many other Internet search engines; several of the blog sites such as Mullings.com, TheDailyHowler. com, Wonkette.com, DailyKos.com; and the sites for the Democratic and Republican National Committees. Check out opposite sites so you will know what is being said on both sides of an issue, and look at the most popular broadcast and cable shows and movies that people are watching. Newspapers often list them in the Nielsen ratings.

Yahoo! and Lycos list the top searchable terms—the buzz indexes are buzz.yahoo.com and 50lycos.com. Also available is the Lycos 50 blog, which details which bloggers are being read. Google lists the most-searched public figures, and most newspaper Web sites will post their frequently e-mailed articles. Add Snopes.com to your search to see which urban legends are making the rounds. Also, check out the Word of the Year, a product of the American Dialect Society and the Linguistic Society of America.

Log on to Talkers.com and look at the top ten issues discussed in the talk-radio industry that week. It is often different from the search terms and based on the research of actual talk shows.

Right after the Super Bowl in 2003, the top searchable term was *Janet Jackson's breast*. Needless to say, it made its way onto many talk programs and hearings on Capitol Hill.

Some of the media are connected. The *Washington Post* now owns a radio station, so sometimes the same stories are covered in both places. You can be sure that the host and the producer have reviewed the media before the interview, and so should you. You can't afford not to. If you really are too busy, have a trusted staffer do it for you, then give you a complete set of notes. It will make a positive difference in your interview.

Any producer who has been around the barn a few times can smell a talk story a mile away. You could put a hundred producers in a room and let them read the same five newspapers, and you could bet the farm they would list the same top five stories people will want to discuss on the air. They may be in different order, but they will be the same stories.

Give yourself a test. Early one weekday morning scan the media listed above and write down your top ten picks. Then tune in to some national and local talk programs—both on television and on the radio. How many of the topics did you pick correctly? If you missed several, keep trying until you are able to get the talk mind-set.

As a spokesperson you will need to be able to talk about those topics as well as your own. If you have time, go to the local diner or coffee shop early in the morning and ask people informally what they think about some of those topics. You will then have your own watercooler poll, and it will help you coordinate your issue with the issues of the day.

Give the background.

One poll indicated that only one in four Americans follows the news closely. Many people get their news and views from radio and television, so give a short background or history of your issue. You will need to paint a more complete verbal picture on radio than on television; you can work with the television producer beforehand on presenting the images that will illustrate your story or your issue. In addition, do not assume that just because someone reads the newspaper and surfs the Internet, he or she will have any idea of what you are talking about—give the background.

Following are some suggestions for providing background information:

- Use terminology people understand—no abbreviations and no acronyms. If you must use either, say the complete form the first time, then use the abbreviation or acronym. Repeating "Central Intelligence Agency" instead of "CIA" all through the interview would be annoying.
- Paint the picture and make it totally understandable for someone in Oklahoma as well as in New York City. Whitman-Walker Clinic in Washington, D.C., sent out a fund-raiser for their AIDS food program. They had brown paper bags with their pitch on it. It was clear to the press and to the donors; fill the grocery bag, and provide healthy meals. A better picture could not have been painted.
- People love to hear a great story. Watch the late-night talk shows for some examples.
- Give results. Make sure your explanation shows action and outcome.
- Be animated when giving historical background.
- Make your story important. Why is the background relevant to what you want to accomplish in the interview?

Be specific.

Political and corporate drivel is just that—drivel. Maintaining a loyal audience, getting ratings, selling ads and sponsorships, and increasing audience time spent watching, listening, and on a chat is what it's all about. As soon as you are predictable, you have lost the audience. Be specific and you are likely to keep the audience. If you are defending a policy you believe in, get ready to name names.

One of the best ways to prepare for your interview is to adapt some of the behavioral interviewing techniques to your preparation. Behavioral interviewing is not about hypothetical questions, but about how you or your organization actually behave.

These tips are adapted from the University of North Carolina's behavioral interviewing techniques:

- Recall recent situations that show favorable behaviors or actions involving leadership, teamwork, initiative, planning, and customer service.
- Prepare short descriptions of each situation; be ready to give details if asked.
- Each story must have a beginning, middle, and an end. Describe the situation, your action, and the outcome or result.
- Be certain the outcome or result reflects positively on you (even if the result itself was not favorable).
- Be honest. Don't embellish or omit any part of the story. The interviewer will find out if your story is built on a weak foundation.
- Don't generalize about several events; give a detailed accounting of one event.

Some of the behavioral interviewing questions that can be adapted are:

- Tell about a time when you solved . . .
- Give a specific example of . . .
- Describe a situation when . . .
- What steps did you take when . . .
- What was your role in . . .
- What was the result of . . .
- How do you . . .
- What did you say when . . .

Speak from your heart and experience while being specific. In preparing, answer the question, "So what?" for the impact of any examples you use.

Put your best foot forward.

One former congresswoman appeared on C-Span one morning wearing a workout outfit. Her choice of clothes said she did not respect the audience or the privilege of being on television. Even if you are doing a radio interview or are on-site for an Internet chat, dress professionally. There may be an Internet camera on you, or your attire might be mentioned by the host. You or your issue should be the topic, not the clothing you wear.

Build bridges.

Building bridges involves more than just using bridging words—it is a matter of using ideas to bridge your differences. Find areas that the right and the left both agree on, such as the limits of the Patriot Act, or taxing access to the Internet, or excessive government in the lives of citizens. You do not want to be too far in either direction if you are trying to move the middle. There are ways to build bridges even with the most contested of issues, and it often makes sense to move the discussion in the direction of building bridges.

Use the techniques of active listening. Find common interests and goals. Make a list of possible areas of agreement on your issue and use it when it is appropriate.

Get energized.

You and the host are talking to your constituents together. It is not the host's job to be passionate about your issue—it is yours.

Be sure that you are not low on energy or sleep. When Howard Dean made his now dubbed "I have a scream" speech, he was not feeling well and he was exhausted. He overcompensated, and it possibly contributed to his losing his bid for the presidency. Lack of sleep is one of the biggest dangers facing public figures.

If you are not in the greatest of moods before your interview, do something to psych yourself up—listen to your favorite music, read a funny book, call an upbeat friend, or watch a tape of your most disliked opponent. Do something that gets your juices flowing.

Convince the host by your words and demeanor that you care about your issue, it relates to the audience, and it is something you believe in passionately. Communicate that.

Choose an in-studio interview whenever possible.

This applies to radio interviews as well as television. Even though radio interviews are easy to do over the telephone, it will be to your advantage to be in the studio—and it is imperative for local issues. It can be a pain, but it is worth your time, even for a short interview. You will develop a relationship with the host and producer and this can prove to be beneficial for future interviews and other issues you might have.

Other reasons to do an in-studio interview and some helpful tips:

- You have a better chance of getting longer airtime.
- Your host (unless it is a shock jock) will be more courteous, if only because of social convention.
- You have a better chance to assess the show and plan a future strategy.
- You may be able to bring supplementary materials that will help make your case to the host, who can then help you convey your message over the air. Have something available to summarize your points at the end of the show.
- If you would like to have a tape of the show, your chances of getting one will be better if you bring a blank tape, disk, and CD with you. You need all three because some stations seem to have equipment from the Civil War era.
- Inform your base and like-minded organizations that you will be on the air, and ask them to call in. This will help counter negative callers.
- Have some drinking water available.
- Before the interview, avoid carbonated beverages (which could

cause you to burp at the most inopportune time) and chocolate (which can thicken your speech).

- Bring a camera. You might be able to use a picture of you and the host or one of you in the studio for future publicity. But always ask for permission—it might be a bad-hair day for the host.
- Shake hands with the producer and the host when you meet them.
- Take them coffee, doughnuts, bagels, or, if the interview is late in the day, some great cookies. The studio staff will love you for it.

Understand the consequences of success.

Be ready to articulate what would happen if your position on an issue became policy. Similarly, be ready to speak about the likely consequences if the opposing view became policy. Lay out the issue in concrete terms.

The average American does not give two hoots about a spotted owl when they are perceived as a threat to jobs. As a result the spotted owl became a familiar talk-show refrain. Environmentalists could have couched their position in a number of appealing ways: projected job creation, the importance of national parks, alternative ways of harvesting forests, renewable natural resources, and positive effects on the economy would have been much more audience-appealing methods of promoting the protection of spotted owls.

Karl Rove, senior adviser to President George W. Bush, is an expert in understanding the success of the other side. In an interview with *Men's Journal* he said that you should "kill with kindness" and have respect for the voters as well as for your opponent. He also suggests that you should not let yourself dislike the opposition—people will pick up on your hostility and it will hurt you.

Gail Norton, President Bush's former Secretary of the Interior, looked like an environmental hero when she made a speech and had a photo op with condors that had been saved from extinction. It took over the oppositions' agenda and presented the administration as being environmentally friendly, even though they had been under intense criticism for their environmental record.

Explain clearly what you think will happen if your opponent's plan is implemented. Beware of the gloom-and-doom strategy—if it does not turn out to be the case, you have lost your credibility.

Howard Dean used the war in Iraq to propel his candidacy to the top during the 2004 Democratic presidential primaries. He spoke about the consequences of the war and he was extremely successful—for a while. He did not understand the consequences of his success. It put him out front so he continued to use it, not realizing that he needed an additional message. This is an example of poor success planning.

And what about the failed 2004 presidential campaign of consumer advocate Ralph Nader? Although no one knows what his real intentions were, he said early in the campaign that he would not seek the support of the Green Party, which had propelled him to more than one million votes in the 2000 presidential primary. He did not plan on the backlash from his former supporters—or perhaps he did. One columnist referred to him as a megalomaniac. Maybe that explains why he didn't seem fazed when he received such a pitiful number of votes in 2004. Unlike the success he had in 2000 in seemingly derailing a campaign (Al Gore's), he could not be blamed for the Democrats losing the White House again in 2004.

The more specific and concrete the example, the better the chance of making a home run. In a debate situation allow the opposition to talk themselves into a corner with their misinformation and half-truths, and then respond concisely with the correct information.

One of the reasons you might be invited back again and again is that you produce a reaction. Producers love that. However, understand what it will do to your relationship with your base as well as with the middle.

Know your opponent.

Be able to quote the other side exactly. Understand their thought processes. Know their arguments. Read the papers, listen to their interviews, attend their lectures and speeches, and read everything they write. Watch their body language.

If you look at the early road-tapes of presidential candidate George W. Bush in 2000 and compare them to President Clinton's, you will see that although the words were very different, their body language was quite similar. Someone spent hours watching Clinton tapes and was an effective coach for candidate Bush.

Listen to people outside your organization. Find out what they like about what the competition is saying, how the competition looks, and what grabs their attention.

In the documentary *The Fog of War* former Defense Secretary Robert McNamara stresses how important it is to understand the needs, hopes, and goals of the enemy. In order for you to win the public relations war you must understand that as well.

Here are some must-do's to become familiar with the opposition:

- Run an Internet search. Use more than one search engine, because the information can vary. Spend the money for a one-day rate on Nexis-Lexis—a deep Web search engine providing more information than other search engines have to offer.
- Log on to the opposition's Web site and do it frequently. The changes made are worth noting.
- Get on their e-mail list. If you would rather not use your own address, use that of a friend.
- Have their quotes on cards, ready and accessible. It is best if you do not read on the air, but the station can make a graphic of it or you can have the host read it. You can also memorize the quotes.
- Know their sources. A church denomination used a quote on the death rate of homosexuals. It turns out that the source was from a study of obituaries from newspapers—very creative, but not exactly scientific. The opposition was able to make mincemeat of the "research."
- Understand their persuasion strategies and what media they typically use. Learn how they argue a point, and make a chart of their techniques—it might come in handy on the air. Most people are consistent in their approach and delivery, so learning about their persuasion techniques can give you a distinct advantage.

- Keep a physical clipping file in addition to a computer file. Keep them in chronological order. It is easier to flip through a file than it is to run a search every time you need to refresh your memory.
- Find out if they have been involved in any scandals or legal issues regarding publications, past spokespersons, or decisions.

Be succinct, clear, and descriptive.

Compose your words ahead of time as if you were writing a long article and then memorize the main points. Remember how much you liked those teachers in college—the ones who told a joke, didn't take themselves too seriously, and were well prepared? It will also work for you.

A basic taboo in journalism is, *Don't bury the lead.* You know the main idea you want to get across, so get to your point and your theme in the very first sentence. Have three message points ready to go, plus words or phrases that you can use.

The Associated Press is now giving two different leads for many of its news stories. One is the traditional straight lead that begins with the main facts of what took place. The other is the optional (or alternative) approach that attempts to draw the reader in though imagery, narrative devices, perspective, or other creative means. It is designed to give people something other than what they have read on the Web.

Clear your mind before an interview. Meditate or do whatever else might help you to focus.

Don't use big words. Be able to talk to people who have an eighth-grade education, but always keep the audience in mind and never talk down to them. Your words are your artist's palette; paint a picture as you talk.

California Governor Arnold Schwarzenegger was discussing redistricting in his state and said, "Some of the districts look literally drawn by a drunk with an Etch-a-Sketch." It was a great description and was repeated by the local media and talk personalities. It painted the picture and made his point.

Talk Radio News Service embedded Iraq War correspondent Cholene Espinoza was able to describe the desert so effectively that the audience had a clear understanding of what it felt like to be there. In describing the biological weapons protection gear (the chemical suit) she said, "It's like wearing a snowsuit for three days and nights in the hot desert." It was a great analogy and one that was easy to imagine. Develop analogies that work; field test them before you go on the air.

Neal Conan, host of National Public Radio's *Talk of the Nation*, says there are two kinds of guests, "people who are accustomed to being interviewed and those who are not." He said that a subset of those accustomed to being interviewed is the messengers, and they are not going to be comfortable until they get their message out.

There will be times when the spokesperson should not be clear or succinct, but should be emotional and human. This would be the spokesperson that has been through a war, a ride in space, or something that really pulls at the emotions. The more the better—bring it on!

Use the rule of three to assess on-air performance.

The rule of three is a handy guide anyone can use to judge what is said on the air. Michael Albl, the executive vice president of Critical Mass Media, explains that you can ask three questions to determine whether an item or piece used on the air is funny, compelling, interesting, informative, or any other adjective you care to insert in the questions. Using the word *funny* as an example, the questions to ask are:

1. Is (or was) the element funny?
2. Is (or was) the element really funny?
3. Is (or was) the element really f***ing funny?

Answers:
No to number 1—Don't use the element because there is stronger material.
No to number 2—Don't use the element because there is stronger material.
Yes to number 3—It is a killer bit—use it! If it is a story, anecdote, or a piece of data and it does not measure up to number 3, then it is not strong enough to be used. Find something else.

Prioritize your talking points.

Decide on the most important points you want the audience to under-stand and to remember. Find two to five points to get across in every interview and make a checklist. Practice working in your points without appearing to be reviewing a checklist. Don't sound rehearsed; let it flow naturally. You have reached your goal when you can make all of your points during an interview and can do it with ease.

Do plenty of practice interviews with a practice host asking questions—some of which may seem off the point. Work on bringing your agenda items into the conversation naturally. Don't be obnoxious or say, "I'm really here to talk about X rather than Z." Victoria Jones of Talk Radio News Service says, "The host may have one specific issue of interest. The more you try to go to your talking points, the more evasive you sound." You can and should get to your talking points, but you must link them to the ongoing conversation.

Be positive, and avoid negative words. Write your talking points in order, with the most important ones first. Change any negative words into positive ones. Stick to your agenda so you won't be thrown off your game. It takes skill and practice to keep your agenda while answering all of the questions in the most effortless and comfortable way possible.

Let it be known that you have a Web page, e-mail address, and/or a toll-free phone number. Ask the host to announce it, or request that it be shown on the chyron on television. If you are the one giving the informa-tion, say it slowly or say it twice.

Put together a bag of options and have it with you, even if it stays in the green room during your interview. This should include position papers, your mission statement, and articles you want for reference. The best way to keep them together is in a briefing book—a notebook that you can review before your interviews. Your staff may have valuable ideas to con-tribute from something they have seen, read, or heard. Let them partici-pate by adding to the bag of options, and give a group lunch for those who contribute.

Get your point across by using *sliders* like, "The most important point (or fact) is . . ." or, "I would like to take this opportunity to add . . ."or, "I'm not sure about that, but what I can tell you is . . ."

Kill two birds with one stone.

Make use of your free time when you are on the road. Pack some extra press kits or have access to a printable electronic press kit from your Web site. Call local stations and offer to drop by. Local hosts, anchors, and producers are often looking for something different for their shows and would welcome out-of-town guests. Make a few cold calls. You might just wind up with a great discussion on the air, or perhaps you could tape something for use at a later date.

If you are a semicelebrity, the idea that you would even consider dropping by might be newsworthy and would probably get quite a bit of coverage in the local press. If you are going to be in a town for business, to visit a friend or family, or to give a speech, consider having your PR department call the local TV and radio stations.

7

BEING ☆ ON! ☆

Helpful hints for the spokesperson.

The sheer force of personality can carry you for miles. Tell stories and relate to issues on a personal level, but you must still be ready to answer what is asked of you.

During the 2004 debates a *Talk Radio News* staffer, Adam Sharon, decided that you could go up to anyone in spin alley, say to them, "Eat s**t," and they would just go on with their prearranged spin. Hosts hear spin all day and all night and it goes nowhere—a lot of it gets recorded on tape and camera, but very little of it gets used. You will not be invited back, and your sound clip will not be used or someone is going to make fun of it. Yes, keep on message, but do it in a fresh and personal way.

Remember, a message is something that you craft beforehand, whereas spin is how you take bad news or something that contradicts your message and turn it around so that it serves your message. For example, the Bush administration's message is that they are keeping America safe and fighting terrorism. The Dubai Ports World deal appeared to contradict this message. So the administration went into spin mode by claiming that the United Arab Emirates is a critical ally in the war on terror and that to renege on the deal would make America less safe.

When talking to callers use their first names. Barry Lynn, the executive director of Americans for the Separation of Church and State, recommends addressing callers by their first names because it shows respect for them and humanizes you. His example: "Marcy, you've got to listen to what I'm going to say, because you have some wrong information."

You can interrupt the host/anchor if he or she talks constantly, but be polite in doing so. You may even be respected more for the interruption.

Use the name of your organization whenever you can. Say it often, but within reason. You are there to sell your cause and if you do not use the name of your organization, no one will know who you are. If you have just written a book tell the host or anchor that you will not plug the book if they will mention it. Usually they are all too happy to agree to that arrangement. It will then look like you are a guest with the information, and they can do the selling for you.

Some additional tips:

- Relate to the moment—pay attention to the topic of discussion right before going on the air. Think of a natural transition to that discussion. For example, a host was talking about going to the dentist, and what a painful experience it was. The next guest was scheduled to talk about the possibility of Ralph Nader entering the 2004 presidential race. The guest segued with, "Send him to the dentist." It got the intended laugh and made it easy for the host to move on.

- Research has shown that television viewers switch channels as often as every seven seconds, so it is imperative that you give your issues impact with descriptive speech.

- Use I statements whenever possible, but unless you are the candidate, remember that it is your *issue* being promoted— not *you.*

- Never read from talking points. In fact, never read on the air— period. It is always obvious when someone is reading a statement or information instead of speaking spontaneously.

- Emotion kills the message. Unless you are talking about a tragedy, avoid raw emotion, but don't become emotionless, like the R2D2 robot from *Star Wars*. Work to achieve a balance. Never lose your composure. Do what is necessary to remain calm, and come prepared with strategies for this. Do not let the host or other guests rattle you.

- If you have a personal tie to the local area, use it. "My husband and I love skiing at Mt. Sunapee. . . ."

- At the end of the interview ask if you can provide additional information or if any follow-up is needed.

Avoid answering hypothetical questions or speculation. It will get you into trouble every time. Be wary of questions that would cause you to make an either/or choice, or the current version of "Have you stopped beating your wife?" Let the question you answer be the question you are prepared to answer. If it is too far-reaching, say so. "This is too far-reaching, and it's difficult to answer." If you are asked some way-out-of-the-ballpark question and you think it is just meant to get to you, it probably is. Don't take the bait and do not repeat the outrageous statement or question.

Your eye movements, your body language, and your words should all convey that you are trustworthy. Maintaining eye contact is crucial. Look at the radio host or television host or anchor. If you are in a remote satellite television studio do not take your eyes off the middle of the camera. Do not look at the monitor—if necessary, have it moved so you will not be able to see it. (See specifics on this subject in the Tips for Television appendix.)

If you are on television ask the producer to let you know via your IFB (earpiece) if you are looking down during the interview. In the studio it can be difficult to know if you are balancing looking into the camera with looking at another guest and the interviewer.

Again, do not go on the air when you are hungry, angry, or tired. Do not agree to be on a show at a future time when you think you are going to be hungry, angry, or tired.

Master interviewer Terry Gross says that a good interview is a subject's ability to talk about his or her craft in such a way that offers some insight. She says that if the person she is interviewing is funny and conversational, that is good enough for her.

Thomas Rankin Associates developed these tips for handling callers:

- Remember that you are the expert. It is beneath you to get into an argument with the callers. Let the host take control of the show—that is what they are paid to do. If it really gets out of hand you might say, "I would like to answer the question," or, "I would like to respond to Sally."
- Never lose your composure.
- In answering questions, use phrases that underline the points you want to make. "The point I am making is . . ." or, "The important thing to remember is . . ."

The three *Be's* of a good guest:
Be amusing, be likable, be honest.

If you have no sense of humor, go to a local comedy club and ask a comedian to punch up your material. Mark Katz of the Sound Bite Institute, and the author of *Clinton and Me: A Real Life Political Comedy*, is a master of this. See his Web site, soundbiteinstitute.com, for ideas.

Know your hot-button issues and be ready to deflect them with just a bit of humor. Have one or two jokes you can comfortably use on the air and that make people laugh with you. Be sure the punch line makes sense and is funny.

Use a cartoon if you can explain it well or if it can be shown on television or on a Web site. Be *real*, and do not be a smart-ass. Always take responsibility. You are being interviewed because you are the spokesperson, so unless you are representing a political candidate, stick with the *I's* and forget the *we's*. Take ownership.

The best hosts are excellent at pithy quotes and sound bites. Talk host Jim Bohannon tosses them off readily. Once while listening to a boring politician he said, "There's a minor tropical storm from that spin." If you can get an arsenal of these quips, use them. But the technique needs to fit your unique personality. A technique that works for one person may bomb coming from another.

Larry David of television's *Curb Your Enthusiasm* wrote a very funny piece referring to President George W. Bush's National Guard service and how he no longer had to be embarrassed about signing up for the National Guard to avoid Vietnam. It earned him a lot of buzz. Written material can often serve as the take-off point for a great interview. If you can write something that can serve as your base for on-air media, go for it.

Larry King was interviewed about what he looks for in guests. He said a passion for what they do, a bit of self-deprecating humor, an ability to explain what they stand for, and a little bit of a chip on their shoulders. (Notice he said a *little* bit of a chip.) This does not mean sarcasm. Sarcasm comes across quite differently on air than it does in person-to-person conversation.

I once sat next to the late Peter Jennings on an airplane, and I took the opportunity to ask him what he looked for in a guest. He said, "Be clear about what you think and what you wish to convey. Tell me when you don't know the answer—a faker insults the questioner and the audience. Moral rectitude and certainty makes me nervous—people may not hold the keys to the kingdom." Jennings also cautioned against the use of sound bites; he said they are often too short and should be used as punctuation.

On the other hand, writer and political commentator David Horowitz said that in political war, "Sound bites and emotions beat argument and reason."

In an interview with *The Washington Post* an ABC News reporter said, "Don't let yourself be intimated; don't let yourself be charmed." Be familiar with the types of questions the host likes to ask.

Some reporters will study their potential guests to ascertain the best way to conduct the interview. For instance, the reporter mentioned above assessed President George W. Bush and realized that he was more likely to completely answer questions that are focused, forceful, and direct.

The *New York Times*' David Sanger finds that he gets better answers from not asking the news of the day, because "no matter what the question is, you are likely to hear the message of the day."

Be upbeat—unless, of course, it is a time of national crisis. Media consultant Jim Tazareck says that people do not tune in to radio or television to have their day screwed up and to make them depressed. Humor can carry you and your issue a long way. Think about the interview as an adventure—as a chance to get to know and to like the person you are talking to. Keep a light touch, even with difficult subjects. If world hunger is the topic, talking about the extraordinary resilience of people in the face of adversity can lighten up a tough story.

A spokesperson willing to relax and have fun can make quite an impression—even if they don't get to all or any of their points. It could also result in an invitation to come back.

Senator Joseph Lieberman appeared on an FM personality show with the goal of talking about his crime program. He really never did get to talk about his program, but he did discuss the Yankees' farm team. He sang the Yankees' song and he talked about how rough it was to represent Connecticut, a state split between the fans of the Boston Red Sox and those of the New York Yankees. He had fun, he was well liked, and he was a tremendous success. If he had been able to infuse his local persona into his presidential campaign, he might have had more success.

Karl Rove, the architect of President Bush's 2004 win, said it is important not to be phony, as voters can smell it right away, and that if you make your campaign about the issue that your spokesperson believes in, it will come though to the public.

Some bonus pointers:

- Have some good quotes ready to go. People like to hear quotes from famous people they can identify. It also makes you appear smart! Check out Bibliomania.com and Bartleby.com for some quote ideas.
- Write down some illustrative stories. Say them out loud and then shorten them. You will be ready to put them on the air at that point.
- Be humorous, but be accurate. Do not let humor serve as a smokescreen for inaccuracy or for not being prepared. The audience will see though it and so will the host.
- You can be biting and funny about your opponent, but don't let any real longtime grudges show though. It will seem like sour grapes.
- Practice some good analogies and metaphors. Work on them before the interview. Inspiration is great, but preparation is even better.
- If you notice your mind is wandering during an interview, so will the audience. Find ways to stay on track.

Be flexible.

A short interview where you can make your points, and make them well, can be much more memorable and often gets more play than longer interviews that drag on and on. Shorter interviews can easily be incorporated into later newscasts. Plan to be on the air for a short three-minute interview, but be prepared with enough different and interesting material to make it for an hour.

If you want to get on the show again, offer to provide the producer with new and different angles.

In times of breaking news—the war in Iraq, a presidential impeachment, a terrorist attack—be prepared to live in the green room. At these times you could be asked to do one segment, but to be available for another segment in two or three hours. This is your time to be seen as helpful and flexible.

Be brief.

Practice making your answers twelve to fifteen seconds long. Even thirty seconds can seem like an eternity on the air. Imagine typing thirty seconds of answers into an online chat. It would take a lot of typing to make thirty seconds of airtime.

Do not be long-winded, but don't be monosyllabic either. Can the host get a question in between your answers? Does he or she have to go to a break to shut you up? On the other hand, perhaps your answers are so short the host or anchor has to work to get you to say anything. Pay attention to the flow of the conversation between you and the host and between you and other panel members. This will help you discern whether you are talking too much or two little.

Try to identify a tangent—yours or that of another guest. Be able to call down another guest pursuing a tangent. On radio and on television, watch the producer, host, anchor, or floor director for clues to wrap it up. A professional knows when to hit a hard break.

There are times when an interview is designed to be part of a radio or television package. These are pieces that can be as short as thirty seconds or as long as four minutes, but only a short sound clip of what you say will be taken from them. Find out before the interview how it will be utilized. Will most of the interview be used, or only a sentence or two? If it is to be a package, hone your answers so you will get the most bang for their buck.

Leave your ego at the door.

There is a difference between a little bit of a chip on your shoulder and arrogance. Monitor everything you say and make sure there is not even a hint of arrogance. Some signs of arrogance on-air are boasting, looking affected, making grand gestures, looking as if you are not really listening, and actively putting down your opponent. For example, Howard Dean referred to himself as the front-runner, and even though he was the front-runner at that time, he never should have said so.

Rush Limbaugh can pull off having a grandiose ego because he has a relationship with his audience, but not everyone can. Microphones magnify and large egos get picked up faster than the speed of light (or sound).

First and foremost, be human. A radio guest from the Clinton administration was on the air right after he had been robbed at a cash machine. The host asked him what it was like to be robbed and he said, "I'm here to talk about the president's agenda." The more he was pressed for information about the robbery, the more arrogant he became. Had he bridged with, "It was very frightening and that is why the president's agenda of crime control is so important," he would have made his point and the audience would have been sympathetic toward him and open to his agenda.

The host will skewer you if you sound like a stuffed shirt, if not in front of you, then after you are gone.

Do not make the mistake of underpreparing for an interview or underestimating the host. A good host or call-in listeners and viewers can provide quite a challenge if you have not adequately prepared. The Alcoholics Anonymous organization has a great expression: "There are only two people who get me in trouble—the poor little me and the great I am." These are wise words to remember when dealing with the media.

A few nights before the Iowa primary, Governor Tom Vilsak said, "The candidate who wins will be the one who, in the days right before the vote, tells the people of Iowa who they are." This is one of the best ways to view a campaign. People don't want *ego* to represent them or to sell them something. They just want an unvarnished look at who you are.

Give your voice a tune-up.

Arthur Joseph, creator of the Voice Awareness Method, says that when we communicate with spoken language only 8 percent of that communication is received through words, the actual language of communication; about 37 percent is gathered from the sound of the voice, and 55 percent is understood from body language. Therefore if you are speaking on the telephone or over the air, 92 percent of your information is communicated solely through the sound of your voice.

Lynn Pritchard writes in *American Way* magazine that she met a blind couple in a hotel who loved her descriptions so much they asked to go on a helicopter tour of the Grand Canyon with her. After they landed Pritchard asked how they enjoyed the trip. They exclaimed that it was *beautiful.* "How do you know when you don't know the colors or shapes?" she asked. The wife answered, "We could hear how beautiful it was by the resonance and tone of your voice." Take care of your vocal instrument. Your voice is crucial.

It is much easier to tell how someone is relating to you and to others when you can observe her body language. You are gathering data on how to proceed and whether or not you should continue with your line of discussion or change directions. This is difficult to assess when you are on the phone.

Body language can tell you a lot. Watch politicians in a room or on television. Good ones have mastered this and you can learn some tricks of the trade from them. If you can get video of them on television or a B roll of them working a crowd, watch it with the sound turned off and write down your observations. Then watch tapes of yourself with the sound turned off. Contrast and compare.

Are you believable?

How often have you heard a speaker, a radio or television guest, or a politician and thought, *They are lying!* Analyze your reaction and you will probably realize what makes them unbelievable. Perhaps it should not be the out-front spokesperson making the case; sometimes a more believable surrogate, or what is called a third-party validator, should present your point.

Political consultants study hours of tape to help make their candidates more believable. Put together your own informal focus group to study your tapes and those of others to find what works.

If there is any question concerning how your issue is going to play, find some concrete ways to make it more believable. A study done by The Times Mirror Center indicates that the news media believes politicians are more honest than the listeners do. Therefore politicians need to do something in the initial few minutes of an interview to establish their honesty with the audience. It is imperative that it is done in a non-defensive way. If you have a record of doing what you have promised, weave that into the conversation and make it one of the main points of the interview.

If you are in a contentious or oppositional situation, smile—genuinely. Be respectful. Moreover, if you want to question someone's credibility, be strategic.

Al Gore's credibility took a hit during the 2000 presidential campaign when Tracy Mayberry, a tenant of Gore Realty's property in Carthage, Tennessee, spoke out against her famous landlord's refusal to improve the plumbing and other equipment in her ramshackle house. It created a media stink not soon forgotten.

Empower the audience.

Reach out to the audience. Let them know they have influence, that they matter, and that they can make a difference. Make statements such as, "Some of the mail and calls I have been receiving lately have impressed me to . . . " or, "I went into the office with this in mind, but my constituents felt . . . ." or, "We had this policy at our agency, but after hearing from the public we took another look at it and . . ."

Invite the audience to write, call, and e-mail you. Let them know you are aware that their donations pay your salary. No one likes a lone-ranger politician or organization.

Empower the audience and begin by remembering what it was about your issue that motivated *you*.

Mind your manners.

People listen to the radio or watch TV at work, at home, and in the car—you and your issue will most likely be broadcast throughout these locations. Your audience may be comprised of several generations of listeners, including children. What is appropriate for one person may not be for another. Unless you are trying to promote a lounge act, there is really no need to launch into a raunchy routine. Keep it simple, clean, and polite.

Your on-air performance is not the only time you will be judged. You cannot be a devil in the green room and a sweetheart on the air without someone—the producer, guest booker, makeup person, or catering crew—commenting about your Jekyll-and-Hyde approach. Be very careful about how you treat those responsible for your makeup; you could wind up looking like a clown.

As you wait for your appearance, be nice. Even if you are nervous, anxious, or angry, do not take your frustrations out on the people around you—especially if you don't know who they are. One man started mouthing off in the green room about a guest on the air, not aware that the other person in the room was the best friend of that guest.

Offer to return.

Be the come-back kid. If there have been many callers and some of them did not get on the air or a subject is unfinished, make an on-air offer to come back. This isn't something to do routinely—save it for when you know you have been a winner on the air or in the chat room.

If the host or producer says, "We have to have you back," take the opportunity to clarify what they mean. It could be in two weeks, a month, or a year. Try not to bug the producer, but do get an honest assessment. Ask for a time when you should be in touch. Find out what subject they would like to discuss when you come back and then follow up by sending some more information about that topic—not so much that they won't need you, but enough to maintain interest.

A potpourri of advice.

The distinct advantage of having a radio or Internet interview over a television interview is in not having to work in sound bites. Having more time for the interview allows for calls and e-mails, permitting interactivity with the public in general and with your base. It can be much less expensive than television, which requires time for makeup, wardrobe, and so forth. Because radio and the Internet can function like the Wild West, you can slip in information concerning upcoming events or other items of interest that would not make it on sound bite television. A word of caution: Before committing to an interview, get a phone number and call to be sure that the reporter or host is legitimate. You do not want to give free interviews to someone who is just trying to discover your position on an issue.

Although much of what follows has been stated elsewhere in this book, the following are some favorite pointers from Cliff May, the former RNC Communications Director—also known in Washington as the man who *lives* in green rooms:

- Treat a television appearance like a lively debate. TV hosts don't want a Jerry Springer, and they don't want a PBS Charlie Rose type.
- Green rooms are like a club. The coffee and food are not good, but you will have some of the most interesting conversations and you will learn more about what is going on than anywhere else in the city.
- Talk radio is a different format. You have more time to develop an idea and you don't have to rely so much on a sound bite.
- Make an effort to show you have the credentials to talk about the topic at hand. Be creative. Have a foundation on which to speak. *Note: Cliff is so creative that he had his organization's attorneys file an amicus brief at the Hauge to provide a platform for his organization.*
- Make an effort to be brief, succinct, and punchy. The way you express yourself on air is different than in print. It is frustrating, but reality.
- Tell the producers ahead of time if something is not your topic. They will respect you for it.

- The rule in the talk media is to go as far as you can without breaking a limb. They usually want the black-and-white, not shades of gray.
- Send your writing to producers and hosts in advance of your print date. However, don't send something more than once a week.
- Make sure you know who you are before you go out there as a commentator. Are you an analyst or a pit bull?

8

UNDERSTANDING THE MEDIA

Learn the ins and outs of the media business.

If you want airtime and Web chat time, you have to adjust to media hours—the times the shows are broadcast or streamed on the Web. Larger stations with a news or talk format may have producers that work only after 8:00 P.M., and television networks often have an assignment editor who works from 11:00 P.M. to 7:00 A.M.—remember to include them when you are pitching, and provide your cell phone number and e-mail address.

For news formats, much of the news information for morning drive is put on in the wee hours of the morning. If you live in the same city as the late-night folks, send over doughnuts, cookies, or even pizza as a thank-you. You can order pizza online, so even if you do not live near the producer, consider this as an option.

Most public-relations professionals forget about evening and late-night pitching because that is not when they work. Also, be conscious of sleep cycles. Jim Bohannan is a nationally syndicated radio talk-show host who is on air from 10:00 P.M. to 1:00 A.M., and then does the news show *First Light* at 5:00 A.M. You do not want to call him late morning or early afternoon, even if you do believe you are his best source for guests.

Talk media is about ratings. Most shows work daily to increase their viewers' and listeners' time spent listening and to increase the advertising base by gaining new viewers and listeners. Public radio and public television stations operate on the same basis. They sell sponsorships and need more people for their fund-raising drives. Public radio and commercial radio have the same goals. Keep those goals in mind as you make your pitch.

Unless you know the age demographic of your media outlets, aim your message at the population between the ages of twenty-five and fifty-four.

This age group interests sponsors and programmers the most, which is unfortunate because older audiences listen to the talk media more than do younger audiences. However, people in the advertising business don't see it that way, and they pay for the airtime.

It is also important to know media deadlines and the editing time needed for broadcast. Make yourself a *beat chart* so you will know which reporter and producer cover which issue, and pitch them accordingly.

The media you are trying to reach may have different timetables. Newspapers and magazines may have long lead times; blogs will have very short lead times, perhaps even half a day; radio and television will be just a couple of days.

Here is a checklist of basics:

- Who are the reporters, hosts, bloggers, and producers who have an interest in your topic or issue?
- Whom do they work for and what are their interests and needs?
- What plans do they have for covering an issue? Will they be traveling with you? Are they doing a series?
- Who is part of their universe? What are the names of the bookers? The secretaries? The line producers? The camera people? The researchers?
- Can you help them with any of their needs?
- What audience do they serve?
- What are their deadlines? When do they go on the air? What material do they need?
- How are decisions made in their organization? How often and when do they review what they are putting on the air or Internet?
- Can you tap into any specials or remote broadcasts they are doing?
- How do the media want to be contacted if you have something breaking? At home? E-mail? Through a producer?

Remember, politicians and heads of organizations come and go, but the media tend to stay around for years.

The care and feeding of the media.

Invite the press and the producers to your events and social gatherings. Internet chat hosts, bloggers, podcasters, webmasters, and online editors have traditionally been left out because most people do not know their names and they are often not listed on any beat sheet. In addition, include news directors, assignment editors, cohosts, and makeup artists. Do your homework—find out who they are and then extend the invitation.

It is important to note that much of the blogging, podcasting, and talk media do not consider themselves traditional journalists. Make the distinction when deciding to invite them to an event. Your like-minded friendly media may want and expect special access.

Remember your friends. If you are friends with opinion media, such as talk hosts and columnists, support them. Case in point: Howard Monroe is a well-known Democratic host broadcasting in Ohio and West Virginia. Both states were important in the 2004 presidential election. He was invited by the Bush-Cheney camp to ride the candidates' bus and sit on the podium when the vice president was in town. The Republicans bought a lot of ads on his station. And the Kerry campaign? Only after they heard about how the Republicans had treated Monroe did they offer him two tickets to a Kerry event—no Kerry interview, no photo op, nothing. To add insult to injury, a new talk station had just started up in the area, and Senator Kerry cut a promo saying he always listened to the new station.

Along these same lines, Sean Hannity cut a video promo welcoming delegates to New York for the Republican National Convention. It was good for the RNC and great for Hannity's visibility. The Democrats ignored their hosts.

Always remember the care and feeding of your hosts—literally. It is common knowledge that you will be fed at Republican events, but make sure you attend Democratic events on a full stomach. Most events sponsored by Republicans include provisions for the press—not so at Democratic events. There is no substitute for good, old-fashioned hospitality.

Consider hosting an event for the media. If you cannot afford to stage an event on an annual or semiannual basis, then consider staging an event with other like-minded organizations. Introduce them to your board or spokesperson or give an award to the program or journalist who represented your issue in the best light. It is a great opportunity to meet and greet, and you and your organization will be remembered.

Learn the names of news directors, producers, associate producers, and production assistants so you can address letters and phone calls to them directly. Get to know the interests of a reporter or host. Two hosts, Doug Stephan and Neal Boortz, can spend hours talking about airplanes. This is useful knowledge on two levels: pitching stories to them and topics for conversation. Send them an article or book that relates to their area of interest.

Media professionals are people—they vote, they go to religious services, they coach Little League, they take vacations, and they have families. Learn the names of their children and ask about them. Be willing to engage them in conversation. They may not be willing to tell you, but they have opinions and views on almost every issue.

Have a holiday party for the local media. Invite them to a nonpress event, such as the opening of a new office. They might not come to something like that, but they will appreciate the invitation.

Don't be a know-it-all.

Listen to the ideas and suggestions of those in the media. On large political campaigns there is often a van for the press. Ride in it with them. This is where you will hear things that your staff will never tell you. The press have been around the barn a few times, and if they suggest something, you really should give it consideration.

Someone in the media told a former State Department spokesperson working for the Kerry campaign that he was smart, but that on radio it came across as arrogance. It made him furious. A few weeks later, his arrogance got out of control and he was taken off the Kerry campaign. He should have listened to some friendly advice.

Be open to suggestions. Not, "I'll take it under consideration," or, "We are already doing that," but, "Thanks, I hadn't thought of that," "What a great idea," and "Very good observation."

Be real with the press. If you are having problems in your organization, tell them. They will find out anyway. People talk to them, e-mail them, and leak information to them.

When you are previewing a new campaign, initiative, or ad, show it to them. Call them personally. Ask them to take a look at it. They can write about it and talk about it, but they can also give you a pretty good idea of what the reaction will be. Make sure that anything going out to the public is going to the press first or simultaneously.

You can also be the go-to person they feel comfortable talking to, or your organization's off-the-record contact. In turn, the media will often share off-the-record industry information with you.

Make friends with those who work in the newsroom. A lot of business transpires between friends. However, never presume on your friendship, thinking that they won't toss any hardballs your way while you are on the air. They have a job to do and so do you.

What can you do for the media?

You are getting something from them—airtime. It is a big mistake to think that your interview time is merely free media or a free gift. You have to earn it. If you question what that is worth to you and your organization, simply call the station or network and ask them for their rate card. Suppose that a thirty-second television spot is worth four hundred dollars. Let's say that you have been asked to appear as a guest for a six-minute interview. That is $4800 worth of free advertising. Or if you can get your spokesperson on a weekly radio program for ten minutes and the sixty-second spot time is worth fifty dollars, you are getting twenty-six thousand dollars' worth of media in one year that you did not have to pay for. It is a win-win situation because you probably do not have a promotion budget that could allow for a twenty-six-thousand-dollar commercial buy, and it is good for the station because they have filled ten minutes of airtime.

Your appearance should be treated as a meeting between clients. What do you need, what do they need, and how can these needs be accommodated? Do they need national stories or local stories? Do they need stories with a local hook? Do they need backup material? Do they need research? Do they need guidance on how to pronounce the name of your spokesperson, your organization, or acronym?

Listen for *needs* phrases such as *we need, we want, we are looking for, we are interested in,* and so forth. Use time-honored sales techniques to point out what you or your organization can offer to the program, the benefit they will receive, how you plan to support them and meet their needs, and then close with your commitment to them.

On-air personalities need to keep their jobs; if a mistake has been made, address it with them personally—do not go above their heads to the supervisor. Several years ago, a certain person went above a reporter's head to complain about the way a story was being handled. It got back to the reporter, the reporter told all the other reporters and producers, and that guest was not booked on any show at that station for well over a year.

Remember to be very, very sensitive to the media's needs. They are your customers and they should be treated accordingly.

Make the producer's job easier.

For starters, do not drive them crazy by asking for tapes. If you want something taped, bring the tape with you.

There are some guests in the business who are known as high maintenance. They demand a car to take them to the studio, they freak out if it is not on time, they treat the makeup room as if it was a beauty shop, and they are usually the ones who go bananas if their segment has to be canceled because of late-breaking news. One guest who was canceled called the vice president of the network and complained loudly with a threat to sue. He has never been seen on the network again.

You should be as easygoing as possible. You do not want the driver, the makeup artist, the floor manager, or anyone else to remember that you were the high-maintenance guest.

There is another way to make producers' jobs easier: Provide them with fun and witty material. Producers loved it when Mark Pfeifle of the Republican National Committee made the CD "The World According to Gore." They were able to utilize the one-liners.

Think about what a producer might be looking for and be creative. Provide quotes, audio, video, pictures—anything that will make the producer's job of filling airtime easier.

Note: When you are a guest on national television you may be offered a residual payment. Never take it. This is especially good advice if you are a politician. All you need is for the opposition to find out that you were paid to make an appearance. Unless you are a card-carrying media union member, do not opt for the easy money.

Judge not.

Just like some teachers and mothers, hosts and producers have eyes in the back of their heads and their ears to the ground in their local communities. It is not a good idea to call around locally to find the political spin of the host or program. They will be annoyed if they find out about it. If you really must call someone locally, call the media critic at the local paper. He or she knows the talk media and will be happy to give you the score. You could also just listen to the show or read reviews.

It is generally safe to ask the producer what the host's take is on a particular topic, but anything you ask might be written in the notes given to the anchor or host. Hosts understand the First Amendment well, but most are willing to honor off-the-record requests. Nevertheless, be on the safe side and assume *everything* you say is on the record. Remember also that whatever message you leave on an answering machine could end up on the air, and any e-mail message you send could end up as a document on a Web site.

Spring a leak.

Yes, it is quite wonderful to have the information you have leaked to the media appear on the front page of a newspaper, but it is also important for you to leak to broadcasters and to your media friends.

Victoria Jones of Talk Radio News Service says that the advantage of leaking to the talk media is that they will make it a multiday story. "The talk media is like a TV serial," she says.

It is quite amazing how many politicians choose to leak to a newspaper or to a television station, but forget the power of radio and its captive driving audience. Politicians will even leak to the Internet's Drudge Report but will not give a heads-up to a radio host whose show they have been on weekly. If you give a scoop to a broadcaster he or she will be your friend for a long, long time.

Radio stations owned by media groups may have a sister station in the same area that might also be able to broadcast your information, and radio and local television allow you to target your audience much more effectively than newspapers. You might get more coverage, even if there won't be the long-lasting effect of print.

Be prepared to back up your leak in case the validity of the information is ever questioned. Leaks are best done in person or by phone. Be careful of anything in writing, such as an e-mail. It took only one week for a strategy piece written for one of the 2004 primary campaigns to make it into print in a major magazine.

9

CRISIS MANAGEMENT

Be up-front: acknowledge, apologize, and act.

If there is a credibility problem with your organization or spokesperson, be up-front about it. If you are called about a situation do not avoid it. Do a preemptive strike and put out your version. Dig up your own past as if you are the opposition. What will they find? How will you respond to it? Who are your enemies and why?

Monitor bad news carefully. Never let a one-day story become a two-day story. Do not try to answer what you don't know—find the information for the reporter or show seeking it, and then get back to them. This might mean approaching the problem as if you are an investigative reporter. Do the research and find the facts yourself so you are not hung out to dry.

Ask for clarification. Use words like, "Can you tell me again what you are saying about . . .?" Take notes and write down exactly what they are saying so you can respond—exactly. If the news is bad, respond immediately, even if your response is "Unavailable for comment." This is different from "No comment." You are just *unavailable* for comment.

Decide who will be available for comment and when and where this will take place. Give that information to the press.

Do not feel compelled to immediately respond to an attack. Victoria Jones of Talk Radio News Service says, "If the host comes straight at you with an attack, use it to recoup: 'Whoa, I've got to catch my breath after that—you're pretty passionate!'"

Just as in any interview or debate, body language and voice tell it all. Take a lesson from the duck on the pond. All may look serene on the surface, but under the water he is paddling like crazy.

Responding does not mean answering questions repeatedly. When Congressman Barney Frank was questioned about his private life he had several press availabilities. He gave the press time to ask questions, but when he felt he had answered all the questions he said that was all he was going to do and they stopped hounding him.

Planned Television Arts's Rick Frishman suggests that when you are under attack, you should always take the high road. Never stoop to your assailant's level by being combative, defensive, or nasty. Stay focused, remain dignified, and stand tall. If you leave with nothing else, leave with your dignity.

In addition:

- Find ways to keep the story from having legs. Meet with the press—not as a group, but individually. Talk to your friends in the media. Keep them informed first. They can be your best advocates or your worst enemies.
- Release the information yourself before the other side does. It helps tremendously when you are willing to be up-front about it.
- Microphones magnify. When the press is on your front lawn and at your front door, be aware of everything you say and do. Take care of yourself. If you are tired, you might say things you will later regret. Boom microphones are incredibly powerful. Think of all the off-color, nasty comments you have heard from reality-show participants and overconfident politicians.
- Take responsibility. During the Waco debacle when Attorney General Janet Reno said, "The buck stops here," she made great strides toward gaining the confidence of the press. Some still attacked her, but she had instilled confidence that she was willing to take the heat. Conversely, Vice President Dick Cheney was quiet after his hunting accident until insider Republicans told him to get out in front of the story. A few days later he gave an interview to Brit Hume at Fox News Channel.
- Be truthful with yourself, your attorney, and your surrogates. Choosing the person who will be available to the media for you is crucial. For example, if you decide on a well-known criminal attorney, even though you might need one, it could give the impression that you are guilty—and impressions matter.

- Get your support lined up immediately. If respected people are willing to vouch for you or your organization it makes a huge difference in how quickly a situation is diffused.
- Be humble, look honest, and express concern over damages for which you may be responsible. An example of not following this guideline is, "I did not have sex with that woman."
- Have a sense of humor, but do not be flippant or arrogant.
- Keep history just that—history. If something took place in the past, remind people that it was long ago and move the agenda to now.
- Make a list of what is being said about you. Compose a response for each item. Decide what you will answer and what you will not. Provide answers that make sense, and speak in complete sentences. Silence speaks loudly and breathes oxygen into a story.
- Don't go looking for trouble, but be careful not to be so legal about something that you wind up saying things like Bill Clinton's "It depends on what the definition of *is* is," or Al Gore's "There is no controlling legal authority,"(concerning his breaking of the law regarding solicitation of funds from federal government offices). That will only make it worse. Answer the question and anticipate what the press will find out next if you do not answer the question.
- If your opposition is on a "fishing" expedition, make them produce the fish. You may know they are after something, but make them prove what they think they have. Counterattack (no free hits) and bring the issue back to what your campaign or issue is about.
- Everyone makes mistakes and everyone says stupid things. Admit you are human and appeal to the public's sense of for-giveness. Address any new mistakes or gaffes within the same news cycle they happened.
- Turn your negatives into positives. Did your staff all quit? You might say, "It forced the organization to be better at recruiting and developing human resource policies."
- Do your research on the opposition. Understand the attack

and the attackers. Is their house clean? Why are they bringing this up now? What can you throw in their direction to shift the attention to them? Be careful, though, that you do not start something that has all the characteristics of a food fight. The press will wind up covering the food fight and not the issues.

- Make the behavioral interviewing techniques work for you by not answering the hypothetical questions. It will only take you into uncharted territory. Stick to what you know.
- Inundate the media with facts, figures, and information—even minor details. Provide so much information they will not know what to investigate first. Keep the information flowing, but never fabricate anything just to placate journalists hungry for a kill. Lots of Web! Lots of Web!

Do not panic. If you have hit a crisis, this is the most important thing to remember. Bad decisions are made when people panic. Remember the three A's: acknowledge, apologize, and act. You can design your response around these three basics.

If you are labeled by an interviewer or you are asked to discuss something another person has said about you or your organization, ask for clarification of what is being said before you respond. Otherwise it could appear that you are buying into the label.

Try to weave your agenda into every answer. This is where your top three talking points come in. Work at least one of them into every answer if at all possible.

Don't blame the media.

Unless this is the purpose of your organization, the oldest and most tired rant of all is to blame the media. Journalists are on a par with lawyers in public opinion polls. Many radio hosts have a great time going after the media, even though they are a part of it. However, they own the microphone—you are only the guest.

It is often a sweeping generalization and a cheap shot to blame your troubles on the media. If you have a strong example of a specific incident you might decide to use it. Otherwise avoid that strategy. The media is powerful whether you like it or agree with it or not; you do not want to create enemies.

Prepare for the tough questions and welcome them.

The Republicans have perfected "the murder board" as a tool to ready their spokespersons for public appearances. The staffers hammer the spokesperson as viciously as possible before an interview. Anything thrown at them on the air will seem like a day in Disney Land after the staff has finished their preparation interviews.

Compose your own murder board. Have them ask you the questions you least want to answer, and then have them use some journalistic techniques designed to increase the squirm factor. Make sure they focus on questions that have no attribution, such as, "People have said . . ." hypothetical questions, questions you can't answer without backing yourself into a corner, and questions that are impossible to answer—like questions about the future. Have your murder board point out any inconsistencies in your presentation, anything that does not ring true, or if the emperor really isn't wearing any clothes. Coworkers do not want to be the bearers of bad news, so offer a free lunch or other incentive. Make it safe to critique.

Before your interview write down the questions you think might be asked. Look at them afterward. How accurate were you? When you can anticipate most of the questions, you can say that you understand that particular media.

Sometimes spokespersons are afraid of certain types of shows. Prepare by fortifying your points with action that has or will be taken, and that is relevant to people's lives.

Project Vote Smart, which tracks all congressional voting records, put together a National Political Awareness Test to find out how many candidates filled out issue questionnaires. Surprisingly they only got a 53 percent response rate, but it fell to 44 percent when no local news organization contacted the candidates about filling out the survey. Many of the consultants to these candidates advised against filling out such a survey. You might be able to get away with not filling out a survey, but you will not be able to escape on the air and you will most likely be asked the very question you refused to answer on paper.

Answer all questions as nondefensively as possible. "I'm glad you brought that up," or, "I'd be happy to answer that," or even, "That's a tough question and I'm glad to have the opportunity to answer it" are all appropriate responses. It can also be helpful to say, "You can quote me." Practice, practice, practice until you can answer as easily as you can say, "Good morning." A host or anchor will invariably bring up some fact, law, or article that you did not know about. If you do not know the facts or statistics, that's okay; just be honest about it and then get back to them with the information.

Use bridging words. Examples may include, "Another point of view on this issue is . . .," "This is an example why . . .," "I appreciate your views on this, but I have my own viewpoint," "You make a very interesting point," and "My take on this is . . ." Also, ask for clarification: "Are you asking . . .?" Try active listening techniques such as, "You are saying . . ." or, "I am understanding that your position is . . ."

Be prepared for all kinds of tricks to make you say something that you had no intention of saying. Reporter Connie Chung crossed the line when she said to Barbara Bush, "Just between you and me . . ." and then went on to air Mrs. Bush's answer on television.

Media people are adept at getting what they want. They know what will set you off. When Senator Zell Miller was asked some tough questions by Chris Matthews on *Hardball*, he became unhinged and started screaming, "Get out of my face. I wish we lived in the day when we could challenge someone to a duel." His losing it made him the subject of ridicule on Comedy Central's *The Daily Show*. From a small audience at MSNBC, it took off and was seen all over the Internet—not the kind of publicity Zell Miller was looking for.

Hosts and listeners admire loyalty. As Victoria Jones of Talk Radio News Service says, "They [hosts and listeners] want you to stick by your people. They want you to be frank as well."

Sometimes interviews will begin with compliments and softball questions just to take you off guard before they start asking the tough questions. In print media, you might find that there is no forthcoming question or conversation. Journalists use pauses, silence, and even playing stupid to get what they are looking for.

In press conferences and on the air there may be times when the host talks over you or asks several questions in one. Another technique is to keep badgering you and never relinquish a point.

Be ready and willing to defend
your board and your supporters.

Think of your board and your masthead of management as your billboard. If you are running a political campaign, everyone who is on your payroll (and even some who are not) or who donates to your campaign in large amounts is fair game. Keep a short bio on each member of your board, along with notes about any possible questions you could be asked. If there has ever been some question about a member of your organization, you will be prepared. When you least expect it, someone is going to ask you about that person.

Try to use any negatives about a board member to your advantage. An ambassador was asked during an interview if being a political appointee was a disadvantage. The ambassador countered that because he had political experience, he was able to help that country's prime minister understand why the administration had to make certain political decisions.

Be ready to disclose where your money comes from and how you spend it. The media and the public want to know who your large contributors are. With the passing of the McCain–Feingold bill on campaign finance, there is no longer as much special-interest money directed to campaigns. However, interviewers are a wily and savvy lot and they know which affinity groups (527s) go with which candidates, so be able to answer questions along those lines, as well as questions about out-of-state contributions.

There will be times when you do not have the answer or you feel that you cannot give one. Just say so if it is proprietary, involves litigation, or above your pay grade. Offer to find the answers to questions you do not know and then get back to the main point of why you are there. Try not to give the on-air equivalent of pleading the Fifth by saying, "No comment." The audience will automatically assume the worst.

Frequent questions for advocacy organizations concern the source and spending of income. Another question at the top of the list is the cost of operation. How much is spent in acquiring the funds? Be prepared to discuss the salary of your top staff, even to the point of having printed material available. Review this information with every member of your staff who has contact with the public. Be certain that all answers agree with the written material and with what your public-relations department is doing.

Follow up, follow up, and follow up some more.

Call the producer (and host, if appropriate) after you have been on the air. It is not always necessary to speak with the producer, as they may not have the time. You can leave a message, then follow it up with a thank-you note. It never hurts to send two notes—one from the spokesperson and one from the booker. Do not send a form letter. Personalize your note by referring to specifics from the show. Take a tip from host Tim Russert. He sends a picture of the person he has interviewed on the set of the show, and it is a very welcome gift.

On the other side of the microphone, the Republicans have sent out LIGHT UP THE PHONES magnets whenever they have a speaker on a show. It is great advertising and a nice touch.

While you are on the air jot down a few of the questions asked. Can you provide more information? Send follow-up information via fax, messenger, e-mail, or with a package. Let the interviewer know what is going on with your issue without your trying to book a guest. Be her friendly neighborhood resource—one that follows up and follows through.

10

PREPARING FOR THE FUTURE USING CURRENT TECHNOLOGY

Make the Internet work for you.

Ken Mehlman, who ran the Bush-Cheney 2004 campaign and then became director of the Republican National Committee, has pointed out that whichever party masters the latest communication technology wins. In the 1930s FDR was able to get the attention of America with his radio program, *Fireside Chats*. The Democrats won in 1960 because they understood television—especially during the Nixon-Kennedy debates. Richard Vigerie was able finish off George McGovern through his use of direct mail.

Mehlman also states that although the one who masters technology wins, it is not a substitute for the message. As he has said about the Bush campaign, "Cause matters most—the Web is just how we get there," and that a good Web campaign is "a tool, a means—not an end."

By using the resources of the Web to carry the Bush message, Mehlman was able to acquire more than a million volunteers to work on the campaign. He believes that the goal of any Web site should be to maintain a customer as much as it is to make a sale. He says that it should be great synergy for everything else you are doing.

Mehlman created a community for those who logged on to the Bush-Cheney site. He built his organization so that local volunteers using the Web site, like neighbors at an ancient water well, were able to mobilize like-minded people in crucial precincts and also increase donations. He created a community, whereas campaigns in the past had to rely on phone banks and an occasional volunteer knocking on the door.

By creating this community, he achieved astonishing results. Through the Web site, 750,000 volunteers received maps and driving directions to the polls in their areas, and 164,498 people in target states used the Get

Out the Vote location tool to find polling places. As a result of the Web sites Bush.com and GOP.com, they were able to garner almost 20 percent of new registrants

This has not been limited to the United States. Douglas Ahlers of the Kennedy School of Government said the Palestinian elections were impeccably run and that Hamas used technology through action alerts, e-mail, and online political ads to win the election and defeat the Fatah party.

Because of the Internet the recall of Governor Gray Davis garnered five thousand signatures a day. The organizing power of the Internet brought the stock price of Sinclair Broadcasting into a free fall before they changed their tactics. Media expert Doug Bailey was able to track the name recognition of Supreme Court nominee Sam Alito. He found that nine days after his nomination, Sam Alito had name recognition of 78 percent. Television had an impact, but the Internet was responsible for his high name recognition.

ViaNovo, LP's Tucker Eskew says, "More and more households and particularly with younger demographics crave broadband access. It's changing the way they get media at home and at work, and although you don't have to be at the bleeding edge, it is important to be up-to-date on how you use streaming media and viral marketing, as well as to develop richer content."

It has been said about the 2004 campaign that Democrats, beginning with Howard Dean's campaign, used the Web to organize themselves and bring in money, but Republicans used the Web to speak to others. The one possible exception was the brilliance of the Clark campaign blogs, which, as of this writing, are still active.

According to Wired.com's Chris Ulbrich, Cameron Barrett of the Clark campaign echoed a famous movie line when he said, "Build it and they will come." He created the Clark Community Network, which allowed users to contribute content and to organize themselves into groups. Everyone who signed up got a personal blog and was able to post their blogs in several areas of the online community, such as veterans, Alaskans, and so forth. Users were then able to rate the submissions, and the best ones became a part of the Clark official blog. Clark may not have received the nod of the Democratic Party, but what Barrett was able to do will be built upon in campaigns to come.

David Alpert of Cosmopolity.org says that you can drive political action through social interaction, and that using the Internet to get people to do something fun and useful, such as mixers, group outings, and so forth, will help to brand an idea, organization, or cause.

Chris Rabb of Afro-Netizen.com also supports this idea. He coined the term *netizens*—citizens of the Net. Rabb believes that you can create incredible relationships via the power of the Internet, and that civic and other engagement can follow an online experience.

Well-known blogger Micah Silfry says that to influence people you must go to them—go where they are hanging out. According to Silfry, Myspace.com is the largest Internet networking tool and it is creating political networking communities. The challenge is to go where the audience is and offer them something that will scratch their itch. Craigslist.org began as classified advertising and now functions very much as a community.

During the waning days of the Clinton administration and the beginning of the Bush administration, a very interesting book about the lack of community was making the rounds among policy makers in Washington. The book is titled *Bowling Alone*, by Robert Putnam. The author's premise is that as a nation we have become disconnected from family, we have attended club meetings 58 percent less than in the post-WWII years, and our social capital, the fabric of our connection, is disintegrating.

Studies have shown that an individual's increase in time spent online also increases their social isolation. These studies and Putnam's theory may still be true, but there is a possibility that because of the technology of the Internet, from Skype telephone technology to photo sharing and meet-ups, the Internet may break the walls of isolation in ways that were unexpected when Putnam published *Bowling Alone* in 2000. As media converges we will continue to see shifts in how people interact with each other and with organizations.

Scott Heiferman, CEO of Meetup.com, talks about five big societal trends. They are:

1. Isolated culture. People can put an iPod in their ear, order food via phone or the Internet, go to the ATM, communicate via e-mail, and get through the day without having to deal with others in person.

2. We live in a world that is more controlled because of the Internet. Meetings, members, and chapters of organizations are messy, he says.
3. We are much more partisan. Townhall.com, organized by the Heritage Foundation, is one of the most successful meet-ups.
4. Many people have a sense of entitlement.
5. People feel less powerless.

Heiferman says that the power of the Internet lies in the ability of someone taking pictures in an Iraqi prison and getting them around the world. It is like Little Brother looking at Big Brother.

He also says that the Internet gives people collective power and that people are beginning to see themselves as members of sprawling group networks. Heiferman believes that our engagement with others through Meet-ups, blogs, and so forth is also our response to media consolidation and control. At a recent conference he posed the question, "With seven hundred Meet-ups forming an emergent network of moms, what happens when they begin to say that they care about what happens in Darfur?"

Another Web expert, Kaliya Hamlin, says that we don't simply pick the most popular or most available like we do with much of our media-based information—we pick the most salient connections.

Martin Kearns, cofounder of Green Media Toolshed, says that to build new network strategies you need to have strong social ties, a rich communications grid, common strategies, shared resources, and clarity of purpose.

Understanding how the Internet has changed our relationships with each other as well as with the broadcast media is challenging for anyone in broadcasting or public relations. For instance, blogs have made a large imprint and deserve attention, but they are not really a special culture. They are the means by which a generation of seventeen-to-thirty-five-year-olds orient themselves around information.

Where e-mail is the choice of communication for many on the Net, younger demographics rely more on instant messaging. A long-distance phone call in 1982 cost forty-five cents per minute; college students instant message each other while in the same classroom, and use the same technology to communicate across the country.

Skype technology, on the other hand, is new in how it carries the phone call itself, according to media expert Todd Townsend. "In normal voice-over Internet, or VOIP, the call is carried by the Internet. Skype utilizes a software that allows computers connected to the Internet and running Skype to act as the gatekeeper and traffic cops for the calls. This kind of networking, using interconnected computers, accomplishes the task without a centralized location. It is called peer-to-peer, or P-to-P. There is no need for buildings, infrastructure, or support staff." Skype has also added video phone call capability, and by the time you read this Skype will have added video to its software, allowing you to become your own global TV broadcaster for the price of a computer, camera, and high-speed Internet connection. Microsoft is integrating this feature into its toolbar menu. EBay recently purchased Skype.

Townsend believes that the key to success in this new distribution model is targeting the correct audience and developing quality content. He says, "As the barriers to entry drop, the amount of content will grow and quality content will gain viewers and potential revenue through subscriptions, advertising, and online syndication. Nonquality content will quickly be forgotten."

Podcasting and vcasting will challenge some terrain of the traditional broadcaster, and finding ways to make a splash in a sea of information—written, video, and audio—will become more difficult. We will move away from a broadcast model and toward a more interactive model. There will be convergence of all of these more traditional forms of media as bandwidth increases (via emerging technologies) and it becomes more viable.

Kaliya Hamlin says it best: "We define broadcasting as transporting content, not as transporting speech. Broadcasting moves content through media. Speech happens in place." Hamlin also says:

1. We move content through a medium with a transport protocol. So it's about shipping.
2. We "architect, design, construct, and build sites" with addresses and locations with traffic. So it's about real estate.
3. We write or author pages and files of writing that we browse. So it's about writing.
4. We perform for an audience that has an experience. So it's about theater.

You know the information revolution has taken hold in our society when Supreme Court Justice David Souter asked a question during an oral argument about stealing music for download on to an iPod.

Hypertext links will become even more prominent and important for getting the message out, as they will allow anything to link to anything. Add to hyperlinks the XML (extensible markup language) and RSS (really simple syndication) and you have a lot to keep up with.

Online media now consists of text and voice as well as moving visuals like video clips, pictures, and animation. Much of this can be localized so it can be geographically aimed and categorized by interest and the like.

We are also quickly moving forward in what we call the semantic Web, where there is a content- and agent-related information exchange. For instance, when the semantic Web is fully operational, a Web page for a doctor will not only give you the office hours, but it will make an appointment for you, book your lab tests, and so forth. A good definition of the semantic Web is "technology for enabling machines to make more sense of the Web, with the result of making the Web more useful for humans."

There is also the contextual Web, in which the Internet behaves like a good neighbor. The contextual Web search service will allow you to search the Internet for Web pages using a context-based query. As of this writing, it is in beta tests (testing of a computer product prior to commercial release). An example of this is KartOO.com, which performs an analysis and contextually places the results of a search.

The Internet neighborhood you are in becomes important as individuals, corporations, and organizations ask, "Is my neighborhood Queens or is it Madison Avenue? Who are my neighbors, and how are we going to work together? Where do I want my e–real estate to be?" Ninety-eight percent of people using search engines use Yahoo!, AOL, or Google. The sites that come up when a topic is searched can help or hinder your agenda. Your neighborhood and your e–real estate are powerful. Businesses and organizations have often stood alone, but now advocacy, links, and sharing have forced people with similar agendas to come together and work in a different way.

As fast as we are writing this, the Internet and its applications to the world of talk media are changing. Sound and video clips can be seen and heard through your cell phone. Newscasts now have viewer responses sent via cell phones that are aired on the local evening news. XM and Sirius Satellite say they will be able to deliver their content by cell phones, PDAs, MP3 players, and similar technologies. News and talk broadcasters may even be behind the technological eight ball as the Internet itself (and therefore, Internet broadcasting) will be available in venues that are more accessible.

One thing is clear—radio and television programming will be Internet-accessible and the point of entry will no longer be just the big program-mers of television and radio. They may have the edge in the market, but there will be multiple entry points for multiple suppliers of content.

You do the math.

With more than two hundred million Americans online and 81 percent of all consumers having access to the Internet, its incursion into our daily lives is virtually ubiquitous. It is estimated that by the end of 2006 more than 65 percent of American Internet users will have broadband, and global Internet users will number greater than one billion—one out of every six inhabitants of our planet. According to Internet World Stats, the average person visits fifty-three domains in a month. As in so many other areas of daily life and commerce, the Internet is significantly influencing all media; news and talk radio are no exception.

According to research conducted by Arbitron and Edison Media Research, 45 percent of Americans have listened to radio programs online and they expect that number to double. Their research also states that as of 2005 the monthly Internet radio and Internet video audiences repre-sent 55 million consumers, and that more than 20 million Americans watched Internet video in the last week of the study.

This research, which is confirmed in a study by the Online Publishers Association, indicates that the most popular online viewing is of news clips—a whopping 66 percent! The amazing part of the OPA study is that 59 percent of the viewers found the video by random surfing. Links, blogs, and e-mailing among friends were other major sources of finding online sound and video. Imagine what will happen when the technology becomes so user friendly that it will be a simple matter to obtain the video clips, audio, and other multimedia on a variety of technologies such as phones and PDAs, as well as on computers.

Services like iTunes, TiVo, and others are beginning to link online multimedia content to conventional media devices like your car radio and home television set. Nonmainstream media audio podcasts, video vlogs, vcasts, and other multimedia content like Flash cartoons are becoming as easily available through your radio or television as your computer. Convergence, and thus real content competition, is becoming a reality.

Evening and weekends are the most popular times to view online video, reinforcing research that suggests that Internet content is truly giving more traditional media sources like broadcast television a run for their money. OPA also found out that the phrase *content is king* was important, as more than 40 percent of online time was spent reviewing content. The sum of all of this? Americans are as or more likely to read, listen to, or watch their daily news online as they are using traditional media. A *U.S. News & World Report* magazine columnist echoes the oft-repeated claim that mainstream media is dead, and notes that the Internet, blogs, and talk radio are the emerging kings.

The future heirs to these thrones are young people and organizations smart and aggressive enough to realize today that it starts online. The Pew Internet and American Life project reports that half of all teenagers age twelve to seventeen have created content for the Web. Their principal online mediums are blogs and podcasts. Video bloggers, or vloggers, and vcasters are among the fastest-growing content developers online and have a Web site, WeAretheMedia.com, that openly proclaims "We are the media!" The site catalogs and promotes video content online. Advocacy groups like Consumers Union and People for the Ethical Treatment of Animals (PETA) have divisions and Web pages dedicated to hosting and promoting their online video content, which now circumvents the traditional journalism filters, providing feeds directly to connected consumers. Gallup and other polling organizations repeatedly find that consumers report this online content to be "more credible" than reports on television and traditional print media.

Traditional radio stations are also among these early adopters getting a boost from Internet broadcasting. The more than ten thousand commercial and public-radio stations have Web sites, and more than four thousand of those offer some form of online broadcasting. Web-radio.com lists upwards of 950 news and talk stations online, with links to their various live broadcasts. These are supplemented by a growing number of online-only news and talk-radio programs or podcasts that range from general to highly focused special-interest or regional topics. Newstalkcast.com is the aggregator for talk programs. One can find programming for seniors from the AARP at aarp.org/fun/radio, or visit the World Paranormal Forum at nightsearch.net for broadcasting news relevant to extraterrestrial watchers. Apple's iTunes directory now lists more than twenty-five thousand pod-casts available on virtually every imaginable topic, making this content portable to iPods and other MP3 devices—many of which are now con-nected to car radios. The variety is endless.

The Arbitron/Edison study listed the top reason people listened to audio on the Internet as audio content they could not get elsewhere. The study also found that 57 percent of weekly Internet radio users listened while researching a product or service online. They point out that Erwin Ephron (known in advertising circles as the father of modern media plan-ning) said Internet radio advertisers often get the last word before a con-sumer makes a purchase.

It can work in the other direction as well. Hitwise.com found that during Super Bowl XXXIX, GoDaddy.com, which had the most provoca-tive ads, got the most online hits, followed by hits for Cialis.com. Bill Tancer, Vice President of Research at Hitwise, said that although adver-tisers like GoDaddy.com were criticized for their provocative spots, "it's clear that the campaign generated significant awareness beyond the stan-dard reach of the paid television placement."

The use of cell phones and the desire of consumers to personalize them led Purina to provide ring tones for cell phones that include barks and meows.

The power of the Internet was clear with the Live8 concerts, designed to motivate the leaders of the G8, to do something about the poverty in Africa. The target audience was eight world leaders. More than 26.4 mil-lion people sent text messages the day of the concert to support the cam-paign—26.4 million people converged to influence only eight people. It surpassed the *American Idol* record of 5.8 million.

With more than fifty million viewers, the most popular video during the 2004 presidential election cycle was JibJab.com's "This Land is Your Land." The Institute for Politics, Democracy, and the Internet (ipdi.org) determined that the content was relatively mild, but by television standards it was edgy. The Institute's Carol Darr believes it was popular because it poked fun equally at both parties. Karen Jagoda, president of E-Voter, said, "TV-obsessed ad strategists don't get the fundamental shift JibJab portends for political programming. This change means that a couple of hundred thousand dollars spent wisely online could translate into a windfall for candidates equal to a TV buy in the millions. That is, if you do it right."

If there are still doubters, the Swift Boat Veterans for Truth were able to take a small television ad investment and, using the Internet, turn it into a major problem for John Kerry.

Virtually every industry from pharmaceuticals to food is being similarly impacted by online multimedia. Jay Byrne, an expert in online-issues management and marketing whose firm, v-Fluence, represents dozens of multinational corporations, says advocacy groups and other interests such as labor unions, litigators, and alternative-products companies are beginning to use the Internet to circumvent mainstream media, lobby government officials, and directly reach consumers. He notes animal rights activists like PETA now run a "PETA-TV" broadcast online, while others produce cartoon animations critical of drug companies, which are being used as campaign commercials for antipharmaceutical industry ballot initiatives. Often the commercial interests they target are blind to these activities or using ineffective traditional responses.

"We see very sophisticated use of multimedia and other online tools by interest groups which previously had marginal influence," says Byrne. "The Internet is enabling diverse interests to combine their efforts and resources, avoid traditional opinion-leader and media scrutiny and analysis, and directly influence consumer attitudes and behaviors. Most industry groups lack similar sophistication when it comes to understanding and using the Internet."

There is a ready-made audience online. Of equal importance for talk radio, study after study shows that opinion leaders and the media go to the Internet first when looking for information. Those online who will influence your issues and generate buzz include guests discussing your issues as well as news directors, program hosts, show producers, and other journalists. *Online* can also include other delivery systems. Satellite producers XM and Sirius have concluded that by 2010 they will have twenty million subscribers listening from cell phones, PDAs, MP3 players and other handheld devices.

Actual numbers for visits to specific sites is still a problem, with the technology from the different rating sites producing very different numbers, although there is push to develop an industry standard for numbers are collected. Tracking actual traffic is further challenged by the trend of using RSS/XML (really simple syndication via extensible mark-up language) which enables subscribers to get your content without actually visiting your site. This content is then often resyndicated through multiple other networks and online channels. This can be difficult when making a judgment call as to what sites to target for outreach, content placement, and advertising, although you can get generic site statistics from a number of tracking companies. Other Internet monitoring services offered by such companies as v-Fluence or Buzz Metrics provide detailed targeting information and can track the syndication and distribution of your content or advertising in more detail.

What does news, talk-radio, and other media convergence online mean for promoting your issue or organization? It means exposure for your issues and the increased likelihood that news and talk-program hosts and producers might cover them. It means getting your issues and positions in front of those opinion leaders who are frequent talk-show guests and commentators. It ensures that your supporters will add volume to and participate in programming related to your issues.

While all journalists and opinion leaders today are online, radio offers an excellent case study for planning your online outreach strategy. News and talk-radio media personalities, reporters, directors, and program producers are relying more and more on the Internet as their principal source for news and program topics. News Generation, Inc., which has conducted surveys about the importance of the Internet in radio newsrooms across America since 1997, reported that news and talk-show producers and assignment editors are online an average of seven hours a day, using the Internet as a global Rolodex for potential guests. In addition, the Internet is now more important than mainstream news media reports for story sources.

Not only is influence important, but also equally as important is the bottom line—the cost. If you could attract as many listeners or viewers through your Web site as you could via traditional radio or print with more control and less cost, where would you put your energy and your dollars? Knowing the Internet audience and making real comparisons to traditional media will allow you to make strategic decisions about your media campaign.

Broaden your horizons: optimize the search engine.

There are three ways a Web site can be found, but one, says Jay Byrne, stands out as most important: search engine placement. "People can only come to a Web site through a search engine result, following a link found on another page, or by typing a complete URL address into a browser," notes Byrne. "Current research shows that over 98 percent of all Internet experiences start at a search engine, thus making this the most influential point for establishing your online presence—a presence which must extend beyond your own Web site."

Organizations should view search results beyond just the placement and positioning of a Web page, including which results appear around your site's. The premise of a white paper published by WebOptimizer and Market Sentinel notes, "Whatever a person finds out about a brand on the Internet is part of that brand experience—and a crucial factor in its integrity and assets." For example, at this writing, Eliot Spitzer, the attorney general of New York State, is running for governor. His campaign has paid for a sponsored search engine link so that whenever someone searches for a major company Spitzer is investigating, a link to his campaign is provided. There has been some question about the legality of such smart tactics, but it is a very creative use of paid search-engine advertising. Spitzer's campaign appears to want his political brand to be that of an anticorporate crusader, and ensure that his name is on all search results linked to companies his public office has targeted. This strategy ensures that anyone searching for these companies will see that they have been a target of a Spitzer investigation, thus branding them. Similarly companies targeted by advocacy groups, socially responsible investment interests, competitors or, as Byrne calls them, "opportunistic feeders," online have their brand's value at risk when negative information is found as a result of associated keyword searches.

Proper and effective search-engine optimization (SEO) is paramount to ensuring your Web site is visible and easily found during online searches. Reinforcing your online brand by similarly optimizing other supportive destinations—something v-Fluence calls online environment optimization (OEO)—can be equally important. Identifying industry- and audience-relevant language online is the first step and acts as a foundation for the process. Such language is often referred to as *keywords* or *key phrases*. Does the public come to your issue using language devised by your marketing department, or more commonly used terms? For example, immediately following the first case of bovine spongiform encephalopathy (BSE) identified in the United States, monthly searches on that issue shot from ten thousand per month to nearly two hundred thousand. However, the term people were using was not *BSE*, but rather *mad cow disease*—a phrase the industry had avoided using because of its strongly negative connotation. Thus the BSE-language-oriented destinations of the Centers for Disease Control, U.S. Department of Agriculture, and cattle associations were simply not being found and had to incorporate *mad cow* into their online content and site coding to have an effective public presence against the animal rights group PETA and other special-interest groups seeking to springboard from the BSE case.

Online tools can show you how often a certain word or phrase is searched, as well as offering additional language recommendations. Utilize tools that cover the top search engines, such as Google, Yahoo!, MSN, and AOL. One such tool for this type of search is offered through searchmarketing.yahoo.com/srch/index.php, formerly overture.com. These keywords should then be appropriately integrated into Web site HTML tags and copy. The title and description HTML tags are most important, followed by integrating a keyword three to four times in the copy. Exaggerated, continuous repetition or inappropriate use of keywords may cause some search engines to blacklist your Web site, so three or four mentions should be sufficient. Given frequently changing search engine–related rules and best practices, seeking out expert advice for effective SEO and OEO is a good idea.

Once you have properly optimized your site, you should submit it to the major directory listing in relevant search-engine library categories. Yahoo!, DMOZ, and Zeal (LookSmart) are the current top directory destinations (Google is an index, not a directory, which uses the DMOZ directory services). Yahoo! offers an express service for reviewing your Web site at a cost of $299 per year. There is no guarantee Yahoo! will add your site to its directory, so be sure to read the guidelines carefully. DMOZ and Zeal, edited by volunteers, do not offer an express service. DMOZ and Zeal typically take longer for review and placement, but are worth the wait because they are associated with Google and LookSmart, respectively.

Links from other Web sites also factor into your search-engine ranking. Forming linking partnerships with other Web sites is highly recommended, especially if they currently have a high ranking in the search engines. Other SEO tactics to consider are pay-per-click and pay-per-inclusion engines. Again, consider where these ad programs place your listing. Searchmarketing.yahoo.com, FindWhat (now Miva), and Google AdWords are recommended.

Yahoo! and Google now have video searching mechanisms. Since millions of people download multimedia online every week, it's worth considering including your own video optimized for keyword search results. Google is also adding a print search capacity for books. Did your CEO write a book? Want it to get maximum search-engine exposure? All of these will require specific strategies to make sure your content catches eyeballs in the search process.

People listening to talk radio are likely to visit that program site or a site recommended during the program. A 1999 Arbitron study found that 29 percent of people with Internet access have visited a Web site as a direct result of a recommendation they heard on the radio. Yet while most news and talk-radio programs are online, only a few engage in the best practice for promoting their own sites—that of providing searchable content on key topics. For the Internet, content in the form of searchable text is king. Ensuring relevant and easy-to-find content can significantly broaden the impact of any program appearance.

Provide station contacts with short background information and biographical data on your guests and your topic, and let them know it can be used on their Web site. Include a selection of relevant and easy-to-read

Web site links for them as well. If the program does not post them to its Web site, the host might mention them as part of the program. Your guest should be prepared to mention these links during interviews as frequently as possible.

Search-engine and online environment optimization expert Chris Clark of v-Fluence (v-fluence.com), has put together the following to maximize search engine success:

Ten Tips for Search-Engine Optimization Success

People are spending a lot of time and money on Web site development, search-engine optimization (SEO) and keyword purchases. While it sounds complicated and expensive, achieving high rankings in the major search engines is not as daunting a task as it might seem.

The following tips will help you build a strong, effective, and strategic Web presence that is a must in today's online environment.

- **Choose the right Internet-oriented language for your Web site.** You must understand how people are searching for an issue, product, or service to ensure your site can be found where they are looking. You may be surprised to find that keywords you thought best described your issue, product, or industry are silent compared to terms used by those surfing the Web. Ignoring terms, even when undesirable, can cost you thousands of visitors a day. Wordtracker is the industry gold standard for such research, while searchmarketing.yahoo.com and Google both offer free tools to help with your keyword selections.
- **Map the individual pages on your Web site.** Review your keyword list and select two or three popular keyword phrases that make sense for a particular page of your Web site. Remember, it is always preferable to use phrases instead of single keywords.
- **Title tags are key.** A major factor in search-engine rankings, the title tag should consist of five to ten words and contain the targeted keywords for that particular Web page. It is best to

avoid placing your company or organization name in every title on the Web site.

- **Pay attention to your body copy.** While it is best to write copy from scratch based upon your keyword selections, you can easily incorporate keywords into the body of existing Web page copy. Aim for two-hundred-plus words, incorporating your elected keywords three to four times, or once a paragraph. Update about a page of text daily.

- **Use META keyword and description tags.** Although they are no longer major factors in search-engine rankings, META keyword and description tags should be used; principally the description tag, which search engines use to describe your Web site in their natural results.

- **Build your links pointing in (LPI) over time.** A Web site's linking popularity—other Web sites that link to yours—is quickly becoming a major aspect in high rankings. The best places to start seeking quality LPIs are the major directories (Yahoo! and DMOZ). Be sure to pay close attention to the submission guidelines! Secondary directories and search engines also offer excellent opportunities for LPIs. Hunting for linking partners using language research is also a great way to boost your Web site's linking popularity. Focus on sites that enjoy high rankings in the major search engines and request links from them. Proper etiquette implies that you should link to a potential partner before asking for a reciprocal link. The best way to ensure high linking popularity is building a great Web site. If you do it right, chances are most of your work will be done for you. If your site is less than appealing, you may find it difficult to find linking partners, much less acceptance in directories and search engines.

- **Measure success with the big boys.** Deciding on which of the several hundred search engines you should pay attention to can be nerve-racking—don't let it be. Together, Google, Yahoo!, and MSN account for more than 96 percent of searches conducted on search engines. Focus your attention in these online spaces.

- **Use pay-per-click advertising if possible.** If you can afford it, use of Yahoo! Search Marketing and Google AdWords is highly recommended. On a budget of even one dollar a day, you could attract leads and brand your issue, product, or service to upwards of 96 percent of the search engine's public, even if it is on a limited basis. Use of these services also offers a great stopgap while you are waiting for improved search-engine rankings results and, in most cases, will be live in a matter of days or even minutes.
- **Don't cheat.** Using tactics like keyword stuffing (repeating keywords over and over), hidden text, and participating with link farms, among others, are dangerous propositions. Make sure that you do not duplicate content from one site onto another. The search engines know these tricks, and they know them better than you do.
- **Patience is a virtue.** Obtaining top-ten rankings can often take months. Don't panic if you don't see noticeable changes over the span of a few months. Constantly tweaking your site copy every month can do more harm than good.

Also, keep up with changes. One site to monitor is SearchEngine Watch.com.

Phone not ringing? Put the Internet on your payroll.

Maintain an e-mail list of news directors, program hosts, and producers. Provide them with updates on relevant topics and recommended guests. Numerous services such as Bacon's and Burrelle's offer online lists of key radio and television programming contacts, including e-mail addresses. A range of software programs from companies such as Vocus, some of which integrate with services like Bacon's, are also available to assist in managing your ongoing media contacts. As with all media pitches, keep your information tight and to the point. Numerous Web sites provide best practices recommendations for e-mailing journalists. Forrester Research suggests that e-mails perceived as ads are opened at a rate of about thirty-three percent.

Other studies show that the rate drops to as low as two to ten percent for e-mails without a recognizable name or subject. Some examples include:

- Make your subject line relevant to your topic.
- Avoid attachments, HTML, and heavy graphics (many media personalities read their e-mail on personal digital assistants like the BlackBerry, which works much better with text-only content).
- Provide all the relevant contact information necessary to reach you, regardless of when the e-mails are read.
- Research your target outlets and the topics they cover to ensure they are relevant before sending your pitches.
- Contact forms don't work for hosts, reporters, or producers on deadline. They want phone numbers that lead to real, live people who can provide them with background information and potential guest interviews. If they cannot easily find your contact information online, they will go somewhere else for their information and interview. A good rule of thumb is that anyone should be able to locate the information they want on your site with three clicks or less. For media contact information your goal should be *one click and you're out*. It is also important to make sure there is a live person to answer the phone. Take your cell phone to lunch if you have to. Make sure the media can reach you.

Although influentials were discussed earlier in this book, their relevance to the Internet bears repeating.

Roper ASW and the *Washington Post* report that 10 percent of the population shapes the attitudes and behaviors of the remaining 90 percent. Their annual research surveys indicate that these influentials now rely on the Internet more than any other source for news and information. Influentials spend more time online (not including time spent on e-mail) than any other medium, and a majority will likely forward information of interest they find online to others. What is most amazing about influentials is they know how to activate people off-line as well. In addition, they are the first to adopt a trend—often three to five years before the general public.

The Pew Internet & American Life Project (pewinternet.org) reports that policy makers and elected officials are also online, relying more and more on the Internet in making policy, regulatory, and legislative decisions. Influentials, policy makers, and elected officials are frequent guests on news and talk radio.

Understanding where influentials go online and what they're likely to see and from whom is an essential first step in developing a successful outreach strategy, says Jay Byrne. "Evaluating the online environment you seek to influence in the context of your target audiences is a necessary first step for effective Internet-related investments," says Byrne. "Unfortunately, too many people today jump into the Internet with a Web site or other outreach strategy without an adequate understanding of the space into which they are throwing their time, money, and other resources." Web site best-practice evaluations are done by industry trade journals like Ragan's Web Content Report (which offers this service free to subscribers) and by firms like v-Fluence, which will evaluate both your Web site and your target environment (or online neighborhood).

Maintain e-mail lists of supporters and other stakeholders. Inform them in advance of upcoming talk-radio show appearances. Provide appropriate details, including the name of the show, the time it will air, and markets in which it will be heard. Give program dial-in numbers or e-mail addresses so supporters can interact by sharing appropriate comments.

Testing to ensure a successful outcome is crucial. Make your e-mail or instant message "bite-size" so people will read it and, as one expert said, "will not be scared off."

The Kerry campaign was very successful in raising money and they did this by testing everything about their e-mail and Web campaign. They did the math and realized that with more than a quarter of a million visitors a day, small changes to their Web content could make a vast difference in the amount of money that could be raised.

In an interview with the *New York Times*, Josh Ross, director of Internet strategy for the Kerry campaign, said that fund-raising letters did poorly on Monday, that e-mail messages are best sent around 11:00 A.M.(after people have cleared their mailboxes), and that contributions swelled around lunchtime on both coasts. Ross also said that the campaign researched what e-mail subject lines worked best. On the last day they raised money, they found that *last chance* worked better than *this is it* in the subject line. In the same interview Ross said they tested thirty versions of their home page and several photos and headlines, finally choosing MAKE HISTORY WITH US.

Many sites have a sign-up process for getting on their subscription lists. If you have one, make it easy and quick. Jakob Nielsen, known as the guru of Web page usability, found that the average subscribing process took five minutes and the unsubscribing process took three minutes. Try to shorten the time for each to one minute. In addition, e-mailed newsletters must be designed to facilitate scanning, as only 23 percent of the newsletters in Nielsen's study were read thoroughly, and 27 percent were not even opened. One of the study's most important findings is that users have highly emotional reactions to newsletters, which have a much more personal feel than Web sites. Nielsen found this was because "they arrive in your inbox; you have an ongoing relationship with them." The younger demographic probably relates to instant messaging the way older citizens feel about snail mail.

Following are some tips for connecting to producers and your target audience via e-mail and instant messages:

- Try to send the e-mail from recognizable names. Develop a relationship between you (your campaign) and the public (or producers). Ari Rabinoff, who worked on the Kerry campaign, said people would approach campaign manager Mary Beth Cahill on the street as if she were a friend, because they had received regular e-mails from her over an extended length of time.
- E-mails work best for sharing new information and mobilizing your base. Producers like valuable and fresh information. E-mails do not work for changing the opinions of the recipients. The Bigfoot Interactive/Roper study found that the highest delivery rates were from media editorial efforts.
- Present the most important material first. Don't make the recipient go on a treasure hunt.
- Ask producers and journalists what kind of information they need. Find out from your base and other interested parties what they want most from you.
- E-mail now delivers content in various ways. Find out if people want an RSS feed, HTML, and so forth.

- Target the e-mails. One campaign e-mailed local influentials the telephone numbers of their neighbors so they would contact them. On national campaigns, when trying to reach the local media, do the homework for them by providing lists of local contacts they can use for stories and on the air. Find out the local Internet sites and target them as well with information and contacts.

- Keep your e-mail lists updated. Find a reason for people to respond to your e-mail, such as a giveaway, and send e-mails often. Somewhere between one-fourth and one-third of e-mails don't reach the intended destination. A recent Bigfoot Interactive/Roper study found that more than 13 percent of all recipients had changed e-mail addresses in the previous six months.

- Create expectations and keep them. If you say you will be sending a weekly update, then make sure you do. People look forward to receiving regular updates and information. If producers know to expect leads and contacts, they can plan around them.

- Set the tone. Influencers as well as producers want to be part of the conversation. They don't want a rant or a lecture.

- Link, link, and link some more. Link to your Web site. Link to photos. Link to documents. Link to other Web sites. When sending something to the media give real links to the hot stories on news sites that back up your position and support the timeliness of your story. Provide as many good Web site links as you can. By directing people in this manner you are allowing them to participate in the journey of getting to the source of your information—and it will increase the likelihood of their buying into your cause. It will save producers valuable time and provide the backup to give to their bosses.

- Put together online events for your e-mail lists. Producers and hosts may want a small conference call; some on your larger lists may want a onetime online chat or a Skype conference call.

- Make certain that anything you send out via e-mail is safe, in case it gets into the opposition's hands. E-mails can spread like a virus—they can multiply beyond what you ever thought possible.

- Spam filters work, so use words that will avoid them. Also, ask the recipients to add your e-mail address, the name of your organization, and the person sending the e-mail to their address book. Generally that will take care of the spam-filter problem, but you might also send your e-mail newsletter to your staff to see what gets through without the above information in their address book.
- The subject line will (or will not) cause people to open your e-mail. Spend the time to develop it for each e-mailing.
- Limit the subject line to fifty or sixty characters. Many servers will not allow more than this.
- Try to measure click-through response with e-mails. Tweak your e-mail newsletters until you have a greater click-through response.
- Thank-you messages work when your e-mail list has responded, but send them out even when they have not, just for opening your e-mail.
- Use short surveys. People will respond—especially if you are able to share any of the results with them.
- Set realistic goals about how long it will take to respond to e-mails. Twenty-four hours is a great goal to have. Track your response time.
- Last but not least, only put in e-mails what you are willing to have on the front page of the *Washington Post*. It is too easy to send what is written to the opposition.

Neighborhood watch.

Most people know to monitor Web sites that are contrary to their own point of view, but are not vigilant about looking for other sites, blogs, and so forth that may influence how people view them and their organization. The legitimate sites are one thing, but the rogue sites and sites that harbor urban myths should be monitored as well. Communications professional Charles Pizzo says, "You must monitor the Internet for references to your organization's name, its brands, products, services, and people. Failing to do so can leave your organization's reputation vulnerable to attack." He suggests several tactics for countering online threats. Some of Pizzo's suggestions include:

- Contact the person revealed in the *who is* search to learn more about their beef and try to intervene with a remedy.
- File a complaint with that person's ISP provider, if what they are doing is over the top.
- Post counterinformation.
- Ignore it.
- Handle it with a sense of humor.
- Mount a full-scale truth site.
- Register domain names such as (your company name) sucks.com (org, net, etc.), so that no one else will.
- If you decide to go legal, understand that the attacker might document all of your efforts.

There are several benchmarks for evaluating your site. Online benchmark mapping and Web site evaluation services have been developed by v-Fluence to help people evaluate their online environment and response options. Some of the elements v-Fluence recommends that you should evaluate for your own site include the following:

Some elements you will want to monitor on a regular basis:

Technical
- Download time—Pages should load in five seconds or less.
- HTML errors for coding—This may create a problem with your page displaying properly.
- Browser errors—You are looking for incompatible tags or attributes with those who visit your page.
- Dead links and domain-name server errors.
- The impact on typical users of the use of Flash, frames, dynamic HTML, Java script, and other tools used on your site.

Content

- Is your site's purpose clear? This should be your overriding concern when evaluating your Web page.
- Is your title tag optimized against the language most frequently used by target audiences?
- Does your description META tag incorporate target language and offer an accurate review of the content on your page?
- Do you have any interactive features or multimedia? Used appropriately, these can allow for a richer experience of the site.
- Look for ease of navigation on your Web page. Are the link words relevant? Do your navigation elements complement the site structure?
- Does your site logo-link to your Web page?
- Do you use *breadcrumbs*? These allow the user to go directly to a higher level of the site and come back to the starting point with ease.
- Does your home page show the best and most recent content?
- Do you want it to look like a directory? If so, does it accomplish your goal?

Style

- Do you use Web-safe fonts?
- Do you use Web-safe colors? There are 216 colors for both Macs and PCs.
- Are you using your space effectively?
- Do your page dimensions fit onto the screen of most computers?

Press Content

- State that you do not monitor your press Web space, indicating that all page viewings are confidential.
- How recent are your press releases? Nothing will make you seem more irrelevant than having an outdated press release.
- Does your press page provide information about the organization? It should be easy to read, fact-filled, and have good links to the rest of your site.

- Can you make media inquiries from your Web page?
- Does the Web page have transcripts of speeches and the like? Reporters often quote from this kind of text.
- Do you have downloadable photos and sound? Are the photos high resolution? Is the sound professional enough for use on the air?
- Will your in-depth information meet a reporter's needs? Are there links to backup positions, and could they take the place of a press briefing?
- Is your online press material as complete as your press kit?
- Upcoming events calendars should be updated a minimum of once a week
- Is your logo available for download?
- If you have TV spots or radio spots, are they online?
- Do you use RSS feed for this content?

Beyond your own Web site, the Internet has changed the playing field, fundamentally altering how individuals and organizations receive and transmit information and influence others. Engaging in good media relations and having an effective Web site are no longer good enough. The dominance of centralized marketing tools like mass media is increasingly eroded by an often bewildering array of decentralized communication channels and players operating online.

To be effective, you must conduct benchmark research that evaluates the online environment and key stakeholder linked to your organizations issues. Then continually monitor that environment to make the best ongoing decisions for action. v-Fluence recommends evaluating:

- Developments and trends in online discussion
- Developments in e–real estate, including changes to relevant Web sites or the creation of new ones
- Trends/changes in Web search-term language for the major search engines (a reflection of the online perception of key issues based on terms)
- Trends in related content being used and found online
- Changes in competitor activity online

- Client- or topic-related stakeholder activity
- Related online mainstream and trade-media coverage syntheses
- Analysis of online activity, including interpretation of trends and actions taken by stakeholder groups

Must-haves and must-do's!

There are three must-haves—sound, video, and a regularly updated calendar. These should provide a good experience and content supportive of your goals each time someone gets online to learn about you.

More than five million people download multimedia content online each week, and this number is growing with increased sales of iPods and similar devices that allow for both audio and video portable content to be downloaded. These musts should fit in with your overall goal of providing a great experience and content that is supportive of your goals every time people go online to find out about your subject matter. Multimedia should not be forced upon site visitors, but offered as clearly defined (include the download size!) options for visitors to access. And all content should be tagged with relevant, searchable keywords and title tags so it can be found by the search engines and indexed by multimedia directories.

Games and interactive features are very appealing. The plan should be to engage as many of the senses as possible of those who visit your site. If you have any doubt about how to make a Web site interactive, go to the Public Broadcasting Web site (pbs.org) and see how they have won the hearts and minds of the kids. Divided into different categories of games, stories, music, and coloring, the site has something for any interest. It keeps the kids on the page longer and ensures their loyalty to the Web site and eventually to PBS.

Run a contest with giveaways. Give logo items such as T-shirts, hats, and so on to those who send in interesting content you can use on your Web site. Ask for tips about the opposition. Ask people to write songs, a jingle, or anything else that would cause them to participate in your site and organization.

Sound clips are different from podcasting, but just as important. They are a means of reaching another of the five senses. Books can't do that, newspapers can't do that, but your Web site can. Sound allows a person to form their own mental images as they are listening.

Video also appeals to the senses and is another channel for reaching your audience. It differs from sound in that, like the emotional medium of television, it allows you to present your entire package.

These two mediums can be utilized in different and strategic ways. They also have more appeal for the eighteen-to-thirty-four age demographic than print.

Washington, D.C.–based company Free Range Graphics developed a funny and well-done video for the Organic Trade Association titled "Store Wars" (storewars.org). Vegetable characters based on the popular movie series *Star Wars* included Lord Tater, who represented the evil, nonorganic food. The video was downloadable and included individual segments such as "Meet the puppets." In a very short period it had millions of viewers. The timing was excellent—it appeared on the Web right before the release of the *Star Wars* film *Revenge of the Sith*.

Whatever you choose to do on your Web site, it is imperative that the quality is professional. Sound that is too loud or too soft or video that looks like amateur hour will negate all your hard work. Several of the media watchdog sites are now providing actual clips of the radio and television they are monitoring. Sound and video on the Web that cannot be downloaded because of poor quality are missed opportunities.

When appearing on a radio program, include relevant content and a link to the program on your organization's Web site. Following appearances, post a brief summary or program highlights to your site with a link to the related program site, and note when and where archived program audio files exist.

Nearly every organization or issue has a network of supporters who can enhance your talk-radio and other media experiences—but only if they know how. E-mail, chat rooms, blogs, Listservs, and Usenet discussion groups are only a few online dialogue opportunities to inform relevant online communities about news and talk-radio appearances or program discussions regarding your topic of interest.

More than one trillion e-mails are sent each year. There are 280,000 listserv discussion groups and tens of thousands of bulletin boards and chat rooms—a portion of which, at any given time, can be leveraged to magnify your news or talk-radio appearances.

Provide audio files (radio actualities) from key events on your Web site. While few news programs or stations use *canned* news, talk shows and some news outlets will occasionally use audio clips or actualities. Most programs prefer audio provided in MP3 file format, which can be downloaded from your Web site. Break up longer audio pieces into multiple, shorter (thirty-to-ninety-second) segments. Be sure to provide text highlights for each actuality indicating who will be speaking, the topic, and where and when it was taped.

When appearing on programs that do not provide streaming audio and audio archives, ask if you can tape and reproduce part or all of the program for access on your own Web site. High-quality digital audio recorders with telephone recording-control devices can be purchased at any consumer electronics store, with software enabling you to easily convert portions or all of a program into MP3, WMA, or other Web-friendly formats.

Your calendar of events is the compass that allows others to find you. Many Web sites of national organizations do not have easily accessible calendars. People who want to attend a live event featuring you or your organization need to have that information available to them without having to make a phone call or send an e-mail. If events are open to the public, post them on your calendar. If you will be making an announcement, let people know when that will take place. Use your calendar to inform people of any organized Meet-ups through Meetup.com. Meet-ups have actually increased in numbers since the 2004 election, and according to Meetup CEO Scott Heiferman, the number one use of Meetup is for stay-at-home moms.

Opt to be an online opportunist.

Choose possibilities for submitting or posting information about upcoming programs, or recent programs where archived content is available. Jay Byrne counsels to also evaluate direct versus indirect participation based on the type of community and content you're seeking to influence.

"In some cases you are better served giving up some direct control of content and letting established online influentials spread the word for you," says Byrne. "Online sneezers—people who share ideas like colds—who have established credibility can become effective conduits for your content."

Byrne's company v-Fluence identifies online discussion "sneezers" and categorizes them as either "prolific posters" or "traction talkers." Prolific posters share new content broadly and repeatedly in the discussion spaces in which they are active. Traction talkers, according to Byrne, are the "E. F. Hutton's of the Web; when they speak people listen." Traction talkers' postings generate other discussion threads and are frequently cut and pasted to be shared by others. Identifying the sneezers and evaluating the opportunities for sharing information with them can often be more effective than directly participating in a discussion space.

Here are some types of discussion channels that are available on the Internet:

> **Usenet newsgroups.** Usenet newsgroups are discussion forums that individuals access according to their area of interest. They are *threaded*—meaning an initial posting will lead to a number of ensuing posts or threads.
>
> Google acquired the Usenet discussion service from Deja.com in 2001. The acquisition included its archives of more than 500 million posts, expanding Google's functionality to provide more sophisticated browsing options, incorporation of current postings directly into the searchable archives, and a host of other features that have given Usenet one of the largest dialogue options on the Web.
>
> Doing a search for relevant keywords will also indicate the newsgroups where the messages are posted and where potential stakeholders and audience members exist.
>
> **Private bulletin boards.** In terms of usability, bulletin boards are similar in concept to Usenet groups. The discussions occur on the Web, are accessed through a Web browser, and are thread-based. The discussion on most bulletin boards revolves around the general theme of the host Web site, although there are bul-

letin boards (sometimes referred to as communities) that exist independently of any static Web site. A searchable listing of many different bulletin boards can be found at ezboard.com.

Community blogs. Community blogs are Web logs compiled by a number of participants and normally include a discussion function that is arranged similarly to bulletin boards. BlogSearchEngine.com offers a searchable directory of thousands of blogs, many of which are community blogs.

Listservs. Listservs use e-mail to facilitate discussions. These discussions can be more focused and action-oriented than Usenet newsgroups. Lsoft.com maintains a searchable catalog of more than 250,000 Listservs. Additionally, the top three portals—Yahoo!, MSN, and AOL, all offer the ability to join and create groups that contain an e-mail component (among a host of other features). Doing a keyword search in these areas can identify appropriate discussion opportunities.

Although the above dialogue options encompass intrinsically different types of audiences and participation, here are some guidelines you may want to consider:

- Review discussion rules and archives before posting materials. Nothing will cause you to be ignored more quickly than disregarding the etiquette or protocol of a specific discussion channel.

- Communicate through established members. Groups will often have hosts or owners; if you are not a regular member it is a good practice to submit content to them first, requesting that they post the information for the group, if they deem it appropriate. Content that is posted from established members if far more likely to be read than content posted from newcomers or unknown individuals.

- Respond to your respondents. If you merely post and vacate the premises, your posting will be disregarded as spam. If someone posts and you respond to their ensuing thread, you are far more likely to be taken seriously.

• Monitor related discussion threads in these groups—they can often be more influential than the radio program you are promoting. Treat these groups and their participants with the same respect and professionalism you would any mainstream media.

Social networking. There are many sites for finding, keeping, and adding networks of friends and business contacts. Friendster.com, AOL's ICQ Universe (icq.com), and ryze.com are primarily for social networking, while LinkedIn.com and ZeroDegrees.com are business- and work-focused.

Understanding how these networks help people to connect and communicate can get the word out in less formal ways. If you view it as a party or community get-together, the possibilities for impact are endless. This works best when you and those in your organization have a trusted network that can be relied upon to help spread the word in a more social, friendly manner.

Wikiprojects. Wikipedia is an online encyclopedia that includes entries written by the online community. These can include corrections of misinformation as well as additions to entries by any one who happens to have knowledge of a certain topic.

One example of the Wiki online strategy was the Principles Project (PrinciplesProject.org), chaired by Congressman Harold Ford, Congresswoman Jan Schakowsky and former Democratic National Committee Chair David Wilhelm. It created online space for a six-week discussion aimed at "creating a single-page statement of progressive principles." They began by asking participants to critique a working draft of a statement, then took the input from the online community and posted three subsequent drafts. They then had a final online vote, culminating in a conference to develop strategies articulated by the final statement.

BlogCalls (often called BlogCon). Bob Fertik of Democrats.com developed BlogCalls. Using freeconfrence.com he took issues being discussed in the blogosphere, put the hot bloggers-related guests on, and essentially had a conference call. The software limited him to the first one hundred callers. It was an inexpensive way to have a large conference call, because the incoming callers paid for their own charges. With Skype technology, it is now becoming possible to have large numbers of participants for minimum cost.

Meet-ups. Although Meet-ups (Meetup.com) are an online activity, only the organizing of them takes place online. Meet-ups provide the advantages of a hybrid model—the benefits of a virtual community, plus face-to-face contact.

Research has shown that Meet-ups are very appealing to women who want the face-to-face contact, and that the folks who attend them are generally different from the influentials and those who are solely Internet users. People often find out about Meet-ups directly from the organization they are interested in, but then use the Meetup site to find other meetings of interest.

Flash mobs. A variation of a smart mob, the term first coined by Howard Rheingold in his book *Smart Mobs: The Next Social Revolution*, is, according to *Adweek* magazine, a cell phone act of mass performance in which people show up at a place in droves, unannounced, do something weird, and leave.

Ford Motors was first out of the gate to use flash mobs. They are using text messaging to give last-minute locales and times for a series of unannounced multicity concerts with emerging artists. They teamed up with Sony and JWT to promote the concerts on a Web site (fusionflashconcerts.com) where people could register to be "insiders" and get last-minute notifications, or could key in a number on their mobile phone. Ford offers a chance to win their new Fusion car.

These are just some of the many ways to promote your issue and information online. Knowing how to use the Internet—both for gathering and for dispersing information—can go a long way in getting your messages heard over live and virtual airwaves. Additional information, links to useful articles, and tips on using the Internet for radio and other outreach can be found at v-fluence.com.

Blog, blog, blog.

The Internet is about empowerment—power to communicate, power to
get information, and power to turn traditional ways of disseminating
information on their ears. For example, we saw the entire political universe change with the Howard Dean campaign "People-Powered
Howard," which was, as one campaign operative termed it, "one big virtual ATM."

For many people blogs and the blogosphere are at the center of the
democratization of content, wrestling control away from mainstream
media and other traditional influencers. One author has gone so far as to
liken blogging to the Reformation, and having an impact similar to the
opening up of the mysteries of the Catholic Church to the masses and
causing a revolt that spawned the Protestant movement. Some see it as
following and amplifying certain kinds of information and that the
Wikipedia revolution will be a continuation of the blogging phenomenon. Still others see it as an ecosystem with traditional media—that
blogs are not able to exist without the traditional media.

Today blogs and bloggers are joining forces and similarly tearing down
mainstream media, political, and corporate institutions.

Some claim blogs are a simply a fad to be ignored. In some very narrow
ways that may be true; however, what underlies blogging and technology
elements incorporated into blogs is here to stay and is defining the future
direction of the Internet. These technologies present significant opportunities; ignoring them is done at significant risk.

Blogging thought leader Glen Reynolds, who published Instapundit,
has aptly characterized the blog phenomenon, noting, "Bloggers have
very little power. What they have is influence." Reynolds suggests that the
blogosphere's impact only occurs when multiple bloggers agree and con-
verge on a topic, drawing attention and influencing search-engine results.
When this happens, something called a blog storm or blog swarm can
occur. Examples of blog swarms include:

Kryptonite lock failure. Bloggers exposed and promoted a flaw
   in Kryptonite bicycle locks, resulting in a ten-million-dollar
   product recall.

CBS News "Rather Gate" scandal. Bloggers claimed documents used by CBS news anchor Dan Rather raising questions about President George W. Bush's military record were forged, resulting in Rather's resignation from CBS news.

Trent Lott racism allegation. Bloggers latched on to comments that the then Senate majority leader made at a party for Strom Thurmond, resulting in Lott's resignation from his leadership position.

Terry Schiavo case. Blog interest and discussions eventually brought massive media attention to the Schiavo case and the general right-to-die issue.

Bloggers are now creating their own blog swarms by having informal conference calls and even working with their readers to increase their power. The Daily Kos bloggers have their own annual conference. Metablogs are indexes or aggregates of other blogs, which also increases a blog's amplification. Other ways to amplify a blog is by linking to other blogs.

Bloggers influence other media as well. Tucker Eskew, former George W. Bush White House media director, says, "You can't really work effectively with talk radio and talk TV without understanding the blog phenomenon, and knowing that blogs tend to reach small audiences, particularly compared to the larger talk media. But they do draw influential audiences, even if those influencers are sometimes in the mainstream media themselves. And what I find the most fascinating is to hear someone in talk radio, and even someone in the newspaper, commenting about something they've read that I know they've seen it first in the blogging world."

No matter how you see and understand blogging, Technorati (technorati.com) states that the number of blogs doubles every five months. As of this writing there are more than sixty million blogs, with ten posts every second. The Pew study found that 44 percent of Internet users publish their thoughts in some manner or create content online—many on blogs or responding to blogs.

Technorati is one way to track the blogosphere, and there are other sites (Google has recently begun to index blogs) that do that as well. One site that offers some helpful tools for blog navigation is blogpulse.com. This index contains the full conversation of recent Weblog posts and offers useful advanced searching options. Blogpulse's Conversation Tracker relies on the ability to segment blogs into posts and to identify permalinks. It creates a threaded view of the conversation graph being generated by blogs on a particular topic—one of the few places you can see the content syndication and associated impact blogs can have on a particular topic or organization. Others, like v-Fluence, offer customized services for their clients to track blogs and their impact while providing options for response and other interactions.

There are many, many opinions out there and, as columnist John C. Dvorak says, "Everyone has an opinion, but many of them are worthless." The job then is to make sure that any blog created by you contains information people want or insight no one else has. Obviously if you are the President of the United States or a megastar, people are going to want to read your blog. If you are not, it had better contain something of interest or it will have the impact of a leaf falling in a canyon.

Authors Susan Herring and Lois Ann Scheidt developed definitions about types of blogs and have divided them into several categories:

- Filter blogs, in which the blogger supplies interesting content found elsewhere online and in the media.
- Personal journals are just that; however, they may include photos, links, and so forth.
- K-logs, or knowledge logs, can be educational, contain scientific information, and the like.

EMarketer did a study on why people read blogs. The top two reasons given were "News I can't find elsewhere" and "Better perspective," closely followed by "More honesty" and "Faster news." Other reasons included "More personality," "Transparent biases," and "Latest trends."

Several of the television news organizations have added blogs that comment on their televised news content and allow for viewers ask questions and to comment. This gives the viewer a chance to feel a sense of ownership and connection with the news brand.

Blogs can also be a source of revenue. Forrester Research found that 64 percent of advertisers in the United States would advertise on blogs.

The Pew/Buzz Metrics study points out that blogs often contain features interlacing them with other blogs. These connective features include a *blog roll* of favorite blogs; a *permalink* identifying a blog entry or post ready for reference elsewhere; a *trackback* capacity, whereby outsiders who link to the entry are listed and given a reciprocal link; and *RSS feed capability* to deliver an entry automatically to those who have just requested its type. These features ensure that whatever one blog buzzes about, adjacent blogs are readily able to amplify.

Tags are like subjects or categories and allow people to find your blog. However, these have to be broad and specific at the same time. Technorati had 13,145 posts tagged *Live8*. Therefore, to get your blog read you have to use the buzzwords, plus a bit of creativity.

There are some basic rules if you have never blogged. First and foremost, a blog is a personal experience. There is a lot of talk about ghost blogging, and it should be avoided. If you are heading up an organization that wants to blog and don't have time to sit and write, then dictate your blog or turn over the responsibility and "voice" someone within your organization who has the time. The NCAA, for example, has turned this task over to a full-time intern who has a clear identity and voice that resonates with the college audience they are seeking to influence and inform. The idea that it is you, real and in real time. Also:

- Blogs are not lectures, nor are they academic papers. They are not your PR department's chance to put their press kit in a new form. They are often short and newsy. They can be one paragraph several times a day or something that occurs weekly. It is best if someone knows when he or she can look forward to seeing something new.
- Be accurate. Do the research to make sure your facts are correct. If you make a mistake, put up a correction as soon as you can. Even the *New York Times* makes several thousand corrections a year, and they are sticklers for facts.
- Blogs build on each other. This means that blogs can build on what you have written previously or on what someone else has written.
- Read other blogs before you write your own. Make lists of what draws you in and what makes you stop reading. Look

into the topics of current blogging so you will know what is
uppermost on people's minds. Go to the tracking sites to see
how news issues are being blogged.

- Look at other blogs to see what attracts you. Just like a billboard or a book jacket, the appearance of a blog can invite you
in or turn you away. Some of the blog sites have software to
make your site more attractive and more *you*.

- Spend time with the software provided by the blogging sites.
Get to know the lingo of *permalink* and BLOCKQUOTE.
Decide if you want to have comments at the end of your blog
quotes. Decide if you want to archive your posts and for how
long. These are all technical decisions and you may choose to
change them after you have been blogging for a while.

- Make sure that your blog is on an RSS (really simple syndication) feed. This enables syndication of your content and
people to be altered when your site is updated.

- If you do not get a lot of traffic on your Web site, and even if
you do, you might want to put your blog up on one of the
established blogging sites as well as on your own. By utilizing
both, you can get maximum exposure.

- Find a name for your blog and also register it as a separate
domain name so it can be optimized for general search-engine
results. This also provides you with a space to post other content (documents, audio, video, and so on) that might not be
online or that you wish to link to.

- Know your audience. Who reads your blog? Whom do you
want to read your blog? Write for them, not for you.

- Just because it is short and newsy doesn't mean that it doesn't
need to be well written. Spell check it and double-check names
and titles to be sure you have identified them correctly. *The
Drudge Report* made mincemeat of Barbara Streisand's blog for
numerous spelling mistakes.

- Link! People love to find out where you are getting your information and what you think is worth reading. Be sure to check
your links. A link that does not work or misdirects people to
irrelevant information is both frustrating and irritating.

- Make it personal. Be passionate! Be honest! Be direct! Add a little debate and controversy! It is not a carbon copy of talk radio, but rather a way of communicating on a person-to-person basis. If you have a personal story, a vignette, then use it—just as you would in a real conversation.
- Be willing to take the bullet for your views. Blogger/journalist Andrew Sullivan put out three fund-raisers for his blog. When he was pro–Iraq War he took in eighty thousand dollars in one week. When he attacked the Bush administration he took in twenty thousand dollars, and when he slammed the Bush administration he took in twelve thousand dollars.
- Find your own writing style—one that is clear, unique, and consistent.
- Remember that a goal is to get your blog to stand out and show up on the search engine. Write so that others (and the media) can quote you and use the information and opinions presented.
- Think about the possibility of other people in your organization writing blogs. Mary Beth Cahill wrote one as presidential candidate John Kerry's campaign manager. You can have employees, organization members, or board members write blogs. Some corporations have thousands of bloggers! The feedback on their sites allows them to get the temperature of their customer base.
- Allocate the time and the budget. You plan your resources for your printed newsletter; do the same for your blog.
- When your blog is putting out some new, important information, let the world know about it by conventional means—radio, press release, television, and so forth.

The Electronic Frontier Foundation has a "Legal Guide for Bloggers." It is well worth reading. See also appendix 4, John Aravosis's tips.

'Casting your Net.

Almost as soon as people began using the Internet regularly, sites had both sound and video. However, it was only recently that people began to think about developing a platform that would allow entire programs to be heard and viewed on the Web with a quick and easy way to produce and download them. As of this writing, more than a third of the people with iPods or MP3 players have mastered the technology and downloaded an audio broadcast. Video players (MP4s) will soon be as common as iPods and MP3 players, making complete video broadcasts available for download.

Services like iTunes allow users to subscribe to and automatically download podcasts to iPods and other MP3 players. Content can be grouped by subject, source, and other fields for easy sorting and user access. Newstalkcast.com and Podjockey.com are examples of this. Tutorials on new technology are offered by lynda.com. Similar video services are expected to be offered by TiVo and other DVR cable providers, linking Web content directly to your television set. Newspapers, radio stations, magazines, and more are all preparing podcasts that can be downloaded regularly with new content. This allows for content portability and flexibility—listening to and watching what I want and when I want it.

Some of it is free of charge. The various revenue models—paid subscriptions, advertisements, in-program product placements, and free content as a loss leader for corporations and organizations—are being sorted out now. The role of traditional radio and television in developing and owning the podcast/vlog (also called vcast) marketplace will also be something to watch. Will the market be dominated by the traditional media or will, like blogging, an entire new "Fifth Estate" spring up and make a lasting contribution to the media landscape? One group called We Are the Media, at WeAretheMedia.com, predicts that this new media revolution is the death knell for mainstream media.

From the first major political video on the DNC Web site in 2002 titled "Social Insecurity," showing an elderly woman being wheeled off a cliff, to the Republican National Committee's early foray into downloadable podcasts featuring interviews with major figures, to "Democaster" in the United Kingdom, which records government meetings and allows constituents to comment online multimedia technology applications on the Internet, many multimedia broadcasts are having profound impacts on our political systems. Similarly, advocacy groups from PETA to Consumers Union have embraced online video and audio, circumventing traditional mainstream media filters and directing powerful content directly to online consumers. PETA-TV calls itself "Animal Rights Television," and offers critical, professionally developed programs directly to target audiences. Consumers Union produces youth-friendly cartoons that depict corporate targets such as the pharmaceutical industry as evil fiends battled by consumer superheroes.

Wikipedia's definition of *podcast* is "an audio magazine subscription; in that the subscriber receives regular programs without having to remember to go get them, and can listen or watch them at leisure. It can be thought of as the Internet equivalent of time shift–capable digital video recorders such as TiVo, which lets users automatically record and store television programs for later viewing."

Although sites such as audible.com have made downloading of radio programming and paid content possible for years, some companies are quickly jumping on the podcasting bandwagon. Fox News Channel was the first to make their entire news channel available on Sprint cell phones.

EContentMag.com reports that a German publishing group, Langenscheidt, believes consumers want "content to go, and they want to enjoy it on the go." They are distributing travel and language content by mobile phones. They also reported that VOCEL, working with Random House and the Princeton Review, is providing mobile content offerings that allow students to practice drills in math, reading, and grammar via mobile phones. Students can even have their phone call them with questions!

Keeping up with what is new in podcasting, vcasting, and vlogs is difficult. Monitor Adam Curry's Web sites. He offers a log of topics on his radio show/podcasts and is currently the most up-to-date and knowledgeable person in this form of new media.

Depending on your issue, your audience may be willing to pay for content. In one study by RampRate/Synovate (RampRate.com), roughly one-third of consumers were willing to pay for content. Deciding to charge for content must be a strategic decision that will fit into your overall message and marketing plan.

What happens when radio or television is bypassed? Music on Command, Inc., (musiconcommand.com) allows a radio listener to purchase and download music as it is playing on terrestrial radio by calling a toll-free number. And what does the radio station get? Not a cent!

The Swedenborgian Church teamed up with New Century Television (newcenturytv.com) to provide a way to disseminate their older videos and new content and lectures. They didn't put long videos on the Web, but instead broke down traditional videos into short, downloadable segments. They were one of the very first religious groups to understand the power of vcasting.

Topics you can cover on a podcast or vcast would never fly on radio, television, satellite, or cable. Journalist Elizabeth Fletcher reports that condom maker Durex was the first company to pay for product placement on a podcast during *The Dawn and Drew Show*. According to Fletcher, the husband-and-wife team did a taste test with the company's flavored condom offerings.

The great thing about podcasting/vcasting is that if the quality is good and the topic is interesting it doesn't matter if it is produced by big media, a corporation, or an individual. If you have content, if you have quality, and if people know you are there, they will listen or watch.

Radio consultant Holland Cooke did a survey of which free topics people would like to download and try. The answers are surprising: comedy, 82 percent; local weekend "funformation," 78 percent; movie reviews, 69 percent; politics, 34 percent; religion, 18 percent. One of the slogans during the 2000 Ralph Nader for President Campaign was "Don't hate the media, become the media." The citizen broadcaster is an intriguing concept. Now anyone can blog, anyone can put sound on the Web, anyone can put video on the Web. But is the quality good enough for you to have the audience you want?

The professional quality of the podcast, vcast, or vlog is crucial. The cutting-edge content is also important, as is your deciding what, if any, audience feedback you want.

You also need to decide what type of podcasts, vcasts, or vlog you want. You may want to have several available on your site. They could provide information on a product, event, or person. They could provide training of your base or your employees. They could be the means for others to get to know the issues and the people of your organization. They could be a way for people from around the country or the world to keep in contact with others who have the same goals and objectives—and, of course, they are all edited by you.

If you are thinking about a regular podcast or vcast on your Web site you may want to incorporate some of the following:

- Do the market research to understand your audience and develop your programming accordingly.
- Just as in the suggestions for blogging, watch and listen to podcasts and vcasts on the Internet. What works? What doesn't work? Then listen to radio and watch television. What elements do you want to incorporate into your programming?
- Podcasting and vcasting are narrowcasting. You need to know the demographics of your intended audience. For instance, many churches are now podcasting "Godcasts." They view this as a way to reach people who cannot attend their church or to support those who want extra contact with their minister or organization within their religion. Their podcasts may be listened to by the general public, but are aimed at a specific constituency.
- Narrowcasting does not mean you won't get the numbers. Purina put the content of their radio program, *Ask the Vet*, on the Web. It may be narrowcasting, but it can attract millions of downloads.
- Be certain that it looks and sounds professional. You may want to use music and other transitions between segments.
- Consider having a professional anchor/host. How the program sounds in the first thirty seconds will brand your podcast or vcast.
- Decide the length and frequency of your podcast/vcast and stick to it. Ten to thirty minutes is a good length. If you have said it will be fifteen minutes long, make sure that it is. If you have said you will do it weekly or daily, see that you do—your audience will expect it.
- Unless you are a great comedian or prize-winning orator, use guests and minimize monologues.
- Pay attention to the feedback. Look at your numbers where available. Adjust your content as necessary.
- Just as with radio and television broadcasts, do not assume anything. Introduce your topics, guests, and, yes, even callers. Restate the name several times during a segment.
- Divide your show into fast-paced segments. If you find your mind wandering when interviewing a guest, then your listeners and viewers will too. Edit so it is interesting.

- For sound-only programs, the quality of the sound is crucial. No one wants to listen to bad sound, even if the content is great. For vcasts lighting is important in order to avoid shadows or the appearance that the viewer is looking through a tunnel.
- Consider a dual-use vcast. When using public-access television, you may be able to use their studios and put together a public-access television program, which you can then use as a vcast on your Internet site.
- By using Skype and other technologies, you can take callers. You can also provide a toll-free line for people to leave messages that you can integrate into the program.
- You can make a program out of short, regular segments that can be downloaded individually, but when put together make one longer program. Someone might want to hear or watch only one kind of segment, while someone else might want to have the entire programming.
- Watch the length of the segments and the length of responses. If you are doing a podcast/vcast aimed at scientists or philosophers, you might be able to justify long, wordy content. As with talk radio and talk television, most people want information in smaller, bite-size segments.
- Use your sound and video editor to cut out unprofessional sounds and dead air. Those *um*'s and *uh*'s, are vocalized pauses, the brain's way of catching up. Eliminate them.
- Unless it is a religious show, don't preach. Like other forms of talk media, it is a conversation.
- Always include a written show summary. This should have the look and feel of a producer's log and anchor's show prep. It should summarize each segment, provide main talking points, and point to supplemental material such as Web sites, books, or events that enhance your material.
- As in radio and television, consider adding promotions, contests, and the like. It brings people in and builds loyalty.
- The human element is crucial in your programming. People want a person or a story they can relate to—someone or something they are comfortable with wherever they are.

- Arm your constituency. The Service Employees International Union (SEIU) sold computers to its members for a hundred dollars and then taught their people how to use the Internet. With podcasts and vcasts you can now teach your constituency to gather sound at local events and to use their cell phones and video recorders to upload material that you can use to create your programs. In fact, ComVu Mobile Video Broadcasting is a service that gives mobile users the ability to transmit live broadcasts of any length using an automated video network. It is like having an army of individual reporters providing you with content. You can make it more appealing by sponsoring contests for the best material. Make it fun, and you will have content that is unique and far-reaching.
- Keep it legal. Don't steal material. Be sure to attribute the material you use. If you use music, then be ready to pay ASCAP and BMI for it. Be informed about the laws concerning libel. You may not be one of the big broadcasters, but you are still responsible for what you say.
- If you can afford the time or money, transcribe your podcasts/vcasts. It makes the content more searchable and will bring you more eyeballs and downloads on the Internet.
- Cross-promote your podcast/vcast using your site and like-minded sites or the sites of stakeholders. Purchase ads on other podcasts or vcasts.
- Consider buying ads in newspapers, on cable television, or on terrestrial or satellite-radio programs to promote what you are doing on the Internet.
- Make sure any blog, podcast, or vcast has an RSS feed. RSS changes the dynamic from sending something out hoping it gets opened, to the desired result of the consumer wanting your information. As Rick Klau from FeedBurner says, "The person waiting for the information retains all the control. If he does not like it, he can stop subscribing. But you have to provide good content to keep people subscribing. People who subscribe to your information are the best customers; they are the best audience to have." Software will soon be available that will

enable people to find RSS feeds more easily, and the ability to track those subscribing to your feed will become much clearer. David Kralik from the National Association of Manufacturers says that the key to RSS feeds is to keep it short or put it on a separate URL to keep it from crashing a subscriber's system.

Keeping up with the ever-changing technology and the way it impacts how we relate to each other goes well beyond the pages in this book. Knowing the Internet landscape and your willingness to accept new ideas will help you. The basic principles of message development, handling controversy, and all the other issues addressed in this book may remain the same, but where to utilize the new technologies and how to understand the context in which to use them will allow you to spread your message even more effectively.

Appendix 1

TIPS FOR TELEVISION

Most of the information we have shared with you in this book can be applied to your media planning strategy whether you are interested in print, the Internet, radio, or television. However, if you intend to appear on television, the following pages will provide some additional pointers that will make your on-camera experience more enjoyable for you and for the host conducting the interview.

How to dress.

- Dressing in business attire is always safe. Being overdressed or underdressed will divert the audience's attention. You do not want the focus of the interview on what you are wearing rather than on the idea or promotion you are pitching. Keep your audience in mind. Is your interview on a daytime show where the audience is generally female, age twenty-five to sixty-five, or are you being interviewed on a Sunday talk show focusing on national and international current events, for which the audience is of mixed gender? Dress appropriately and not only will you look good, but also you will fit in with the host, set, and audience.

- Studio lights generate a lot of heat, so it is most likely going to be hot on the set. If you are dressed too warmly and have to remove a jacket, you are going to look less like an expert.

- If you have a few days before your interview, select your television clothing. If you will be seated for your interview, have someone photograph you while you are sitting; if you will be standing and demonstrating something, have a photograph taken of that pose. Share the photo with people who can give you an honest opinion of your outfit and how you look. This does not require a trip to the photo lab—you can use your cell phone camera. Solicit advice, but be prepared to accept it if what you are told about your outfit is not what you want to hear. Also, sad to say, but the television camera really does add ten pounds to your appearance.

• Can a microphone be clipped to your clothing? If a woman wears a blouse and no blazer, jacket, or cardigan, the weight of the microphone may pull on her blouse and be distracting. The same is true for men who wear a polo shirt with no tie. Blazer collars and ties are typical places for the sound team to clip a microphone. Note that tie clips and necklaces can create a lot of noise if the microphone bangs against them. Swishy fabrics can also create a noise problem.

• Despite what you may think, it is good to wear colors. Black and white look dull on camera, especially in this age of high-definition TV (HDTV), where colors practically jump off the television screen. There is a long-standing debate about whether men should wear white shirts. Several of the candidates in presidential debates have worn white, but light blue is worn just as often. If you want to look presidential, stay away from brown suits, seersucker suits, and vests. Watch the Sunday-morning talk shows. Almost every male interviewed wears a navy blue suit, white or light blue shirt, and red tie. The interviewers are a little less cookie-cutter in their appearance. Women, think tailored suit. Navy is always a winner, but so are red, yellow, and even pink. Again, look at the Sunday-morning talk shows, or watch C-SPAN and check out what the female senators and congresswomen are wearing. You will be able to pick out who has a fashion advisor, who has her own unique style, and who picks out the first thing she comes across each morning!

• Do not select your television wardrobe based on what is in fashion, but don't wear something that was in vogue thirty years ago. (Although it does seem that every fashion trend within the past forty years has had a rebirth!) It is better to be more conservative in your on-camera wardrobe than to be too far out there. Remember your audience. If you are doing an interview with MTV you certainly don't want to wear the same wardrobe you would wear on *Face the Nation*. Watch both shows and note that when the president does a town hall forum on MTV he takes off his suit jacket, sometimes even rolls up his sleeves and loosens his tie. He would never do that on *Face the Nation*.

- As with your clothing, make sure your jewelry or accessories are not overpowering. Metallic jewelry really shines under those lights. (Think about someone abandoned at sea using a mirror to attract a rescue plane.) If your accessories are huge, your face disappears, and the noise your jewelry makes will annoy the audio team. Avoid heavy chains on the neck and wrist. If you have a huge diamond ring, turn it around during the interview. Sparkling diamonds can be a distraction. Avoid large earrings—they could get in the way of your earpiece if you are being interviewed by remote instead of in-studio. Men, wear a tie, not an ascot or cravat, unless that is really the way you dress.

- Patterns to avoid are plaids, checks, polka dots, and busy geometrics. These all tend to read bizarrely on camera. Have you ever seen someone being interviewed, or even a host or anchor, whose tie or blouse seems to actually move because the pattern is too busy? Avoid wild color combinations for the same reason

- Men, wear long socks. If you are being interviewed on a "living room" set, no one wants to see skin above your socks. Be sure that your socks either match or compliment your shoes and slacks. Women, make sure your skirt or dress will cover everything if you cross your legs during a seated interview. Wear new panty hose to ensure that there are no runs on the verge of spreading up your leg.

- Don't overdo ties or scarves, but don't blend into the sofa either. Bright and slightly bold ties are fine. However, a small pattern could appear as polka dots on camera instead of the expensive Hermès palm-tree pattern that it is.

- To avoid looking scrunched-up and messy while seated, pull the back of your blazer or jacket down and sit on it; this is one of the tricks of the trade. The studio people will probably tell you if it doesn't look right.

- Even men should wear at least a little bit of face powder to tone down a damp or ruddy complexion. Those studio lights are hot, and it doesn't take long to break out in a sweat. The networks have makeup professionals on staff to help reduce the shine. If your interview is in a small market, you won't have the luxury of a makeup artist to help you, so carry a small compact with you to lightly coat your eyelids, cheekbones, forehead, and nose. Men, if you are bald or you have a receding hairline, apply powder there as well. The goal here is not to look like you are wearing powder, but a small amount will drastically improve your polished look—greasy and shiny is definitely not attractive. Before applying the powder, use a paper towel to soak up any moisture.

- Be conservative with eye makeup. You don't want to look like a vampire with dark black circles under the eyes, or like a deer in the headlights from too-light eye shadow that gives you a wide-eyed look. You will need to wear a slightly heavier eye shadow, liner, and mascara than you normally would, but not too heavy. And don't forget to tone it down before you leave the studio after your interview.

- If you are traveling to your interview destination, take a change of clothing. Do not wear your interview apparel on the plane or train. You don't want to be on camera sporting a huge coffee stain, broken heel, ripped jacket, or run in your hose.

What to ask before the interview.

- If you have an opportunity, ask about the angle of your shots. If you feel you have a best side, tell the floor director in the studio and he or she might be able to accommodate your request.
- When you are booking your interview, ask if the interview will

be taped or live. It makes a difference. Interviews are often done live-to-tape, which means the interview will be treated as if it were live. Instead of one long segment that is edited in postproduction, you will be interviewed, go to commercial break (at which time you may only sit there for the scheduled length of the commercial that will be added in postproduction), or you may have an audience that will interact with you and the host during the interview. If the interview is taped, ask when it will air to avoid dating when it was taped. For example, don't use words like *yesterday* or *today*—say *recently* instead.

- If you are interviewed in the studio, ask which camera to look into if you are expected to make direct eye contact with your television audience. If the interview is treated as a cozy one-on-one between you and the host, you should not look into the camera at all; your attention should be on the host. If you are doing a show that takes calls from viewers, such as *Larry King Live*, you want to know which camera you should look at when you are addressing the caller. If there are several cameras, don't be afraid to ask before the interview who is going to prompt you to look at camera one instead of camera two, and so forth. If the cameras are stable, meaning there isn't a cameraman in the studio operating the camera, ask what the angle will be—head and shoulders, two-shot with you and the host, wide shot almost full body, or full studio shot. You do not want to be caught on camera fidgeting with your hands when you *thought* that camera was only showing your head and shoulders.

- If you are at a remote location, meaning at another studio or being interviewed via satellite, always make sure you know where to look into the camera. The camera in this case is your audience or your host. Ask the camera operator how the audience will see you. His or her job depends on getting a good shot. Will you appear to be on the same level as the audience, or looking down, to the right, or above? Looking straight into the camera is best.

- Ask about the total length of the interview and the number of segments. Your actual interview may only be seven minutes

long, but it could take twenty minutes with commercial breaks
or news cut-ins regularly scheduled during your interview
time slot. Keep the overall interview length in mind
throughout the interview. Like a newspaper story, have a
snappy headline (an introduction); a balanced body (the main
reason you are there—the information you are trying to get
across to the audience); and a closer (a summary of everything
you have said in a nice, neat little package). Rehearse prior to
the interview. You don't want to have any dead air during your
interview. Make the most of every second you are on the air.

- If you are unfamiliar with the host or the show, you should
  have been given briefing materials to familiarize yourself with
  the host and the show's format from the person who set up the
  interview. Will the host put you in the hot seat, try to make
  you look stupid, try to make you sound more knowledgeable
  than you are, be fair, be honest, have a personal gripe or personal preference to your issue? If the regular host will not be
  doing your interview, seek the same information about the
  guest host. Also, determine if you will be alone on the set with
  the host. Will other guests be sitting on the couch before you,
  or will they be interviewed while you are sitting there? Learn
  what you can about the host, guest host, and other guests. The
  last thing you want is to look ignorant on television. You don't
  want to see your startled face on the front page of the newspaper, or on the Internet do you?

- Always ask how you will be identified and look at it prior to
  going on the air. You have probably watched an interview
  where the chyron (the text underneath a person's face to identify who she is and/or why she is there) changed midinterview.
  Misspelling of names is a common mistake—we can name at
  least three networks that repeatedly make this error. If your
  name is something like J. Allen Smith, is that the way you want
  to be identified or do you prefer J. A. Smith, or perhaps Allen
  Smith? The name on your business card may be Katherine
  Wilson, but you prefer Kate Wilson. How do you want the
  host to address you, and how do you want to be identified?

The same goes for your preferred title—Vice President (VP) of Business Marketing, Professor (Prof) of Business Management (Mgmnt), and so on.

- How do you want to be introduced? If you are a former beauty queen and now you are vice president of a company, does the audience need to know you were once a beauty queen? If you are vice president of the Miss America Pageant, then it is significant. Otherwise it may not need to be included in your introduction.

- If you will not have an opportunity to see the set before your interview, be sure to alert the producer about your height in reference to that of the host's. If you are significantly taller or shorter than the host is, the chairs need to be adjusted accordingly.

- Will you be the only person interviewed for the segment or will others also be interviewed? If there are others, it will cut down on your airtime, but it will cut down on the other guests' airtime as well. Watching an interview where the guests are fighting for airtime is painful and annoying. The issue gets lost while the audience is watching the guests jockeying for the camera.

- If you are not solo, are the other guests in the studio with you or being interviewed by satellite? If the other guests are off-site, will you be able to see them and appear to be looking directly at them by way of an in-studio monitor, or will you look into the camera as if you are also being interviewed via satellite? Note: Be sure the audio in your earpiece allows you to hear the other guests and that the audio has been patched in from the remote location. You will have a control knob to adjust the audio.

On the set.

- When the host introduces you, acknowledge that you have been introduced. A simple nod of your head, not a ridiculous grin or nervous laugh, will be sufficient. The first verbal or visual impression you make on the audience should be after your introduction. Make a short statement such as, "Thank you, Jim, it's good to join you this morning to talk about [issue]." Right away, you have taken control of the interview. The best follow-up to your greeting is a question from the host.

- If you smile too much, it gives the audience the impression that you are a simpleton and begs the question of why you were invited to be on the show. Unless (a) you really are a simpleton, or (b) you are a dentist and your smile is your business card, just be yourself. Forget about the camera, the lights, the microphone attached to you, and, in some cases, the studio audience and just pretend that you are having a pleasant one-on-one chat with the host.

- If you have to wear an earpiece because another host or another guest is at an off-studio site, wear the earpiece in the ear that won't be on camera (if you are sitting at an angle) or in the ear where it fits best. If you are playing with the earpiece during the entire interview, people will focus on your distracting actions instead of your words.

- Again, it will most likely be hot on the set. Unless you feel faint from the heat of the lights, do not let your voice betray how hot it is in that studio! Conversely, no quivering or shivering if the station has cranked up the air-conditioning too high.

- Watch your hand gestures. You don't want to come across flighty, which can happen if you are always gesturing; especially if they are wide, expansive, and unnatural gestures. Use your hands, fingers, and facial expressions to make a point, but don't overuse them. You will lose impact if you are either too fluid in your movements or if you are too static. Keep in mind that the more you use your hands, the more opportunities there are to knock something over. Do not use facial expressions as your response. Silence is not golden in this medium (or in radio). Silence gives the audience the impression that either you are not knowledgeable or you have nothing to contribute to the discussion. Find a medium range of expressions and review how you come across with these visual responses. Practice until you are comfortable, but not too rehearsed.

- Look at the size of the set. If it is a small one, camera location and the number of cameras make a difference in the way you should address the host and the camera (viewing audience). Small sets mean there is less space between the camera and the guest and host. If you lean in, you come closer to the camera and your features will be exaggerated; not quite as bad as a funhouse mirror, but the effect is still noticeable. You may block a two-shot (you and the host on camera together) if you lean in and block the other camera from taking a shot. The size of the set also dictates how you sit. If it is a small couch, don't sprawl across it or jump up on it like some Hollywood stars have been known to do. If there is a coffee table or end table, don't knock it when you're crossing your legs. (Actually, it is better not to cross your legs at all. The camera is not kind to the front view of crossed legs.)
- If the station has provided you with a cup of coffee or glass of water, remember where they are in reference to where you are. You don't want any spilling mishaps to reduce the on-camera time you have to pitch your issue.
- Don't use your coffee mug or glass of water as a prop and drink constantly throughout the interview. The more drinks you take, the more likely you will spill it on you, your microphone, or the set. Or what if you have a gurgling sound afterward and your voice pitch changes? Worse yet, what if you have to go to the bathroom during the interview? Watching a guest squirm because he or she has to use the facilities is very entertaining, but something you want to avoid at all costs! Unless you really have to take a drink because your mouth is dry, don't.
- Answer questions in sound bites. This requires practice. If you are asked, "How is the economy?" and your response is, "Good," you are making it very difficult for the host or inter-viewer. The worst interview is one in which the guest responds in short yes or no answers. It is important that you present your issue and get your expert point of view across. A good response will restate the question: "Overall the economy is doing well, but there are some concerns in the housing market

[number of jobs created, interest rates, number of unemployed, and so on]." You are the expert—give the good news and the not-so-good news in the same sentence. You are providing the interviewer with a follow-up for the next question, such as, "Is this across the country, or are there regions where the economy is doing well in the sector you just mentioned?"

- If you do not have the answer to a question, don't dance around a response—simply say so. But use it as an opportunity to talk about your issue. For example, "Is it true that the shortage of rice in China will move people to your side?" Answer: "I don't really know about the amount of rice in China, but I do know that if people want to make this world better for their children and their children's children, they should think about what kind of an impact [the issue] will have on them. It may not affect them right this moment, but it will affect future generations. [Look at camera directly.] If you want a better life for your children and your grandchildren, I urge you to support [the issue]."

- If someone representing your opposing view is being interviewed on the same program, there is no TV guest etiquette that requires you to wait until the host asks your position on an issue before responding. For example, the host asks your opponent, "How is the economy?" and she says, "I think the economy is doing poorly," and then supports that opinion. If the show does not break for a commercial, wait until after your opponent finishes speaking and then say directly to the host, "I disagree. I think the economy is doing well because . . ." Or you might say, "I agree that in the Southwest the economy is not doing well, but overall, across the country, the economy is on the upswing." However you choose to handle the situation, do not get into a screaming match with your opponent—unless, of course, you are on the *Jerry Springer Show*, where it is expected of you. The best advice is to be professional and to remain calm.

- Will your issue make an impact on the viewing audience? If so use the camera to help you get your point across. Let's say that eminent domain is your issue—the right of the government to take your property for its own reasons. Look into the camera, pretending that you are looking directly into the face of John or Jane Public. Paint a picture of the home your children grew up in—the home and city where you feel most comfortable. Then tell how it could be taken away from you by that very city because more tax money can be generated from a super-big-box business than can be generated from your residential or personal property taxes. If your issue can have an impact on individuals, let them know it, and let them know what they could do to help sway the decision the other way. Suggesting they contact their members of congress about an issue is often a good practice.

- As mentioned previously for radio interviews, keep your audience in mind. If your interview is on a station that targets a younger audience, don't act aloof, superior, or *old*.

- How can you impress upon your audience that you are believable, that you are sincere, and that you are looking out for their best interests? Pretend you are talking to a friend or family member, or pretend you are talking directly to the constituency you are trying to help. In other words, practice. Be careful not to practice too much, because if you come across as too polished or rehearsed in your presentation, the audience might not trust you. On the other hand, if you come across as uninformed, why should people believe you really care?

- We cannot overemphasize the importance of practice. Ask a friend or colleague to act as the host and have him fire questions at you. Be ready to think on your feet and keep the key points in mind at all times. If you can answer the questions of who, what, when, where, how, and why, you will be able to get all the important details about your issue out there. As an example, let's say you are the spokesperson for an annual fund-raising event and you are trying to drum up interest from the community. "The American Heart Association is sponsoring a mountain hike on Saturday, October seventh, at nine o'clock in the morning. We're going to start from the campground at the base of Lone Peak Mountain and we'll hike up the mountain to raise awareness about heart health and the importance of taking care of your heart. There will be trails that every one can use. You don't need to be a mountain climber to join us. Take advantage of the tips our doctors will share on how you can keep your ticker ticking! This isn't a race against a stopwatch, but it is a race against time—the amount of time you'll still be around if you have a healthy heart!" This is an example of getting all the facts out there right away and then expanding on each. Who? The organization. What? A mountain hike. When? The day of the week, date, and time. (Don't forget to add a rain date if your event is outdoors.) Where? The location. How? Walking up easy trails. Why? To improve heart health. These are the same rules you should follow in your press releases and every time you or someone else has an opportunity to promote the issue.

- Be constantly aware of the length of the interview. Time is not on your side. Answer the question, get to the point, and don't embellish. Expand on details only if it is necessary. Long-winded answers ensure you will not be invited back for another interview! Keep in mind that commercial breaks are a necessity. Take your cues from the host unless you have been advised prior to the interview to take your cues from someone else. Watch the host's hand signals. He or she should be able to give you a heads-up when you need to wrap up your comments, extend them, or cut them off immediately. If the host starts fidgeting because your answer is too long, do not get upset if he or she has to interrupt you. You may not realize it, but the host is often connected to the director with the earpiece and receives cues throughout the interview from the control room, as well as from the floor director.

- Don't be distracted by floor directors, camera operators, and sound people. You would be amazed at how many conversations take place among the technical people during an interview, or how often someone drops something off-camera. Keep your focus on your issue and your attention on the host.

- If you are in a remote location, the camera is the audience or your host. Look directly into the camera. Unless the station has a two-way monitor, you probably won't see the person asking you a question. In any event, whether you are looking at a camera and pretending that is the host or you are actually seeing the host on a monitor, don't forget to stay focused. It requires a great deal of concentration, but don't overemphasize how much you are trying to stay focused. Practice by listening to radio interviews or to television interviews while not looking at the screen. Maintain your energy level, even when you are not talking. You never know when they may cut to a two-shot—the technical term for when the TV screen is split so that one-half shows you in the remote location and the other half shows the host/interviewer in the studio. Reaction shots are important, and you never know when they may cut to one. To be safe, always look engaged, interested, and alert. Never look bored or talk off-camera to someone in your remote location.

Miscellaneous TV tips.

- If you are given a choice between an in-studio versus a satellite interview, choose the in-studio interview. You will be able to react to the interviewer much more easily. Observing body language will tell you whether he or she is really listening or interested in the interview; if not, take control of the situation and make your responses more interesting. Face-to-face interviews are always better and are preferred by the interviewer or host as well. The television station may offer you transportation to the studio by sending a car if you are local or, if it is a network and you are in another city, they may pay for airfare. If this is a possibility, ask and then work out the details. However, there is a fine line between a demanding guest and one who is just trying to make the best of a logistical problem.
- Be sure the host or producer has information about you and your issue well in advance of the interview. Backgrounder papers, releases, op-eds, FAQs—anything that will make it

easier for the host to understand the issue and why you are the spokesperson. If your previous experience is part of the hook that is getting you on the air, use it. Scripts for the show teasers are written well in advance. A teaser is a sort of mini commercial: "Coming up Tuesday, we'll be joined by John Doe, a world-record holder in _____ and cancer survivor. He'll be here to talk to us about cancer prevention." Unfortunately, the hosts seldom have time to be thoroughly informed about your issue. They will have prewritten questions, and too often they use those questions as a guide for the interview, never straying from them. Those are tough interviews—but if you have provided all the information for the researchers to write the questions, you should come across well informed, poised, and interested in your issue.

- Have a spokesperson who presents a nice appearance. We aren't talking drop-dead gorgeous or handsome here, but rather someone who is well groomed and appropriately dressed. Your spokesperson is the face of your issue. Do you want the audience to remember the topic of the interview or how inappropriate the spokesperson looked?

- If you hear about a story or an issue that your local station may be covering and you have a viewpoint other than the one being presented, it never hurts to call the newsroom or senior producer for the show and ask who the contact person is for that issue. Try to pitch your point of view. At best, you will be invited for a point-counterpoint type interview; at worst, the station will use all your points and ask the questions of the opposing position themselves. Even though you may not be invited to appear on the show or be asked for an interview on the issue, you can fax or e-mail clear talking points about your position. Remember that talking points are not press releases. You may not get credit for your side, but if you are satisfied that your position will be addressed during the interview, you have succeeded in getting your viewpoint across.

- Remember green room etiquette. The green room is the waiting area where you will be sitting prior to your on-camera interview. Depending on the size of the station, you may be treated to food and drinks. Green rooms of the networks are always stocked with fruits, vegetable trays, pastries, deli meats, soda, water, and occasionally alcohol. Although the treats and sweets may be tempting, try to refrain—especially from alcohol. Don't blow your fifteen minutes of fame by slurring your words and coming across as a lush. Raspberries, blueberries, broccoli, and the like are foods to avoid. Don't spend your entire interview with food lodged between your two front teeth!

• Above all, enjoy yourself. You have nailed a television interview where people will not only read or hear about you and your issue, but they will see you and put a face behind the issue. Don't get uptight about the weight your television interview may have, but also don't ignore how important this window of opportunity can be. Good luck!

Appendix 2

TIPS FOR PRINT INTERVIEWS

- Unless the reporter is on a very tight deadline or is a wire service reporter with more frequent deadlines, print interviews afford you more time to compose your thoughts than do broadcast interviews. As the interviewee, you don't have to rush to get your sound bite in at the top of the interview. You can be more pensive and reflective when you respond to questions. No one is annoyed when you say, "In other words," or "Let me put that another way." Print interviews offer you the opportunity to present more angles to your issue—almost as if you are thinking while you are talking. This does not mean you shouldn't prepare for a print interview without rehearsing what you are going to say. Regardless of the interview format, be prepared to answer the basic questions of who, what, when, where, why, and how.
- Be honest. Again, this is a tip for every interview, but it seems even more disconcerting to pick up a newspaper and see in black-and-white some glaring lie attributed to you. You can try to blame it on the reporter and say he or she misunderstood, but print reporters are even more careful to present quotes accurately than some broadcast reporters are. No one benefits when you tell a lie—especially you and your issue. Your issue gets lost and your lie becomes the story.
- Avoid being misquoted. Tape the interview yourself. Don't present your wanting to tape it as mistrust of the reporter; present it as a tool to help you refine your message, prepare for other interviews, and so on. In addition, if your assistant tapes the interview it will seem less like "your word against mine." However, ask for permission—especially if the interview takes place at the newspaper. You are on their turf and they may not allow outside recording devices. If you are being interviewed over the phone, ask a colleague to listen in. Advise the reporter that you are having Adam listen in to the interview because he

may be able to translate some of the technical details for you. If you have the technical ability to audio tape both sides of the interview do so, but alert the reporter that you are taping the conversation. Be aware of wiretapping concerns. In some states, only one party has to be alerted that the conversation is being taped. If you were taping the interview, that one party would be you. Other states require that both parties must be aware that the conversation is being taped.

- If your print interview is in person, don't be surprised if a photographer joins the reporter. Perhaps the newspaper or magazine doesn't have a photo of you on file and this is the opportunity to take one. Dress professionally and appropriately.

- The lines between on the record, unattributed, and background information can become very blurry over the course of an interview. You are always on the record unless you clearly state otherwise. Think of "off the record" as though it is a conversational parentheses—nothing inside those parentheses can be printed. One example of an "off the record" comment took place during the 2000 presidential race. President Clinton told the White House Press Corps, off the record, that a certain Republican candidate looked presidential. The comment was never reported.

- Unattributed means that the reporter can use the statement but cannot attribute it to a specific person. We commonly see, "a senior White House official, on condition of anonymity, says . . ."

- Think of background as information that fills in the blanks or sets the scene for what a reporter needs to know in order to write a story. Again, always be clear that this background information is unattributed. One technique is to ask the reporter how they plan to characterize you (nameless official, person inside the industry, etc.). Tell the reporter when you are back on record.

- If you desire to leak information, have someone else in your organization make the statement in a follow-up call to the reporter. For example, "Unattributed, about 40 percent of the flying public will be targeted for terrorist profiling." Then instead of having a direct quote from someone who is in charge of terrorist profiling, the reporter can write, *Government officials have indicated that 40 percent of the flying public will be targeted for terrorist profiling.* No one is quoted directly and the information gets out to the public. Don't be surprised if reporters are reluctant to include all the information you have provided them. Remember Judith Miller of the New York Times? Although it is believed that she had the information, she didn't write an article naming a covert CIA operative, yet she was jailed for protecting her source—a source she didn't name in a story she didn't write.

- Treat your print interview the same way you would treat a broadcast interview. Assume everything you say is on the record and going over the air live! No matter how well you think you know a journalist never let them lull you or never let yourself be lulled into the kind of conversation that can come back to haunt you or your candidate, according to Steve Rabinowitz, who was the "master of message" for Bill Clinton's 1992 campaign.

- Speak slowly. Print reporters take notes even when using a recorder. Reporters have their own self-styled form of shorthand. Unless a person is a court reporter or a stenographer, no one can take notes as quickly as people speak. Do not jump from one angle to the next unless you know the reporter is keeping up with you. If your interview is over the phone, you will often hear the reporter clicking away on their keyboard. Pause between talking points. Allow the reporter to read what he or she has just written to confirm what you have said.

- Use your time with a print reporter wisely. Since these interviews are often longer, use the time to emphasize and highlight important points; don't hesitate to use repetition. Summarize your position for the reporter. Treat the interview like an informative conversation and relax. There are no cameras capturing your body language and no broadcast-quality audio recording picking up the quiver in your voice.

- Practice. We cannot overemphasize the importance of rehearsing the points you want to make in your interview.

Organize your thoughts. Don't allow dead airtime between the question and your answer. Even if the reporter has asked a question that is sophomoric or ridiculous, answer the question, but then elaborate. For example, the reporter asks, "Do you really think there's a problem with athletes and steroids?" Your answer could be, "Yes, I do believe there is a problem with athletes and steroids. Let's look at the facts. [Cite the number of athletes banned for steroid use, and so on.]" If the reporter is trying to catch you in a response, acknowledge it. "John, you're trying to get me to say _____. I won't say that, but I will tell you . . ."

- If you don't have an immediate answer for the reporter, don't hedge; be honest and say you don't have that information or fact but you will get it for her. Follow up with the information after the interview, but not so late that the reporter has already filed the story without the information you promised. This is also a good opportunity for you or your staff to reinforce how much you enjoyed the interview. Even if you don't like the reporter, courtesy is always better than belligerence.

- Also, follow up if you find yourself unsure about a fact or figure. For instance, "I told you ten percent of the association's budget goes to operating expenses. I'm aware that our overhead expenses have raised concern with our donors, so I wanted to confirm that figure, and I found that the accurate overhead is really thirteen percent." Then cite how that 13 percent is spent if that was not covered in the initial interview. If you have had to spell something for the reporter, a reassuring call from you that you have checked and the spelling is correct (or incorrect) will be appreciated. If something is printed inaccurately because your information is inaccurate, the editor will hold the reporter accountable when a correction has to be printed in the next issue.

- If something embarrassing happens during the interview, alert your staff immediately. Let us say you are asked who started your organization and you cannot for the life of you remember the founder's name. Try to brush over your temporary memory loss with a comment like, "I've been so focused on this issue I have completely blocked out every other aspect of the organization. I'm sure the name will come to me shortly." A good reporter does research too and may ask questions well beyond what you are prepared to discuss. Offer to have another member of your organization speak with the reporter on that subject. Be helpful, even if you feel you have been set up.

- Do not let down your guard during the interview. As is the case with other news media, the print reporter may try to disarm you by having you believe the two of you are friends. Be friendly but professional.

- Although mentioned before, it bears repeating here: Keep the reporter/newsmaker lines of communication open. This could be beneficial in the future for follow-up stories or even with different issues altogether. Drop the reporter a line when you have read or written an article that may be of interest to him or her. If you have new information about your issue, let the reporter know that as well.

- Finally, don't forget to send a thank-you note after the interview; if not the same day, send it after you have read the interview article. Thank the reporter for their time even if you do not like the angle of the story. "Although I disagree with you on your approach to the issue, I enjoyed meeting with you and I hope we can revisit this issue soon."

BRANDING TIPS
FROM MASTER BRANDER PETER ARNELL

1. Fish where the fish are. You won't catch a fish if there aren't any.

2. Real estate is important. The Internet is a huge example of that.

3. Build an anticipatory mind-set in the consumer. You want your customer to be desirous and awaiting your arrival in whatever you do. You want your customer predisposed to try it rather than be surprised. People don't like surprises.

4. Take the surprise and make it part of the product.

5. Allow the consumer to build the brand with you. Maintain your customer and build from that base.

6. Do not sell the brand to your customers. Let the brand acknowledge their needs. Let them understand the role of the brand in their lives.

7. Explain it. Do not put it all out there and expect them to "get it" without an explanation.

8. Retention, retention, retention: Give them a reason to come back every day. Be part of an ongoing retention strategy.

9. Have good strategies to get feedback from your customers.

10. Research. Exploit the obvious. Everyone wants to give you advice. Take it. Listen to it.

TOP TEN THINGS TO KNOW WHEN YOU START A BLOG
FROM JOHN ARAVOSIS/AMERICABLOG.COM

1. **Have the time.** For your blog to be successful, you need to update it regularly and write good content. That takes time. Worse yet, if your blog becomes popular, you'll need to spend even more time doing it. It's kind of like having kids or pets or plants—it takes nurturing and a good plan to figure out who's going to take care of them during your vacation.

2. **Have the energy.** There's no use starting a blog if you don't have the energy and drive to see it through. Meaning, you need to update it regularly with interesting and new content, even when you don't feel like it. Again, the pet or kid analogy kicks in—your blog needs constant nurturing, whether you're in the mood or not.

3. **Reveal yourself.** Just like good op-ed writing or on-the-air punditry, a blog audience connects with you more when they get a sense who you are, a sense that they're dealing with a real person and not some impersonal dead-tree publication. That means revealing a bit of yourself to your audience through tone and substance.

4. **Say something.** You have to have something to say or there's no point in writing a blog. Of course, you probably already have something to say or you wouldn't be interested in doing a blog in the first place. Be original, having something unique to say, be interesting, give your readers a reason to read you instead of (or at least in addition to) the thousands of other blogs already out there.

5. **Good writing helps.** Blogging is writing, and being a good writer will help make your blog more interesting to your readers.

6. **Interact with your audience.** Your audience will likely feel a personal connection to your blog. Help foster that connection by interacting with your readers via e-mail and on the blog itself via comments.

7. **Know your comparative advantage.** A corollary to point 4 above, write about what you know. In my case, I know national politics, the religious right, and gay civil rights—and that's what I write about, mostly. Not only am I an "expert" on those topics, and thus have something to add to the national debate, but I also love those topics and have a passion for writing about them. That passion hopefully comes across in what I write, and helps make my writing more interesting—it will for you too.

8. **Don't expect the blog to pay the bills.** Yes, if you get enough traffic people will send you donations and you can even sell some ads. But it's the rare blog that can sustain its writer(s) completely off of its own revenue. It's probably best to approach the blog as you would any other hobby—don't expect it to pay your rent, but do it because you love it.

9. **Reach out to other bloggers.** One of the best ways to build traffic is to have other bloggers link to your posts. The best way to do that is to email other bloggers, from time to time, the hyperlink and content of a particularly interesting post that you think might interest their readers.

10. **Shoot for the moon.** It's utter baloney to think that there are already so many blogs you'll never be able to make a dent. Competition is a daily fact of life in any field. If your blog is good, it will get noticed. Just make sure you strive to offer your audience something it can't get anywhere else.

GUIDELINES FOR
PROFESSIONAL-LOOKING VCASTS AND VLOGS
FROM PRODUCER CHRISTIAN CAPOBIANCO

1. Before hiring a cameraperson make sure they are qualified for what you are shooting; look at some of their work. Preferably they will have a reel of their work. Check references.

2. The same goes for the sound person.

3. Have a location scout. Take your technical crew to the location(s) that you will be shooting so they all prepare what they will need to bring (for example, if you're shooting outdoors using existing light, you would need to bring extra c-stands, reflectors, sandbags, camera filters). Determine before hand if there is street noise or other distractions. NO SURPRISES!

4. Decide on a backdrop. You may need to bring a few choices with you.

5. If interviewing, make sure that you get a release form signed by each person before shooting.

6. If you're interviewing more than one person at a time make sure they do not talk over each other. Also, each person should repeat the question. For instance, the interview asks, "Where were you born?" The interviewee repeats the question in the answer by saying, "I was born in Cleveland, Ohio."

7. Make sure your subjects have a few changes of wardrobe. See Tips for Television, Appendix 1. White reflects poorly and washes the subject out. Black absorbs light.

8. Make sure all your batteries are fully charged the night before.

9. Have extra batteries on set as well as other power supplies like stingers (extralong extension cords) and adaptors.

10. Have extra tapes on set. The interview may go on longer than expected in order to get the appropriate information, or you may find B roll that you didn't plan on.

11. If you're shooting a person, ask them if they can bring their own makeup for touch-ups or have a makeup/hair artist on the shoot.

12. Make sure you bring extra wireless microphones; sometime people break for lunch, forget to take it off, and lose it. Also throw in a boom mic, because you never know!

13. Schedule a preproduction meeting the day before so everyone knows what the day's events will be like. Make a list of each other's cell phones, in case someone gets lost or oversleeps and they happen to have the camera. Also collect maps, directions, local phone numbers for lunch, beverages, directions to nearest hospital, posting signs for along the way and for crew parking and unloading.

14. Always have a first aid kit with you. Accidents happen.

15. Check the weather, sunrise, and sunset. If it's an exterior shoot, have a cover set in mind if it rains or if someone cancels. Have a plan B!

16. Make sure you know who is responsible for labeling the tapes/DVDs. Make a written tape chain of custody.

17. Make MASTER tapes. Always have a second set of tapes. You never know!

18. Bring your questions, and make sure someone else, such as the cameraperson, has a copy.

19. Bring walkie-talkies with headsets for those who need them. Communication is key!

20. Bring protective gear for equipment in case of fog, drizzle, and dust (desert shooting), as well as sound blankets. Winds can really ruin dialogue.

PROMOTION CHECKLIST

☑ Preparing your Message and Campaign

1. Is your spokesperson willing to go on the air?
2. Have you monitored the media that you want to use?
3. Have you created, defined, and refined your message?
4. Is your word usage up-to-date?
5. Have you set the goals of your campaign?
6. Is your campaign designed to move the middle?
7. Have you defined your purpose? What is it you want to have happen?
8. Have you personalized your issue(s)?
9. Have you made complex issues understandable?
10. Have you examined your timing and all the ramifications of your timing decisions?
11. Have you looked at which issues you can piggyback on?
12. Have you found ways to rejuvenate your message with a new angle?
13. Does your intended audience feel they are more in control of their lives with your issue(s)?
14. Have you found a way to make your story today's news?
15. Have you crafted a sound bite, something people are going to remember?
16. Are you being creative in your use of statistics? Is your use of statistics interesting?
17. Do you understand the pros and cons of your strategy and message?
18. Can you identify your audience? Would you be able to paint a picture of them?
19. How would people stereotype your message? Are you ready for it?

☑ Marketing Your Campaign, Issue, or Spokesperson

20. Have you thought of creative, wild ideas that will attract attention?
21. Do you have a great printed and online press kit?
22. Are your sound and video easily obtainable?
23. Have you used organization and personal history to increase your credibility?
24. What have you done to bolster your credibility?
25. What are you doing for fun?
26. Do you have real ways to find class in your campaign?
27. Have you found ways to be the source of information?
28. Do you know how your message works today? Have you looked to find out how your issue is being searched on the Internet?
29. Have you found a way to make your event unique and open to the media?
30. Have you found ways to multiply your message and use new venues?
31. Have you found a way to capitalize on controversy?
32. Have you used VNRs and other PR techniques to get your images in front of the media?
33. Is your event calendar available to the media?
34. Do you have a research plan and timeline?
35. How are using traditional and nontraditional methods to reinforce your message?
36. Have you used your constituency to call in to the media?
37. Can people find you? Have you made it easy?
38. What is your cross-promotion plan?
39. Are you willing to debate?
40. Are you allowing free hits? Are you ready to fight back?
41. Do you understand that small markets and niche Web sites can get the job done? Do you have plan for them?

☑ Selecting and Preparing a Spokesperson

42. Is your spokesperson a positive personality?

43. Have you coached your spokesperson?

44. Have you monitored the media before the interview?

45. Did you debrief your spokesperson?

☑ Booking the Spokesperson

46. Have you thought outside your target programs?

47. Are you booking a radio and TV satellite tour?

48. Have you refined you pitch?

49. Have you found ways to provide additional service?

50. Do you know why your campaign and issue matter now?

51. Have you made use of conference calls?

52. Are you completely honest?

53. Have you provided a choice of spokespersons?

54. How available are your spokespersons?

55. Are your facts straight? Are your times zones correct?

56. Do you have a backup plan for cancellations?

57. Do you need to review a radio or TV station's public files?

☑ Preparing to Be On

58. Have you reviewed the current news on the day of the interview? Do you know what the hot topics of the day are?

59. Have you painted the picture? Does the audience understand the background?

60. Are you specific? Have you avoided broad generalizations?

61. Are you dressed and made up for success?

62. Have you found ways to build bridges, areas of agreement?

63. Is your spokesperson energized?

64. Have you chosen an in-studio interview? If not, why not?

65. What will be the consequences of your success?

66. How well do you know your opposition? What words and arguments will they use?

67. Have you clarified your language and developed workable analogies?

68. Have you developed your material to be the strongest it can possibly be?

69. Have you prioritized your talking points?

70. Have you maximized your time on the road?

☑ Being On!

71. Have you walked yourself through all eventualities that could happen on television, radio, or the Internet?

72. Are you able to be amusing, likeable, and honest?

73. Can you be flexible? Can you roll with the punches?

74. Are you prepared to be brief and watch the flow of the conversation?

75. Have you left your ego at the door?

76. Have you warmed up your voice?

77. Are you believable?

78. Have you found ways to empower the audience?

79. Is your green room behavior as good as your on-air behavior?

80. Did you offer to return?

81. Have you decided your style? Are you an analyst or a pit bull?

☑ Understanding the Media

82. Do you understand the ins and outs of the media business?

83. Have you cared for and fed the media?

84. Are you humble?

85. Have you found ways to something for the media?

86. Have you made the producer's job easier?

87. Are you nonjudgmental about the media?

88. Have you decided to leak something? If so, to whom?

☑ Crisis Management

89. Can you be up-front? Can you acknowledge, apologize, and act?

90. Are you taking the blame? Have you avoided blaming the media?

91. Have you created your own murder board?

92. Are you ready and willing to defend your board and your supporters?

93. Do you have a follow-up strategy?

☑ Preparing for the Future

94. Are you up-to-date on the capacity of the Internet and other new technologies?

95. Do you understand what the Internet numbers mean to you?

96. Have you optimized your search engine?

97. Have you put Internet on your payroll?

98. Do you understand the neighborhood of the Internet site?

99. Do you update your content regularly?

100. Are you using dialogue opportunities on the Internet?

101. Are you blogging?

102. Does your Internet site use multimedia?

GLOSSARY

Actuality: Sound bite or feed taped live and disseminated to radio stations over phone lines or the Internet.

ADI: Area of dominant influence in which a particular market denominates, though not to the exclusion of other markets.

Advisory: A brief scheduling notice, change, or addition; often referred to as media or press advisory.

Affiliate: A television or radio station associated with a larger network (e.g., ABC, CBS, FOX, NBC, and NPR).

AQH: Average quarter-hour listenership.

Arbitron: Organization that tracks and provides statistical data on nationwide radio listenership.

Assignment editor: Person in the newsroom who determines which reporters or crews cover which stories. The assignment editor works under the news director and helps shape news coverage.

Audience: The total number of people tuning in to a network or station over a defined period—usually a week or a month.

Audio files: Computer files that contain digitized sound that can be heard online.

Avails: Television and radio advertising time slots still available for purchase.

Blast e-mail: A single e-mail that can be sent out to a large number of recipients by using a bulk or blast e-mail tool.

BLOCKQUOTE: A method of quoting more than a few lines from a document on the Internet. Allows readers to verify the authenticity of the quotation and also find related information.

Blog: *See* Weblog

BlogCon: A press conference for bloggers, often by telephone but sometimes online.

Breadcrumbs: Typically appear horizontally near the top of a Web page, providing links back to each previous page the user has navigated. Breadcrumbs provide a trail for the user to follow back to entry point of a Web site.

B roll: Footage (usually video images, but can also include background sound) that plays over the audio of an interview and links story components together.

Browser-safe colors: There are 256 colors that look the same on all computers and browsers. Other colors may display in unpredictable ways, depending on the computer in question.

Call-in show: Radio or television talk show that allows listeners to call in to the program with questions for guests or hosts.

Call letters: The identifying letters of a radio station. East of the Mississippi River, radio station call letters begin with the letter *W.* West of the Mississippi River, radio station call letters begin with the letter *K.* There are some exceptions to this rule (e.g., WDAY in Fargo, North Dakota).

Chat room: An online, real-time communication between two Internet users. Messages are typed on a keyboard and then sent between chat room users.

Chyron: The lettering on the bottom third of a television screen used to identify guests or interviewees.

Click-through: The process of a visitor clicking on a Web advertisement and being routed to the advertiser's Web site—also called *ad clicks* or *requests.* The click rate measures the number of times an ad is clicked versus the amount of time it is viewed.

Combination rate: Twin AM and FM stations that offer a reduced rate for spots; also called a *combo.*

Contour maps: A map that shows a transmitter's service contours. Radio station maps can be found online at radiolocator.com.

Copyright: A law based on the idea that society will benefit from the creation and dissemination of artistic and intellectual works.

Core constituencies: Supporters aligned with a particular cause; can also be referred to as a *political base.*

Coverage area: A geographic region that includes all the homes covered by a station's signal.

Cross-browser compatibility: Before a Web site is launched, it should be tested on versions of all major browsers to ensure that it can be viewed properly. Once this is done, the Web site has achieved cross-browser compatibility.

Cume: The cumulative amount of listeners or viewers who, over the course of a set time period (usually a week), watch or listen to a particular program.

Cutlines: An explanatory comment or designation accompanying an onscreen pictorial illustration.

Daybook: A schedule of events produced daily by leading news organizations. The daybook is a useful summary that editors and reporters often refer to when determining which events to cover.

Dayparts: Blocks of time on the broadcast schedule usually denoted by the letters of the alphabet (e.g., the A block refers to the opening portion of a program).

Deadline: A cutoff time when a reporter's story must be completed and filed with an editor.

Domain: An Internet domain name refers to an organization's Web address.

Download time: The amount of time it takes for a Web page, audio file, or video to download. Download time varies, based upon the file size and Internet connection.

Dub: A film or tape copy duplicated from the master (the original) and then distributed for broadcast.

E-mail alert: Messages containing breaking news or other important updates sent electronically to subscribers and users.

E-newsletter: A periodic update delivered via e-mail to supporters or subscribers.

Earned media: Free media generated from any news (or other) event.

Effective reach: A measure of audience listenership for radio programs.

Electronic press kit (EPK): A press kit on the Web that can be easily downloaded and e-mailed.

Embargo date: The date at which time-sensitive information can be released by the media. However, the media often possess this material in advance of the embargo date.

Fairness doctrine: A Federal Communications Commission directive requiring equal media time for opposing viewpoints, but repealed during the Reagan administration.

Fax broadcasting service: A service that will fax news releases on demand to multiple recipients.

Feed: A recorded sound bite sent to radio stations over the telephone. It can also be called an *actuality*, implying that the bite was recorded live.

Flash animation: Multimedia technology developed by Macromedia that allows a large amount of interactive media to fit into a relatively small file size.

Format: 1. Media type: Print, television, radio, online. 2. Type of programming: Call-in, public affairs, talk.

GIF: Graphics Interchange Format. A type of image file that is used for photos and graphics on the Web.

Gross ratings point: Called GRPs or points, this measures the audiences for television and radio programs. For example, 1 point equals 1 percent of all televisions or radios owned by the target audience.

HTML: Hypertext markup language, or the computer language used to create content for the World Wide Web component of the Internet.

Internet organizing: Organizing and mobilizing supporters on the Internet for a particular cause.

JPEG: Joint photographic experts group, a compression technique for reducing the size of color images.

Lexis-Nexis: A Web-based information service available for a subscription fee and that offers access to archived news articles, congressional voting records, corporate filings, and other useful information in the public realm.

Listserv: An e-mail distribution service allowing a user to send one e-mail to a Listserv address, which in turn gets distributed to all members of the Listserv.

Live-to-tape: A taped interview that will air as part of a live program.

Log: A second-by-second record of what a channel broadcasts daily. It includes programming and advertising spots.

Logo link: A Web site's logo added to a larger Web entity to broaden Internet exposure.

Lowest unit rate: The lowest rate an advertiser can charge for a given class of spots during the 45 days preceding a primary and the 60 days preceding a general election.

Make good: A station's decision to run a spot for no charge as compensation for failing to run the original spot or failing to run it properly.

Market share: The percentage of all televisions or radios tuned in to any given radio or television show.

Master: An original recording used to make high-quality dubs or copies.

Media kit: Also called a press packet, this is a folder containing information about the candidate, organization, or cause. It usually includes a biography, brochures, press releases, news clips, a CD-ROM or DVD, and so forth.

Media market: Television and radio stations available within a particular geographic area.

Meta tags: Phrases and keywords used to describe a Web site by Google, Yahoo!, and other search engines. When a Web search is conducted, these search engines refer to phrases and keywords to locate related Web sites.

Mult box: A central amplifier with multiple plugs that allows radio reporters and television cameramen to insert recording cables and record a person speaking without having a microphone set up at the podium.

NAB: The National Association of Broadcasters, a leading lobby organization based in Washington, D.C.

Narrowcasting: A form of broadcasting, but to a narrow audience, not to the general public. Sometimes applied to podcasting.

News director: The person in charge of news coverage in television newsrooms. In radio, this person is likely to be more involved in the hands-on work of producing the news.

Nielsen: An organization that tracks and provides statistical data on nationwide television viewership.

One sheet: A synopsis of a press release, pitch idea, or guest biography in a concise, one-page format.

Op-ed: Short for *opposite editorial,* a signed opinion column that appears on the final page of a newspaper's main section, opposite the editorial and letters to the editor page.

Open reel: An older technology term referring to a 1/4-inch magnetic tape, usually recorded at 7 1/2 inches per second (low speed), or 15 inches per second (high speed).

Outlet: A media entity or news organization, whether a publication or a station for television and radio.

Packages: A completed television news story including all reporting, video, and audio work, plus graphics and logistics involved in producing the story.

Parody site (sometimes called a suck site): An imitation Web site that uses humor to criticize the opposition.

Paid media: Any paid advertisement or spot by a political campaign, organization, or cause that airs on broadcast or cable television, radio, or the Internet.

PDF: Portable document format, a file format that allows readers to view documents in their original format. To open PDF files, Adobe Acrobat Reader must be installed on your computer.

Permalink: A type of URL designed to refer to a specific information item (often a news story or Weblog item) and to remain unchanged permanently—or at least for a lengthy period of time.

Pitch: To sell a story to a reporter or producer in a succinct manner.

Press plan: A written plan for garnering earned media; also called a *media plan*.

Podcasting: The online creation of audio files (most commonly in MP3 format) in a way that allows software to automatically download the files for listening at the user's convenience.

Political broadcasting: If programming during an election campaign includes an appearance by a political candidate running for public office, equal opportunities to appear must be made available to opposing candidates requesting an appearance on such programming, provided the request is made in a timely manner.

Political file: Records of political broadcast requests, disposition of requests and changes made, if any, and records of free time provided to or on behalf of political candidates.

Portal: A Web site that provides a central location for audiences interested in a particular subject to view many links relating to their subject of interest.

Public inspection file: Each AM, FM, and TV broadcast applicant and licensee must maintain a local public inspection file that is available at the station's main studio.

Pulsing: A heavily run ad schedule that airs for a period of time, stops, and then runs heavily again for another schedule.

Radio issues/program lists: A quarterly list of programs that has provided the station's most significant treatment of community issues during the preceding three-month period.

Radio time brokerage agreements: A copy of every contract or agreement involving time brokerage of the licensee's station or of another station by the licensee. Confidential or proprietary information can be redacted, if necessary.

Rating: A measure that tracks the percentage of the total television-owning population tuned to a particular program (or station) at a particular time.

Reach: The percentage of people exposed to a media schedule or campaign at least once.

Really simple syndication (RSS): A format for syndicating news and content. The information is delivered as an XML file and can syndicate news for Web sites and Weblogs.

Rotation: The order in which spots air on television or radio. In an equal rotation, each spot plays once and the order repeats itself without change. In a 60-40 rotation, for every three times one spot plays, another plays twice.

Run of schedule: Spots that run during a program but do not follow a set broadcast order.

Satellite: Television technology that allows for the transmission of video from anywhere in the world.

Share: The percentage of the total number of people tuned in to a particular television station or program. Ratings determine a station or program's share.

Site map: A map of all the pages that appear on a Web site. The map can list the Web pages alphabetically or in chronological order.

Skype: A computer program that can be used to make free voice calls over the Internet to anyone else who is using Skype.

Slogan: A single, short phrase used to define a campaign or issue.

SOT: Sound on tape.

Sound bite: A well-crafted phrase, message, or expression that succinctly captures a point of view or part of speech. Reporters use sound bites in their news stories.

Specialty press: Press that provides news and information to media consumers outside the mainstream, and is often tailored to that audience.

Split: The difference between the number of spots a host gets and an advertiser gets per hour. There are twelve to eighteen spots per hour.

Spot: A unit of advertising that lasts either 30 or 60 seconds.

Streaming media: Technology that allows data to be transferred over the Internet. The data plays in a steady stream after a brief download time.

Stringer: A correspondent who is paid by a news organization for each filed story, but is not a member of the organization's full-time staff.

Surrogates: Credible representatives of a political campaign who support, represent, and speak on behalf of the candidate.

Talking points: Brief points that cover the essential information of a news event.

Targeting: To develop a media campaign (political or nonpolitical) tailored to a core constituency.

Thread: In online discussions, a series of messages that have been posted as replies to each other.

TiVo: A popular brand of digital video recorder that allows users to capture television programs to internal hard disk storage for later viewing. (Sometimes called *time shifting*.)

Tracking poll: Brief survey conducted by a polling firm or political campaign to determine voter attitudes on an issue.

Traffic: The names, numbers, and rotation instructions of spots to air on television or radio. This is public information.

TSL: Time spent listening.

TV issues/program lists: A list of programs that has provided the station's most significant treatment of community issues during the preceding three-month period.

URL: Universal resource locator. The global address of documents on the World Wide Web.

Usenet: A worldwide bulletin board system that can be accessed through the Internet or through many online services.

Viral marketing: An informal, word-of-mouth method of message dissemination.

Weblog, or blog: A running online diary providing informal commentary on a Web site. Weblogs are usually written by a single author, but readers can post their comments on the Web site.

Web strategy: A targeted, designed, and written plan for an issues-based Internet site.

Wire: Press associations like the Associated Press, Reuters, and United Press International, which distribute news stories electronically from locations throughout a country and the world.

Wrap: A very short (usually 5 seconds) taped introduction and conclusion to a radio feed.

INDEX

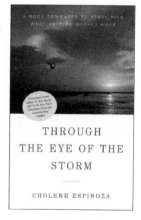